C. Rutenber

The Human Enterprise

The Human Enterprise

AN ATTEMPT TO RELATE
PHILOSOPHY TO DAILY LIFE

M. C. OTTO
UNIVERSITY OF WISCONSIN

The King's Library

1940

F. S. CROFTS & CO. NEW YORK

To
Ernest G. Ehlman
who
When We Were Young
advised
The Steeper Road
and
To the Memory
of
The Conrads
where
We Lived

FOREWORD

One who writes on philosophy is supposed to speak with peculiar finality. Plato set the fashion and his successors followed it. Even William James deemed it the prime philosophic problem to lay hold of "the first *whence* and the last *whither* of the whole cosmic procession."

This makes the situation awkward for the author of this book. To comprehend all things in their totality, or to dig through appearances to the ultimate nature of being, is magic beyond his powers. The reader must therefore expect something different from universal and absolute truth. Should he be tempted to conclude that this leaves no reason to philosophize at all, the answer may be made that the search for all-inclusiveness is the vice, not the virtue, of philosophy. The *spirit* of philosophy is the quest for depth and richness of meaning, for wisdom of life, a quest that is endless; abstract formulas, closed systems, pronouncements on ultimates, these are the *letter* of philosophy.

The intent of this remark is constructive. It is not made in disparagement of philosophy. Too often, however, the claims of philosophy are overstated by philosophers, and philosophic achievements are overrated by the interested public. Such errors can do only harm. It is better that no one be deceived by them. Besides, whatever anyone may think to be the function of philosophy, the reader should not be misled as to the present author's intention.

"It is a good thought of Plato's," writes Marcus Aurelius, "that when we discourse of men we should look down as from a high place." The passage has not been found in Plato, but it is the sort of thing he might have said. It is a wise saying. We need on occasion to look from a height, to see men in relation to the human story and the long evolution of life. We need to look from a hill. Let it be a hill rising out of the topography of daily experience, high enough to afford a good prospect, yet not so high that the everyday scene is lost from view.

The writer of the following chapters cannot claim to be without bias. One kind of bias he is not only aware of, is not only willing to admit, but is constrained to emphasize. It is a militant interest in man's earthly enterprise. As to the advance of this he is neither indifferent nor neutral. An era of human history is running out. A new era will come in. Those who plan to live in the world they have known, modernized a little where necessary but otherwise the same world, "are building castles," as R. H. Tawney has put it, "on land already cut off by the sea." The hard realities and the people who must make the best of them will never be the same again.

In what respects the coming age will differ from past ages will depend upon how the battle goes between the forces working for and those working against the intellectual and moral potentialities of men. The most precious thing that has emerged from the wrestling of the centuries —human uniqueness—is everywhere in peril. No friend of man can stand aloof and wait.

There is one bias that so far as possible has been here avoided. It is the bias in favor of the merely wished-for.

Although the undertaking which the present study represents is impelled by a positive interest in a life of happiness and dignity for all so far as this is attainable, it aims to hold itself to rigorous standards of evidence and truth. And it hopes to illustrate the philosophic method. But since it is intended for people who want philosophy to throw light on life as they know it, the ideas presented must have something to say to them. They may not listen. And the author will be accused of debasing a scholarly subject. Both risks must be run.

It would be a pleasure to acknowledge the indebtedness I feel to members of the Department of Philosophy at the University of Wisconsin, to students with whom I have had the privilege of working, authors of books I have read, colleagues and friends with whom I have talked. That pleasure I feel obliged to forego. I must, however, make an exception of Burdette Kinne, whose critical reading of the manuscript has been of unusual help to me.

A bibliography will be found at the end of the book, where I have also availed myself of the opportunity to thank a number of publishers for the privilege of using quotations.

"And being now at some pause," as Francis Bacon said when he had finished a book, "looking back into that I have passed through, this writing seemeth to me (as far as a man can judge of his own work) not much better than the noise or sound which musicians make while they are tuning their instruments; which is nothing pleasant to hear, but yet is a cause why the music is sweeter afterwards."

M.C.O.

CONTENTS

I know of no more encouraging fact than the unquestionable ability of man to elevate his life by conscious endeavor.

Henry Thoreau

Because I believe in the power of the truth and the spirit, I have faith in the future of mankind.

Albert Schweitzer

To take an interest in humanity and its fortunes and to feel that philosophy exists for humanity, that is surely the greatest virtue a philosopher can have.

Dickinson S. Miller

Let us cherish the domain we have received from the hands of Nature, and in using it for our collective enjoyment manage it wisely and damage it as little as possible. Let us study the pages of its story. Let us sense its romance. And finally, let us receive its benediction!

Harlean James

But for democracy there is no choice. It stands or falls by its faith in the common man. This faith is the only basis on which it can undertake to remold the sorry scheme of things so as to make it conform more nearly to the heart's desire.

B. H. Bode

The submergence of self in the pursuit of an ideal, the readiness to spend oneself without measure, prodigally, almost ecstatically, for something intuitively apprehended as great and noble, spend oneself one knows not why—some of us like to believe that this is what religion means.

Benjamin N. Cardozo

A MEDITATION

i

It was a Sunday afternoon and I had climbed a hill to get a view of the surrounding country. From the base of the hill stretched a strip of oak wood, the billowy tree tops motionless in the mild September sun. Below the wood flowed a broad, greenish-blue river. Across the river a village was visible, almost hidden by maples and elms, and beyond the village a countryside of green and brown, with here and there a white farmhouse and a red barn, stretched away to plum-colored bluffs and to a rim of bright cumulous clouds banked behind them. Now and again an acorn dropped to the ground or the faint cawing of crows drifted up from the valley. A chipmunk coming to inspect scolded under his breath. The downy wood-pecker busy overhead tapped softly. Even the noisy blue-jay, flying back and forth as if bossing the whole affair, seemed to moderate his strident call. And all afternoon the cloud banks lingered on the horizon as if becalmed there.

Seated on this hill, it was easy to indulge a languid half

attention and to mistake this dreamy state of mind for a profound intuition, the intuition of an all-comprising unity behind the landscape's palpable diversity. Awareness of the interrelation of things there certainly was. It was not, however, the mystic's sense of absorption in Ultimate Being, nor was it an excursion into the intellectually simplified world of the scientist. It was more like that feeling with which we are all acquainted when everything seems strangely of one piece. It was a plain man's perception of a unity within and through the rolling expanse spread out from hill to horizon and beyond. For in the experience of the plain man it is heightened awareness, not forgetfulness, of the world and its abundant life which lifts him out of provinciality into perspective. At such times he senses the presence of something vaster, profounder, more ultimate than he deals with in his workaday contacts. As I looked from this hilltop, responsive to the quiet yet animated scene, it appeared obvious that in direct experiences of this kind man touches metaphysical bottom.

Metaphysical bottom? How easy to make big phrases. Is there a metaphysical bottom? Is there a type of reality which may be taken as ultimate, which may be regarded as existing beyond all experience, or as superior to every other kind within the range of experience? Men who busy themselves with such matters talk as if there were. When reckless, they tell you what it is. When circumspect, they quietly take it for granted and merely indicate the steps or stages whereby the thinker may assure himself that he is progressing thitherward.

The thing itself, however, the thing the reckless declare and the timid hint at, has a way of eluding all specifications. Forever it vanishes behind a not-yet.

Psychologically it is understandable why man should rim his thought with an ultimate horizon and misconstrue his own limitation as the ontological terminus of the round of things. But, well considered, what valid reason is there for believing in the existence of some one type of being, some one kind of substance or energy behind or in and through everything? The deepest ocean rests on a bottom, though it has not been sounded; the highest mountain rises to a peak, though no human foot has stood there; but reality, ostensibly sounded and scaled again and again, may well be without bottom or summit. The "universe is wild," as Benjamin Blood once said, "game-flavored as a hawk's wing." Its stuff is rangy.

ii

This is said, let us remember, out of doors, and in the mood of common sense. Ordinarily we snub the lusty world that challenges us every day and all day long. We welcome instead the bloodless apparition which careful training has taught us to prefer. Out of doors it is more difficult to deny audience to the world in its immediate aspect. In childhood, objects were discoveries; they were graphic, vivid presences. But children are soon cured of this whimsy. They are conditioned to respond to things as signals for action, so that objects gradually cease to be appreciated for what they are. This is called education.

Growth in the ability to react quickly to things as signals proves to be of great practical advantage, which explains why the adult is habituated to respond automatically, or with a minimum of awareness, even to the more striking objects of his surroundings. Much time is thereby saved; and since most people believe, as Edison did, that time is the only capital no one can afford to lose, and, with the rest of their fellows, that the best investment of time is in action, they are satisfied to increase the quantity of the investment without examining too carefully into the quality of the return.

Thus it comes about that, judged in terms of appreciation, few adults live in a world of objects. They live in a world where objects are taken for granted, where people act as if there were objects. In the presence of a gorgeous and inexhaustible pageant, men and women are coerced by "practical" considerations into acting as if it were the height of intelligence not to look or listen.

If we wish to remain alive, practicality cannot be dispensed with. Nevertheless the initial step in seeking a profounder acquaintance with the world is to turn back toward an innocence unwittingly bartered away. A curious mortal will take himself to school to his physical environment. He will seek to cure his blindness to the wealth of color and form with which he is surrounded. He will try to hear the enticing sounds inaudible in the workaday clatter and to sniff the news borne on the winds. Over these avenues he will make his initial excursion into philosophy. In a library the suggestion would appear heretical, if not idiotic. In the open air nothing could seem more orthodox or sane. And to get a sense of direction

he will not begin by attempting some prominent land-
mark of speculation, Berkeley or Kant or Plato. Even less
will he rely upon some academic guide to help him master
these famous peaks of philosophic tradition. He will begin
with men at home in lower altitudes, eager spirits sensitive
to the forms and moods of nature—Henry Thoreau, W.
H. Hudson, William Brewster, Henry Beston, Richard
Perry, or others like them.

iii

But we have chosen to meditate on a hilltop, and on
a hilltop the landscape is a disk cut out of a larger zone.
The winding river, which ends suddenly against a sloping
green pasture to the northeast and at a purple-brown sand
bar in the southwest, is not actually cut off at these seeming termini. Since I have tramped miles upstream to an
ancient ford of the Indians, and miles down in the other
direction to a little city once the haven of German revo-
lutionists, my acquaintance with the river is able to step
across the boundaries now set by my eyes. And the river
itself, I happen to know, does better. It glides majestically
beyond the borders of my personal acquaintance. Far in
the north it takes its rise, flows through forests of pine,
slips through marshes and meadows, skirts the habitations
of men and, greeting this hill in passing, searches out the
Mississippi and thence finds its way to the Gulf of Mexico.
"And leagues beyond these leagues," as Bacon said, "there
is always more sea."

This suggests a problem which cannot be limited to
what is seen with the physical eye. Possibly it takes us at

last to Berkeley or Kant or Plato. Indeed much farther. The little hemisphere which any man's momentary experience comprises, the spatial circle he wears like a hoop skirt from place to place, expands, as he thinks of it, into a larger and then a larger one, until his thought is adrift in a cosmos stretching away to infinity. There in that vast sea of space lie universes like shimmering misty islands, farther and farther out, until the eye of the most powerful telescope falls short. And the segment, whatever it may be which confronts a man, is always in one way or another continuous with the limitless ocean of being.

Nor does knowledge extend only outward beyond the horizon of visibility. The process may be reversed. One may turn from the outward range of experience and concentrate upon the minutest spot. One may look with the intensity of the miscroscope. New realms of existence are disclosed, layer below layer, curious in texture and curiously alive. Under the surface of ordinary perception are these ordinarily invisible foundations, as successive tiers of populated basements and cellars support the skyline of New York.

When telescopes and microscopes have done their utmost, the eye of the mind takes up the task. For the moment it detects, as ultimate in the nature of things, minute systems of interdependent forces, each one of which, although incomparably small, is architecturally analogous to a solar system, illustrating, in its infinitesimal scale, orbital motions like those of celestial bodies.

In this subatomic world physical science immerses us.

We eat and drink universes. We displace universes with every breath we draw, with every step we take. Engaged in making a living, absorbed in love or hate, surrendered to the pursuit of pleasure or success, we ignore the hidden floors upon which the stage of our daily performance rests. But meditation entails responsibilities which action can avoid. Begin where we may, meditation pushes on to dizzy heights, to fearful depths, to breath-taking horizons.

iv

Does this sum up the baffling character of the data? Is there not an aspect of the world spread out from river to bluffs which we have so far neglected, but which must be included in the survey, although it multiplies and complicates the facts? What of the human beings who people that world and whose failures and successes make up the drama of life? They are part of the problem, possibly the most difficult part, the part that is hardest to study with reasonable freedom from prejudice.

Yes, men and women help to make up the puzzle and add to the difficulty of solving it. Under their hands the world, already baffling in its natural state, becomes more baffling. Even humble men and women are impressive by virtue of the means they devise for laying siege to things they find alluring. What is any village or village life but the materialization of their devices? And if we push our thought beyond villages to the measure of towns, of metropolitan cities, of the earth, these devices take on enormous proportions. Millions of lives become implicated in them, intricate patterns of routine occupation arise, acts and thoughts are dominated by a man-made order of things, almost as if by physical nature.

Buildings, mechanical power, institutional machinery, all contrived by human art and in that sense artificial, constitute a complex of powerful forces operating objectively over against men, threatening defeat if disregarded and holding out prizes to those who obey. It is not physical nature alone to which man must adjust himself and which he must master as he is able; it is not only in contrast with the noble house in which he labors for a day and lodges for a night that man seems puny and insignificant. He is dwarfed and overawed by institutions which he has himself set up in the lap of nature—the world of business and commerce, systems of economic affairs, industrial, political, professional organizations, and many similar fields of action.

No person can escape living in some relation to this man-made environment or free himself completely from interest in the objects and transactions, the losses and gains, native thereto. He is fortunate if he is not drawn altogether within the circle of its influence, if the world of his daily occupation does not completely determine his activities, shape his mind, and command his heart.

v

More imperious than the means men devise as instruments of their desires are the desires themselves. The art of living would be simpler than it is if men and women had to reckon only with physical nature and institutional machinery. They have to reckon with more. The supreme

fact in a biography is inner, not outer. It is the story of
how desires channel their way through the natural and
social environment and thus set the current of life. Some
persons are at the mercy of acquisitive impulse. Some give
up everything else to preserve their moral integrity. Some
who were frustrated in an elemental hunger are ruled by
a passion similarly to starve mankind. Some are busy pla-
cating ghosts, ghosts of yesterday or ghosts of tomorrow.
Some live in the enjoyment of beauty, in the play of the
mind, in the exercise of power.

So in all hamlets and towns and cities men and women
make terms with desires. We speak of mere desires, as if
they were phantoms, as if one had only to snap one's
fingers to see them vanish. Life is more honest than
speech. It acknowledges desires to be stubborn powers,
powers which play the title role in every human drama.
Although subjective in essence, desires may prove to be
as resistless as the most powerful external forces, lifting a
man to glory or hurling him to disgrace. They fashion men
into saints, they lead them to achievements of incredible
sublimity, they turn them into brutes. The greater number
they persuade to plod faithfully through an existence which
forever promises and rarely fulfills. Desires are the allies of
destiny.

In carrying out tasks at hand few people are downright
failures. We have no reason to be ashamed of our ability
to visualize nearer goals, or of our effectiveness in over-
coming obstacles that lie directly in the way. We may
well be proud of our accomplishments in science, tech-
nology, art, business, and in the instruments of law and

government. The person must be soulless whose speech does not become lyrical, whose emotions do not break through the reserve of intellectual propriety, when he contemplates things done by man—the great cities he builds and operates, the long furrow he turns, the machines he sets in motion over the land, the ships he makes to ride the sea and the air. As exploiter of nature and creator of all that this requires, man has shown himself bold, resourceful, tireless.

This is the hopeful aspect. There is another. The more a thoughtful observer is inspired by the magnitude of these achievements, the more poignant may be his apprehension as he contemplates the total scene. If he asks in what larger program these specific activities have their place, or what great human end is to be served by the feverish activity everywhere conspicuous, the answer is not reassuring. There is no such program. There is no awareness of a great end. Men have lost faith in taking life comprehensively. The great maps of life are gone, as the life is gone which they charted, and the interests which now engage mankind have no place in a larger human venture. At the entrance to the village across the river, at the great ports of our country east and west, we should, were we to tell the truth, set up a sign with this message upon it —unless we should paint it on a giant dirigible as a world advertisement: "Wanted! A Philosophy of Life."

vi

So we are led to think of the philosophers. How are they responding to this need for a philosophy of life? Not so well. Something depends upon the philosopher selected, but certain generalizations can be made. We may arrive at them by way of examples.

"It seems to me," says a distinguished contemporary philosopher, and in a manner thoroughly typical, "it seems to me that I am now sitting in a chair, at a table of a certain shape, on which I see sheets of paper with writing or print. By turning my head I see out of the window buildings and clouds and the sun. I believe that, if any other normal person comes into my room, he will see the same chairs and tables and books and papers as I see, and that the table which I see is the same as the table which I feel pressing against my arm."

This philosopher then proceeds to show that all this is an error, to be corrected by philosophical reflection. We cannot call any particular color *the* color of the table, since it is of different colors from different points of view and under different illuminations. In the dark it is quite without color. For a similar reason we cannot call any shape *the* shape, nor any quality whatever *the* quality of the table. What we have before us when we deal with a table is not a table at all, but a complex of "sense data." And lest the reader fall into a second error, he is cautioned against thinking that "the table *is* the sense data or even that the sense data are directly properties of the table."

The plain truth is, according to this philosopher, that we do not see or hear or touch reality at all, only *appearances*. These appearances may indeed be signs of some reality behind them, but there is nothing on the face of an appearance to bear witness to a reality which it reports or even to suggest that it reports any. "Thus our familiar table," he nonchalantly concludes, "which has roused but the slightest thoughts in us hitherto, has become a problem full of surprising possibilities. The one thing we know about it is that it is not what it seems."

A well-known maiden was of a similar mind, though, not being a philosopher, she mixed her skepticism with unphilosophic humor. She sang her doubts, you remember, in these words:

> Things are seldom what they seem!
> Skim milk masquerades as cream;
> Highlows pass as patent leathers;
> Jackdaws strut in peacock's feathers.
>   Very true,
>   So they do.

There is indeed a kind of humor in the philosopher's own contention. The disintegrating analysis which he practices on the table may, as he argues, be extended to the buildings, the clouds, and the sun visible through the study window. It must therefore be applicable to the chair in which he sits. But in that case he does away with himself. For if the chair goes, he goes. Even a philosopher cannot remain seated when his chair is snatched from under him. The floor which stops his fall may be only an appearance, and the part of him that lands there may be only another appearance, but this will hardly save the appearances for the philosopher, since it saves nothing of him *but* appearances. And when a philosopher has himself suffered the indignity of being reduced to a collection of appearances, the one thing we know about him is that he is not what he seems. He can no longer philosophize tables, buildings, and clouds out of existence. Nor himself. The question therefore arises, "Where do we go from here?" And the answer is, "Certainly not toward a philosophy of life."

vii

Obviously these casual remarks, although pertinent, are not a scholarly critique of a philosophic position. They do not aspire to be. They are meant to suggest why it is that the philosophy of the schools is so generally ignored by healthy common sense. Would a man lost in the woods find his way out by thinking of the trees as not real things at all, only an aggregation of appearances? No person in his senses would believe so. Which shows, perhaps, why problems and solutions that further the profession of philosophy may be nonsense in the conduct of living.

Nonsense in the conduct of living—yet there is no denying that a great many people feel a strong preference for just this kind of metaphysical theory. It appeals to many persons because of the cruel circumstances of their lives. If they can tell themselves that life is after all only an illusion and that all they look upon is a tracery of mythical figures behind which reality is concealed as behind a curtain, things may seem a little less irrational, a little less cruel.

And it appeals to men and women whose interest in the fate of their fellows is of a vague, mild sort, or who are without any such interest at all. So long as they can themselves live in comfort, they are not disturbed by conditions which make life a tragedy for others. Social problems, however, may threaten their peace of mind. Then preoccupation with "higher thought," with a "philosophy" that converts disturbing matters into mere appearances, provides a respectable way of escape. If one enjoys the correct relation to reality, why bother about appearances?

Still other persons revel in "the problematic thrill." They get a peculiar satisfaction from verbal familiarity with intellectual enigmas which they can regard as too deep for the common run of men.

And there are people who luxuriate in an atmosphere of the mysterious or the spectral for its own sake. In short, large numbers of human beings have one reason or another for denying the reality of this or that aspect of empirical experience. A philosophy which helps them to transform the world they see and touch into a stupendous fairy tale is a source of relief, frequently of inspiration.

What makes these fictions seem plausible? Language helps. Some people are not disturbed so long as their words hold out. In this case they put the burden on phrases like "mental fragment," "partial aspect," "point of view." If a man is not too critical these phrases will do the trick. But what if a man is not satisfied with verbal solutions? Well, in that case, the explanation will be unsatisfactory. An "aspect" or "fragment" cannot be used as a means of explanation and then conveniently forgotten; it too must be explained and in terms of whatever is called real.

This fact is not by any means sufficiently appreciated.

If a thing appears it must appear in or to something that is not itself an appearance, and so must partake of that something's reality. When "mortal mind," to take an example, is used to account for "error," it must have some status in reality. For if "mortal mind" is itself a species of error or unreality, how can it be employed as a valid means of explanation? Are we to think of "mortal mind" as the error of another "mortal mind," and so down the line to infinity? On the other hand, if "mortal mind" is to be regarded as real, then whatever view of experience it gives rise to must share in that reality.

Merely refusing to call a reality by its appropriate name, calling it an appearance instead, makes no difference to reality. Reality is not thin-skinned. It does, however, make a difference to the one who thereby deceives himself as to the nature of the world in which he lives. Repugnant aspects of life do not disappear because they are ignored. Cruelty, injustice, degrading environments continue their devastating work even if they are denied the dignity of being real. And everything a man can turn to for help in distress, everything he can set his hope of joy upon, everything he can select to improve himself or add to the happiness of others, has no better claim to reality than the aspects of experience which cause him to stumble or to go down in defeat. In the end men and women are badly served by a theory, whether in a scholarly or a popular form, which furthers the delusion that we see more deeply into reality as we turn away from the objects and thoughts and feelings of our daily experience. It is these which constitute the stuff of reality.

viii

Quite as notorious as the philosopher's reduction of the world to myth, is his insatiable yearning for all-inclusive knowledge. "There is in all men," Mr. Justice Holmes once said, "a demand for the superlative, so much so that the poor devil who has no other way of reaching it attains it by getting drunk." This demand, he thought, is at the bottom of the philosopher's quest for absoluteness. And he was right. Many are the cases of philosophic inebriation which this thirst has resulted in.

It seems obvious to many philosophers that any partial view must, by the very fact of its fragmentariness, distort, rather than report, reality. The august term, reality, so they hold, may in strictness refer only to the totality of things. Individual objects may by courtesy be called real, but speaking with logical exactness, the term must be reserved for the all-including Something from which larger or smaller fragments borrow a contingent appearance. Anything falling short of this absolute totality must be regarded as mythical and thus as in direct contrast to the real. Ever since Plato published his now famous definition, if not before, the philosopher has been ambitious to be "a spectator of all time and all existence." He has wanted, with Spinoza, to contemplate the finite under the aspect of the infinite. Even thinkers of lesser magnitude, whom George Santayana refers to as "those little gnostics," have aimed to become what he ironically calls them, "circumnavigators of being."

Do they accomplish the undertaking? Scarcely. No philosopher's eye has yet envisaged what William James termed "the whole paradoxical physico-moral-spiritual Fatness." To this year of our Lord, and notwithstanding strenuous attempts to visit all kingdoms, and to touch "the outskirts and suburbs of things," the sea of multiple fact rolls majestically over the rim of every philosophic chart.

In this surprising? How can it be? Every sailor, no matter how daring, is wrapped in his shroud and buried in the vast expanse when he has made but a brave beginning in his voyage of exploration. How can we expect that his log shall elucidate the mystery of the sea? Whatever fault may be found with the philosopher, it cannot be that he does not report upon the totality of the experienceable. If he sometimes talks as if this were his intention, it only proves that he is human and can take himself too seriously.

In any case, the philosophical systems that lay claim to all-inclusiveness are not remarkable for what they include, but for how much they leave out. People who come to them for knowledge of the world or of life are rarely impressed by the richness and substance of what they are offered. They are surprised by its meagerness and unsubstantiality. Too often all that is nutritious, exciting, or important in life is found to be missing, while that which is put forward as supremely real seems nebulous or fanciful. The world of the philosopher is found to be a highly specialized way of regarding things, a pale apparition of the world's substance.

Even were a philosopher able to accomplish the impossible feat of observing from no particular station, it would not help the men and women in the village across the river, or men and women anywhere, in the conduct of their lives. Let us assume a person to be relieved from specific organs of knowledge and freed from the bias of time and place. Would he then be qualified to give a true report of reality? It is tempting to think so. Tennyson, not of the profession, but a philosopher in his way and speaking in the philosophic manner, is believed to have neatly proved the case in the poem known to everyone. If he could understand the flower in the crannied wall, so he writes, root and all, and all in all, he would understand man and God and everything!

Would he indeed? Or would he know nothing whatsoever? Cusanus, sailing in the Aegean five centuries ago, asked himself this question and answered it in a way that still holds good. A man can know only when he does not know everything. A flower really known "root and all, and all in all," in a manner involving everything else, would cease to be known as a flower. All other things too—crannied wall, man, God—would merge into one another and lose their individual identity to such an extent that they would no longer be objects of knowledge. Knowledge would consequently cease.

There are psychic states, empty of all describable content because the boundaries essential to knowing have fallen away, which are said to leave behind them an overwhelming sense of one's having been caught up and absorbed in the profoundest and completest reality. And this sense of having been thus dissolved into the unified whole of things may, as a rapturous experience, be forever desired once its savor has been tasted. This does not show that knowledge is possible in the absence of distinguishable objects, for the experience is one of ecstasy, not of knowing. The mystics who claim access to reality by virtue of mystical raptures are the very ones who insist that this is utterly different from knowledge; so much so that they speak of it as ineffable, as unstatable in words, which are the unavoidable media of knowledge.

At any rate, the plain man is interested and must be interested in knowledge of the kind of reality with which he must come to grips in his daily life. It is there that he needs to feel solid ground under his feet. The world in which he must work his way is always a limited world, and his knowledge of even that limited world is always limited. If the mere fact of limitation is evidence of error he cannot make sense of things. Left to himself he is apt to feel, perhaps vaguely, but rightly, that some corner must be found in reality for everything that enters into human life and into which human life enters. Otherwise how is he to account for the events of his experience? They occur. They confront him. He has to deal with them, make his choices, and take the consequences.

What the plain man needs to know is where he may step with safety and where not. Of course if he thinks about life, his own life and other lives, this will lead him sooner or later to the problem of what real safety is, or to say the same thing in different words, what it is that is most worth saving. This, however, does not relieve him from acting in a limited environment or from depending upon incomplete knowledge to guide him. He must choose from among imperfect, transitory goods, must reject evils that are not perfect in their evil character, and make his way from one fragment of experience to another, toward that which is relatively more, rather than relatively less, desirable. There is simply nothing whatever to the notion that to understand anything it must be understood in a setting of everything.

ix

The theme has wandered far from the hilltop, but in the open we are not permitted to remain long unconscious of the widespreading earth. A moment ago the evening mail plane came into view above the skyline. With incredible speed it moved across the valley, disappeared, and rapidly droned its way to silence. How beautiful the countryside must appear from the air in the warm colors of the lowering sun! Who would not wish to see it spread out like a great map below him? This wish fulfilled, does a man then regard the simplified pattern he sees as the truest picture of the landscape? Does he announce that nothing which is invisible from his elevation really exists? Does he suggest that those on their feet walk among "mere appearances"; that to approach "reality" they must go higher and higher until every feature of ordinary experience has been left behind?

Says Captain Stevens, describing what he saw from eleven miles in the air: "Below us was the brown, sunbaked earth, so far away that no roads, railroads, or houses could be made out." Did he conclude from this that the only true view is the view from the stratosphere? The idea never occurred to him. When people look from balloons and aeroplanes they do not pretend to abolish the view from the ground. They believe themselves to have expanded it into the heretofore unknown. Things seen from the air and from the ground interpenetrate and enrich each other. The experienceable world gets the quality of both aspects. The "sky-infected mood," as Christopher Morley has called it, does not take away from, but adds to, "the beauty and strangeness of the globe herself," and to the significance and mystery of mankind in search of happiness.

Except for philosophers. This is a third way in which they fail the common man. Having mounted above the earth, the philosopher swears that heretofore he was blind and that he will not be blind hereafter. Between flights he treasures the memory of what he saw, and so, flying and remembering, he labors to master the pattern of things as they appear to him in the air.

Just now the favored pattern is that of mathematical physics. The philosopher who turns in this direction seeks truth in a system of abstract entities. The new objects of contemplation thus gained, and the intensified intellectual discipline thus demanded, have in some instances vitalized the philosophic atmosphere. Possibly great conceptual feats will be performed by philosophers who concentrate on the construction of a universe as a free design responsible only to mathematical intuition.

Yet the view from the ground remains and remains imperative. Any number of problems can be mastered only in concrete form. Desirable as it is that man's powers of abstract thinking be developed, since its successful practice makes for the happiness of him who does it, and since the intellectual results obtained can sometimes be put to common use, abstract thinking in no way assures a wise and happy course in life. It is individual human beings with characteristics peculiar to themselves, with noninterchangeable interests at stake, who are in need of wisdom in dealing with events, objects, perceptions, feelings, ideas, and ideals in their experienced particularity. How can this wisdom be looked for from a type of reasoning which intentionally disregards those forms of experience? The philosophic technique which models itself on that of mathematical physics advertises its detachment from the effort of mankind to increase the general welfare.

X

So the matter comes to this. As professional philosophers we are not interested in the world spread out before men's eyes. The visible world provides us with the springboard from which we dive into the world invisible, whence we now and again bob up to recover our breath. Or, to use a less athletic metaphor as more becoming to philosophers, we look upon the world of daily experience as a dim vestibule to bright halls of true being. To these we press forward. As we proceed we become absorbed in the technical and abstract; everyday interests and needs are forgotten; everyday objects and values drop from our attention or fade into the background as unworthy of concern.

Is this unavoidable? If it is, then men and women who

have a life to live and who have faith that something may be made of it if they take thought, will do well not to break their heads over philosophy. They will do better to rely upon their own native idealism and practical good sense. Their neglect of philosophy may be a pity, but after all what else is there left for them to do? They cannot be expected to deny the reality of the familiar world about them, the world they discovered in childhood and explored in youth, in which men plow and dig and build, in which winds blow, rains fall, and seasons revolve. This must be for them—for all of us—the world of primary reality. From it under sun, moon, and stars all knowing draws its raw material and thither all knowers sooner or later return to try their conclusions.

Early men lived in that world solely, and it retains its experiential primacy for those who call themselves civilized. Impressions received there, settling into the depths of the psyche, form the leaf mold out of which ideas sprout and by which they are nourished. It is thence, as Emerson said, that the originals of language are drawn and first lessons in relating thinking to fact. Taking hold upon it with muscle and with brain, man has built other worlds or laid them bare. All these are rearrangements, extensions, or refinements of the world originally come upon.

Thought worlds and other man-contrived worlds are marvelous achievements, never to be too greatly admired in their true character; but they no more annul the source out of which they developed than the birth of a child proves the nonexistence of the mother. In this primary world men willy-nilly must live out their lives. There they suffer and are defeated or find a way to victory and joy. And it is precisely there they cannot get along without those "far-flashing beams of light," to use William James's words, which he believed philosophy "sends over the world's perspectives."

They cannot, that is, unless they must. If they must, they can and they will. *For the ultimate prestige belongs to life, not to philosophy.* Men and women will manage to live, even live to a purpose, whatever philosophers interest themselves in. After all, of what advantage to men is a theoretically luminous universe if in their daily lives they must stumble on without light? What has been gained for mankind when the scholar has pictured the harmony, perfection, and beauty of the cosmos, if on our planet millions of human beings must continue to endure squalor, poverty, and strife? Of what human significance is it to win freedom for atoms or electrons if Sacco and Vanzetti move inexorably to death and millions cannot escape from unemployment and poverty?

Or is the hunger of a thinker for intellectual triumph of such worth that the hunger of men and women for a life that tastes good is as nothing in comparison? Possibly. And if it is true that Nero fiddled while Rome burned, possibly he too was justified if his technique was flawless and the music noble.

xi

The conclusion is that we are without any larger ideal of human living, and that without it the details of our lives tend to become ugly, insignificant, and disappointing. Nor can we expect help from philosophers so long as they are indifferent to the nearer goals that are steppingstones to more distant ones. If a reader happens anywhere upon a remark such as this in *Stamboul Nights*—"But the fillip of life, for me, is in the small permutations and combinations of incident that make up the lives of us all"—he may safely conclude that it is not the remark of a philosopher. It was not a philosopher, but Eugene Debs, who said: "While there is a lower class, I am in it: while there is a soul in prison, I am not free."

Must this then be our final word? Is philosophy necessarily esoteric, "designed for, and understood by, the specially initiated alone"? If so, where and how shall the uninitiated attain a philosophy of life?

How naturally these questions lead to William James. For it was he who inaugurated the contemporary movement which would transform philosophy from a tangential influence into a powerful social instrument. It was his aim to do this by changing philosophy from a sense of having arrived in a realm beyond life into a method of direction in the midst of life. The issues made controversial by him were the projection into philosophy of problems actually encountered and recognized as vital by men and women in the venture of living. It is the flesh and blood of things, not their skin and bones merely, which come to expression in his writings.

The contribution made by William James needs to be insisted upon less in the interest of his reputation, which will take care of itself, than in the interest of mankind, whom his philosophic innovation deeply concerns. The lesson which he taught was that philosophy is not solely, nor even primarily, a set of views. Had he offered no more than another schematic picture of the cosmos and another abstract formula of life, "sublime in its blankness," to speak in his own words, we might, as L. P. Jacks remarks, regard the situation with equanimity. "But the change demanded by William James and his sympathizers," Mr. Jacks goes on to say, "is much more vitally near to us than any fresh formulation of the secret of the universe. It amounts to the introduction of a new temper into the whole business of speculative thought, and indirectly into the whole business of practical life. It strikes a new keynote for human experience as a whole." William James turned *toward* men and their needs. He *trusted* their temperaments and desires. He taught that wherever men *struggled and failed or triumphed* was exactly where they touched reality most deeply. Because he taught this, in deed was this, his figure rises before us in these confusing times.

When the whole intellectual and social climate had changed, making the problem of cultural orientation more vast, complex, and urgent, a philosopher of similar temper grew to power whose distinguished leadership has continued to the present. How did John Dewey become the liberalizing force in American life which he is acknowledged to be? He took his own admonition to heart, and changed philosophy from "a device for dealing with problems of philosophy," into "a method, cultivated by phi-

losophers, for dealing with the problems of men." The
sheer mass of his output has silenced those who can be
convinced in no other way. In the eyes of those who are
alive to the growth of philosophic thinking, he has long
ago assumed a place of leadership among the thinkers of
history.

Critics will have their say. The years will outsay them.
The philosophic revolution for which William James and
John Dewey are responsible belongs to the great creative
heritages of mankind. It will be reckoned with until men
no longer ponder the meaning of human existence because their hearts no longer beat.

xii

In the luggage that pioneers take with them on the
journey are memories and habits and attachments acquired in the home from which they set out. Their children, lured by horizons that lie farther along the trail,
find it easier to detach themselves from traditional modes
of living as they seek to overcome the crudity of the surroundings where they settle down. It was indeed a momentous step when William James and John Dewey gave
up all claims to knowledge of ultimate or universal reality; when they decided to rely on a relative and growing
conception of the human scene in its natural setting. One
intimate contact with traditional philosophy, however,
William James and John Dewey did not break. They retained for the philosopher his ostensible pre-eminence in
the domain of ideals. Despite the profoundly changed re-

lation which they aimed to set up between ideals and reality, they left the philosopher enthroned in the domain of value as monarch of all man surveys.

The breaking of that tie with the past is the radical step which is still to be taken. As the advance of the right foot draws after it the advance of the left, so the relinquishment of supremacy in knowledge of reality draws after it the relinquishment of final authority as to the best life to live. The two go inseparably together. Philosophers must be brought on a par with other thinkers who seek to improve man's chances of making the best that is possible of life.

To accomplish this end without sacrificing high standards of workmanship and philosophic range of vision is difficult, yet in some form it is the predicament of everyone. Everyone must make the most of his possibilities through living and working with other people bent on making the most of theirs. How to do a unique kind of work and enjoy life according to one's own tastes and in this way to attain to genuine selfhood, and how, in doing this, to contribute one's share toward the realization of the like ambition of others, that is exactly the human problem.

We are thus brought back to the questions with which our meditation ended. Is philosophy necessarily esoteric? If so, where and how shall the uninitiated attain a philosophy of life?

But the sun has set. Soon the countryside will lie in darkness. A mist will creep into the fields along the river. Pungent odors will scent the cool night air. Whippoorwills will call, owls will hoot, foxes, badgers, skunks, minks, weasels, racoons, all the creatures that hide by day will come forth and enact their nocturnal dramas. Constellations will move across the sky, Pegasus, Andromeda, fiery-eyed Taurus with the Pleiades on his shoulder, and, toward morning, brilliant Orion.

Meanwhile the village will sleep, freed for a time from ambitions and strivings and in no need of a way of life. We too shall put off further thought of philosophy until another day.

❧ II ❧

PHILOSOPHY AND SHIRT SLEEVES

Two questions were left when approaching darkness brought the meditation of the preceding chapter to end. They were these: Is philosophy necessarily esoteric, "designed for, and understood by, the specially initiated alone"? If so, where and how shall the uninitiated attain a philosophy of life?

Since our purpose is not merely to describe conditions but to do something to improve conditions, we must consider what resources there are to draw upon. One of these is easily overlooked. It is the moral and intellectual attainment of normal human beings. Few of them know anything about technical philosophy or care to know anything about it. Only a few more acquire an outlook sufficiently comprehensive or coherent to be called philosophical in any strictness of meaning. Most men and women however do accumulate a collection of ideas which, taken together, constitute an interpretation of the world and a theory of life. The chapter now before us is an attempt to look into this home-grown philosophy.

i

We begin where the philosophy begins which we are
to study—in a segment of the world and its ongoing life.
No segment is too small if it includes a human being, and
one human being will do about as well as another.

This morning a man was seated on a log at the swampy
margin of a lake. Let us begin with him. The ground was
moist under his feet and yellow with buttercups. Cattail
reeds stood ankle-deep in water. A bittern thumped mys-
teriously from the tall grasses. The rumble of distant street
traffic was just audible. Now and again an automobile rat-
tled over an invisible bridge. Far off the factory whistles
announced that it was seven o'clock.

The man arose, bethinking himself of breakfast. The
smell of coffee was already in his nostrils. He took a last
look about him. He noted the wind blowing from the
southwest, and he wondered what the weather would be.
Out on the lake he saw a fisherman casting for pickerel. A
few herring gulls, not yet departed for larger waters, floated
between lake and sky. Tree swallows skimmed over the
pond lilies, almost touching them, and a pair of black
terns beat back and forth on wings that seemed tireless.
He remembered that someone had called terns the swans
of the air.

A step or two, a movement of the head, and this scene
was shut out. But another had replaced it; another assemblage of objects had arranged itself about him—things,
animals, people. Now he faced a row of houses. A dog
had just bounded out of a front door and was attentively

sniffing the air. An Italian workman with a cigarette hanging from his lips was coming along the sidewalk. A milk wagon was moving slowly down the middle of the street.

As the man saw all this he vaguely wished for the dog's sense of smell. He greeted the passing Italian and wondered what kind of a home he had left behind and what he thought of life. He recalled how a few days ago a friend had vigorously denounced all milkmen for "hogging the middle of the road."

No matter how often the man might turn or how far he might walk there would always be something to see, something to remember, something to wish for, something to wonder at. He might have mountains and forests or desks and typewriters; books and pictures, or kettles and pans; he might look upon fields or streets, the sea or the sky, the living or the dead; what he could never do is escape from a round of things experienced in this direct, immediately present way.

ii

There was a period in each of our lives when we did not take account of the complex world known to the adult. As an object of our personal awareness it had no existence. But it existed for other people who were on hand before us. They received us into their world and incorporated it into our dawning awareness. What we, the newcomers did, what we then felt and thought, and so what we became, would have been very different, assuming that we could have remained alive at all, had we not been fitted into an already established arrangement, had

we not been absorbed into an operating world of interrelated things, people, social institutions, and the processes of physical nature.

When each of us first waddled forward on the soles of
his own feet, he merely advanced still farther into the
realms of order which he had ventured upon by being
born. Growing years brought numerous changes, some of
them very profound, but nothing ever lifted us out of a
give-and-take relation with a world. It is surely incorrect
to say, as Julian Huxley does and as many philosophers do,
that the only reality we know immediately is "a chaos of
experience." A chaos of experience is a late and sophisticated conception of "the thinker." It is the theoretical
wreck of experience, not its original living embodiment.
No one starts at the beginning of things or creates an
environing world out of nothing but his own fullness of
being. Everyone emerges out of an ongoing pattern of life
which itself emerged out of another and out of which in
turn other patterns will emerge.

As this is true today, so it has been true in the past. As
it is true of mankind, so it is true of all living creatures and
of every existing thing. No matter how far back we care
to trace human history, whether generations, centuries, or
hundreds of thousands of years, we find that each human
being is born into an environment of people interacting
with each other, with lower forms of life, with physical
things and forces.

Even were we to step over into the animal state, it
would still be true that from the very beginning the individual is adjusted to an outer world and to beings of his

kind and other kinds. So too, if we moved on beyond the organic into the inorganic. Each inorganic thing exists and operates in togetherness with other things. If a mountain, a rock, or an electron attained to consciousness and speech it would talk of objects near at hand, of friends and foes, of cosmic forces and stellar spaces. Nothing is alone and nowhere is there experience of chaos.

iii

The philosophically unsophisticated person takes this familiar world quite for granted. Whatever he does or thinks about, he begins from where he is, in the midst of houses, trees, rivers, seas, clouds, animals, people, and the more distant sun, moon, and heaven of stars. And he begins with these in various sorts of interconnection with each other and with himself. People are building houses and living in them, plowing fields and reaping harvests, fishing in rivers and seas and riding upon them, exploiting insects and battling with them for survival, relying upon helpful occurrences in nature and seeking protection from the catastrophes that cannot be controlled.

In this encompassing world he has friends, perhaps enemies, and besides friends and enemies, numerous acquaintances to warm the edge of encircling strangers. Some persons he seeks out, some he avoids. He has parents on the one side, children on the other. He works for someone and someone works for him. The virtuous and the vicious are his fellows, influencing his career. He is affected in a hundred ways by the comings and goings of men, women, and children, some of whom he knows, most of whom he does not know.

What should make him doubt all this? Why should he question the existence of the social and natural world which coerces, thwarts, sustains him at every step, in which he is so intimately involved, to which he is so inescapably bound? There are moments when the whole business seems utterly without significance, moments when the bottom suddenly drops out of things and all of experience seems strangely like a dream. Normally, however, what everyone does is to accept as the very stuff and measure of actuality the world of things and creatures which he sees when he opens his eyes.

But neither the world nor man is a simple affair. Consequently the life which men and women live cannot be a simple affair. Exposed as human beings are to insistent and varied stimulation, naturally responsive, and capable of multiform behavior, they are sure to become involved in contradictory actions and conflicting interests. This leads to observation and reflection. The environment is scrutinized for clues to successful procedures. Beliefs and feelings are examined, desires are weighed against each other, attitudes are assessed with respect to anticipated results. It turns out that everything is not of the same nature nor of the same reliableness. Effective action is found to depend upon the ability to discriminate between the way things are *actually* and the way they may *seem* to be. Early in life everyone learns that the texture of experience is woven of fact and fiction, and everyone adopts some criterion of distinguishing between the two, at least so far as this is a practical necessity.

iv

Now is there a recognizable first step in the acquisition of this knowledge? Is there a type of fact which is the earliest to be appreciated by the child? Possibly. If there is, what it is remains a secret which the forgetfulness of childhood has refused to disclose. The initial advance against ignorance probably takes place on a number of fronts at once, winning no decisive victory at any one point, but pushing ahead here and there all along the line.

No; we cannot determine with certainty what comes first, but we can make this guess. Bits of information about human nature are probably among the first to be picked up, since so much hangs on the ability of children to detect and deal with the moods and humors of the persons with whom they must get along. The cleverness of children in touching off the foibles of parents and teachers, their shrewdness in circumventing the whims and temperaments of adults, their acute judgments of personality and character, show how early and how inevitably a rough and ready kind of psychological information is a product of the exigencies of life.

Aside from its obvious utility, knowledge of human psychology happens to be fascinating on its own account. For both reasons it grows as a vital interest from childhood on. Gradually through the years, by picking up fragments of information in one place and another, by getting a fact or an idea from a newspaper or a novel, a scrap of theory from a lecture, an idealistic slant on human relations from a sermon and a materialistic slant from business or social contacts, everyone adds to his stock of psychological data until he frames a theory of human nature and becomes after a fashion a psychologist.

This unacademic psychology is often sagacious and wise, and sometimes it is picturesquely expressed, as, for example, by the Wheelhouse Loafer, in the Vineyard Gazette:

People, as a whole, are a great deal like fish. Some are valuable, filled with fine qualities, some are good, but too small to be worth a cuss, and some are just trash and had better be hove over the side. And in amongst 'em all are the sculpins that'll gouge the devil out of you, the Portugee men-o'-war that'll sting you blind and an occasional shark that will gobble you whole if he happens to feel that way.

From the scholar's point of view, that is to say, for teaching or publishing purposes, this homemade psychology may be worthless, but it is an indispensable aid in everyday living. It throws light on what people say and do. Some persons without other training than that which they gain from daily experience become so adept in their judgments of men that knowledge of human psychology almost seems less a matter of learning than of a native turn of mind.

v

As life inevitably makes something of a psychologist of everyone, so it makes everyone something of a moralist.

The newcomer in the world is trained by his elders to form habits considered appropriate. In the order of time, habits of health and cleanliness come first, but even before ordinary language is understood, the child's ears are accustomed to the sound of words that will always remain among the most difficult to define: right, wrong, good, bad, nasty, and others of moral intent. What the psychologists call "conditioned reflexes" are established between such words and the conduct desired.

The indoctrination takes so well that a child that has only recently managed to walk, and is still in the process of learning to talk, will use moral terminology with all the air of an adult, accurately reproducing the adult moral grammar and not infrequently the adult moral intonation. While still so young as to be confined almost entirely to home influences, and without having the slightest notion of what is taking place, every child imbibes a sense of right and wrong and a stock of ready-made judgments on conduct.

The time comes when children pass beyond the confines of the home. They explore the wonders of the street, spend exciting hours on the playground, go to school, are brought under church instruction. Everywhere they bump into rules. Everywhere they must adapt themselves to approvals and disapprovals. They learn what it means to "play fair" or to "cheat," and how it feels to be "isolated" from games or playfellows. They are introduced to the art of leadership. They find that companions can be helped or used. And all this new information seems peculiarly authentic, for children are by instinct naïve realists, ready to accept the busy world of the senses as the real one. Quite automatically the concepts and rules of behavior acquired in the environment beyond the home tend to dominate the expanding outlook.

If at this stage of development all authority over conduct were delegated to the outside world, the lives of children would be greatly simplified. We all know that this does not happen. Home and world exert influence and exercise authority side by side. It is to the clashes which occur between these authorities that children owe a heightened self-interest. They are made aware of interests distinct from the interests of others, especially from those of adults. Often the interests of adults seem not only different, but antagonistic. Logan Pearsall Smith has expressed this mood in a vivid picture:

They sit there forever in the dim horizon of my mind, that Stonehenge of elderly disapproving Faces—Faces of Uncles and Schoolmasters and Tutors who formed my youth.

In the bright center and sunlight I leap, I caper, I dance; but when I look up, I see they are not deceived. For nothing ever placates them, nothing ever moves to a look of approval that ring of bleak, old, contemptuous Faces.

The two schemes of life are not always felt to be so utterly discordant. Still, the pattern of desirable and undesirable behavior has to be rearranged. Choices have to be made between actions which seem right; things have to be done which seem wrong, now from the one standpoint, now from the other; and what is perhaps most important, circumstances entice children beyond the frontier of established habits. As the indoctrinated attitudes and beliefs are put to these tests, conduct becomes problematical. Right and wrong are perforce thought about. The child becomes an embryo moralist.

vi

Moral dilemmas do not vanish with childhood. They grow more complicated and urgent. The effect of early decisions may be far-reaching, may be influential throughout life, nevertheless it is the youth, not the child, who in moral conflict plays marbles for keeps. It goes without saying that the experience is not of the same intensity for all youths. More human beings than we suspect are born morally feeble-minded. And of those who are congenitally sensitive many are made insensitive by extreme material or spiritual poverty. The leaven of hope turns sour within them. The normal ambition to make something of life flattens into indifference or it swells into bizarre or reckless forms of self-seeking.

An appalling number of youths begin a life of crime in their adolescence. They are successful burglars, racketeers, hijackers, gangsters before they are twenty, and incorrigible criminals by the time they have reached their best years. Still larger numbers, who never turn to thieving or strong-arming their way through life, become what they call "realistic," adjusted to the morally ruthless struggle in which, as they say, "dog eats dog" and only a sentimentalist is deterred by humane feeling or social conscience. An enormous quantity of energy is thus poured into human living without regard to its ethical quality or the outcome of the larger human endeavor.

This is not however representative of mankind in general. The next young men or women you are likely to meet as you walk will not be insensible to moral demands. They will make them of themselves and of other people, and they will expect other people to make them in return. We are often advised that this average morality is a cloak full of holes through which animal vulgarity and the brutality of the savage are visible. If this were true, standards of conduct would be more readily put off and on than they are. Nor in that case could the mass of men and women be counted upon to enter co-operatively into the ramifying practical relations which form the material basis of civilized life.

Whatever the behavior code of the average youth may be, it is not a cloak, not something to be put on and off at will. It is an integral component of a living organism's response to his world. And as a rule it includes a willingness to take a hand in the job of preventing everyday conduct from falling to the level of sheer unreflective desire. It bears witness to the presence of a taste, partly instinctive and partly acquired, for the finer kinds of satisfaction.

Moreover, if you walk far enough, you will meet those on the better side of the average, youths of exceptional intelligence and social fervor. They have somehow caught a vision of possible improvements in civilized living and, as they mature, devote their talents to their lifework with something like a great passion. They give luster to any calling, since a calling is not great in itself, but becomes great when greatly pursued.

It is to such idealists that we are chiefly indebted for the rise of man from savagery, and for the recovery of civilization whenever it had been overwhelmed by the return of barbarism. It is upon them that mankind must rely today when the open revolt against civilized ideals has once more broken loose. Older people, battered, de feated, disillusioned, their vitality lowered and their out look colored by a sense of the fewness of the years that remain for the doing of anything, may give up and take programs of life lightly. The young, who are at the begin ning of their careers, cannot but take seriously the prob lem of choosing a mode of life that shall repay the effort put forth.

When these young men and women set out on the high way of life they go with conceptions of right and wrong. This is true in some measure whatever the childhood ex perience has been. They also go with a sense of duty and a desire to put their ideals into practice. Frequently both of these are flickering and wayward purposes, but again they are strong, steady, and intensely sincere. "Out in the world" these habits and beliefs are confronted by counter influences, some of which are direct and aboveboard, oth ers so insidious that their destructive impact may go un noticed until the damage is beyond repair. Unless they are abnormally protected, young men and young women are compelled, and more drastically than children are, to reconsider their ideas of the best course of life to pursue.

Without attending a class in ethics, or opening a book on the subject, the embryo moralist which each one became as a child, matures into a critic of morality and works his way toward a self-conscious theory of ethics.

vii

If this moral ripening is examined, it is seen to have an inner and an outer source, a source in the developing human being and in the enlarging world of experience; or, rather, since the two act in conjunction, the source is in reality one, and it is their expanding interaction. Perhaps a still better statement, in spite of its paradoxical sound, would be that the moral conflict originates in an area lying as it were *between* the human being and the environment, which, however, exists only as their reciprocal interpenetration.

Whatever may be the best form of statement, the facts are clear enough. A widening arena of endeavor and achievement, and a self of increasing complexity of interests, act and react on each other. Latent desires awaken and match their strength against inculcated habits. New ambitions appear, capabilities hitherto unsuspected are called forth, superpersonal projects are taken on, idealistic schemes intrigue the imagination. In other words, interests and activities which were not foreseen, and for which little or no provision was made in early training, assert themselves.

The problem of deciding what to believe and do is aggravated by the discovery of flagrant discrepancies between moral admonition and observed practice. Every youth who has his eyes open and who thinks even a little, undergoes disillusion when he comes into responsible contact with the world of his elders. He learns that cool, self-seeking trickery, and crassly materialistic ambition may win success; that these may be the ruling motives of individuals and groups from whom, if he believed what he had been told, he had a right to expect the most exemplary conduct. He reads or hears about "rackets," about vice, about "breeding places of crime," and finds that frequently they thrive because of the social indifference of the "best people."

He learns that persons of wealth and respectability may owe their privileged status to unscrupulous ancestors. He sees men honored in the community who make it their business to extract all they can from man, beast, and the resources of nature, and to give as little as they can in return. "Law," he reads somewhere, "is like a watchdog that barks only at the man in old clothes," and he wonders whether it is not true. He is forced to admit that there is nothing which someone will not do for money; that "life is cheap"; that money, influential backing, the power to bestow favors, triumph again and again over ability and character. He listens as leading citizens speak slightingly of truthfulness and generosity in human relations. He gets glimpses, sometimes a shocking insight, into sexual hypocrisies, excesses, and abnormalities. All about him and in the wide world it seems to be force, might, power, which rules, not intellect nor character.

Little by little the suspicion grows in him that ethical

conduct does not hold the honored place in personal or community life he had been led to believe. The roots of his moral personality are exposed by the ebb and flow of experience.

If he is one kind of youth he will say, "Well, it's the way of the world; you just have to accept it," and will then do what he can to make good his description. If he is another kind he will take the situation more to heart, as the college student did who wrote these frank words to a former teacher:

> I have tried your theory of life and it doesn't work. Either you are ignorant of what the world is like or—forgive me for blurting it out—you are lying in your teeth. The thing to do if you want to get on in life is to draw the blood from your veins and fill them with ice water, remove your heart and put a cash register in its place, and for the idealizing human brain substitute the cunning brain of a fox. That's the thing to tell college students if you want to tell them the truth.

Tom Corwin put it in this way: "If you would succeed in life you must be solemn—solemn as an ass. All the great monuments are built over solemn asses." Alice Roosevelt Longworth comes to the cynical conclusion with which she sums up Washington life in her book, Crowded Hours: "Anyway, the show is there for us, and we might as well get what entertainment we may out of it." Winifred Holtby burned like a purifying flame to the end, meeting social injustice and degradation in the spirit she ascribed to Virginia Woolf, "as one who looked upon the worst that life can do to man and woman, upon every sensation of loss, bewilderment and humiliation; and yet the corroding acid of disgust has not defiled her."

These are types. In some such way every human being gradually adjusts himself to moral obligation, whether his endowment and background are average or superior. Thereafter many will regard moral idealism as something that is normally outgrown in the course of experience, something which is appropriate and necessary for children, and for adults who remain children in mind, but which only clutters up the road for those who mean to get ahead in the practical world or have a good time in life. There may be twinges of regret that things are as they are, rather than as they once seemed to be, and a verbal morality may linger on after the actuality has ceased to exist which it originally symbolized.

In one spirit or in another, a considerable number of people eventually reach a point where they live and strive for a kind of success that is unhampered by considerations of right and wrong. The older they grow the more they make up their minds that moral idealism is mainly, if not altogether, a form of make-believe. They have adopted a moral theory, such as it is.

The same thing can be said, in a deeper sense, of the men and women who continue to acknowledge moral obligation yet recognize the necessity of reshaping their moral conceptions as they become better acquainted with the world. Their ideas of right and wrong may be liberalized, enriched, and refined, or they may be narrowed and hardened until morality is a question of black or white with no shades of grey between. The direction taken depends upon the individual's endowment of intellect and imagination. A generously conceived moral theory reveals an outgoing, sensitive nature; a rigid morality a repressed, insensitive nature. Hard and fast rules, in their extreme form, scarcely conceal the coarse, brutal impulses which they clothe in noble-sounding phrases and sentiments. Whether inspired by generous or ungenerous impulses, the result is the critical espousal of an ethical creed.

Thus as children, youths, adults move on through the years they settle into established ways of behaving, or, as we say, behaving themselves, and into corresponding ways of passing judgments upon behavior. Deep down inside there may be doubts, or specific situations may arise when no satisfactory solution can be reached; nevertheless decisions and criticisms are based on a more or less inclusive and consistent theory of the right and wrong way to live. Some sort of moral theory is worked out. In the course of time everyone becomes at least an amateur theorist in ethics. And quite a number of persons become considerably more than amateurs.

viii

Possibly nothing seems more remote from men and women in general than a regard for logical thinking, yet life compels them all to take lessons in logic as it does in psychology and ethics. This is true in spite of the prevalence and power of emotional "drives." Persons like Dotty, in Elizabeth Hall's short story, are typically human and representative of the vast majority:

Other people were consistent and logical, but logic had very little compulsion for her. She preferred to put her faith in her emotions, which told her with a good deal more authority what she ought to do. They were astonishingly mobile, and rose to her defense in a crisis, so that she could act with decision while other people tormented their minds for reasons.

There are a good many Dottys in the world. Sometimes it seems as if the "other people" were almost nonexistent. Logic seems about the last thing to look for in human behavior. But the causes of action are so often hidden that it is not easy to be sure. We all know that people can give a good reason for doing a thing when that was not their reason for doing it, although they think it was, while people like Dotty, who believe themselves to act from pure feeling, who "jump to conclusions," may be influenced by reasons of which they are not aware. They have a reason and want to be logical, only they do not elaborate a succession of ideas to connect what they decide to do with the reason they have for doing it. Sometimes they could not do so if they tried.

This does not prove, however, that their action had no rational foundation. Failure or inability to give a reason is not the same thing as not having a reason. Items of information gained from numerous successive experiences may be concentrated in a sudden instantaneous flash of insight. This insight will then appear to have no relation to anything else, although it is actually the condensation of a large number of related experiences from which the connecting links have dropped away. Life is indeed more than logic; at the same time there is more logic in life, in a Dotty's life, too, than is apparent on the surface.

Why is this fact, if it is a fact, not more widely recognized? Probably because logic is thought to be a purely technical subject which must be learned from texts and teachers. And this is not true. The subject which goes by the name "Logic" in books and is studied in colleges, with its syllogisms, conversions, obversions, canons of induction, and all the other dialectical apparatus, is everyday logic refined and, in its most developed form, intellectualized. Any occupation will give rise to problems and hence to problem-solving activities. When these problem-solving activities themselves become problematical and are studied with the purpose of improving them, the information thus gained, in addition to being useful for other reasons, is material for logic.

Logic begins when thinking is critically thought about, wherever and whenever this occurs. The young man who described logic in one sentence was entirely right: "It's using your bean to see that the old bean does a good job." Animals and mentally backward people rely upon trial and error to reach results, and if this fails them, they soon give up. When normal human beings fail in solving a problem, they may turn their attention upon the method they employed. They may try to find out why they failed. Whenever this happens, the problem-solver is giving himself a lesson in logic. That is how unavoidably and naturally everyone engages in a study which appears strange and forbidding as an academic subject.

ix

At what age children first show an interest in logical
validity is difficult to determine. It is not far from the
seventh or eighth year. Before this time, the child's indifference to the logic of an argument is positively charm-
ing. Premises seem scarcely to be heard; the sole test being
whether the conclusion is in accord with what is known
about the world. If it is not, the most compelling logic
will not change its status. One can get a child to agree to
premises which make it logically unavoidable to conclude
that a lion is about the size of a rabbit, but the conclusion
will be rejected on the ground that "anyone who has ever
seen a lion knows that it's ever so much larger than a
rabbit." One may make a glaringly false argument to demonstrate that fire burns, and the child will let it pass, because "anyone can see that fire burns."

Children are more curious and observant, more intellectually alive, than they are likely to be as men and
women, but they are not intent upon producing logically
consistent patterns of ideas. They are ambitious to find
out how things work and hang together. As they grow
older they want to know what the world is actually like,
the world of which they constantly hear and read. As
items of information accumulate, many of them unrelated
and some of them contradicting others; as inferences grow
in number and importance, problems of classification and
consistency must be reckoned with. The adolescent does
not show by any means the young child's delightful indifference to logical connections and categories. He will

make nice distinctions in the meaning of words and evaluate the force of evidence. He will assess a given conclusion in the light of the argument made in its support.

The point is that, by the time adolescent boys and girls have reached adulthood, every one of them has acquired habits of observing, of predicting consequences, of testing evidence which differ only in degree from those of the trained investigator or the professional logician. Proficiency in logic continues to develop step by step with the development of the problems which are met and solved under the stress of living. Modest as the attainment may be on its lower levels, any number of people, lawyers, doctors, editors, government experts, engineers, skilled laborers, show a logical acumen in the field of their special work that is impressive.

If the rank and file of men and women are notoriously illogical, this is at least partly due to the fact that they are educated from birth to use their minds for certain purposes only, and are discouraged from using them at all exactly where the need for careful thinking is greatest. Moreover, people who are illogical in general are not illogical in every particular. Logical ability, like other ability, operates within specific limits. Even professional logicians are perpetually accusing one another of bad logic.

In spite of all opposing influences, and in spite of lack of intellectual ability, which is of course a handicap where it exists, every man or woman manages to pick up a working acquaintance with logic, though it may not be known as such; and every one of them is actuated by a real desire, however unconscious and unsteady, to think logically when thinking has to be done.

X

If human existence were free from hazard and everyone by taking pains could be sure of securing what he desires, and if all things desired proved to be desirable, there might be no lifting of wistful eyes beyond the nearer goals. But man is blocked by circumstances and by himself. He is subject to accident and hindered by weakness and disease. He is the victim of social and natural calamity. Besides, whatever the achievement, whatever the triumph, there is always the longing that will not be satisfied. *"Wo ich nicht bin, da ist das Glück."* Finally death cuts every man down and time brings the noblest enterprise to end. Any number of problems may be solved, but not the problem of problems, the problem of evil. Every man meets it as a child, tries all his life to unravel it, and retires at last leaving it unsolved. Apparently the earth was not made for man, as it was not made for any creature. Its seasons pass over him and its beauty touches him in passing. In the wide-spreading universe life is the ship, and man the barnacle that clings to it until he is rubbed off.

When a man becomes aware of the terms of his existence, he might accept them as offered and make the best of the bargain. Some do. They add up the ills of life and say, in the words of George Cohan, "But it's a great world, and don't forget it whenever you are trying to remember something." Others are just as downright in their rejec-

tion of the world. "The whole business," writes one of
these, "is ashes in my mouth. You may have America for
your Valentine, Man for your Christmas present, all of
Life for New Year's. I hand them over without a shade
of regret."

There is something arresting in this fact that a bit of
cosmic stuff coming to life, attaining to consciousness,
mastering the art of speech, can bring Life into court and
hand down a judgment for or against it. Yet in some degree this is the rule. Relatively few people really accept
life for what it is worth on the face of it. They hunt about
for a theory of things which will make all that happens
seem rational and somehow right. The adopted theory
may do little credit either to a man's intelligence or his
feelings. It may be a thin fabric of superstitious beliefs, or
merely a cosmic justification of cold-blooded egotism. On
the other hand, many persons will do better. They will
rise to a magnificent conception in which the joys and
sorrows of their fellows, the culled wisdom of past ages,
and the knowledge of their own time are united in beautiful expression. An occasional Abbé Jeanne will have ears
"for a song sounding high up in the regions of the soul, a
song like those little organs which are sometimes perched
in the upper gallery of a church, and spill their music
down a slanting ray of sunlight."

One man measures the universe by his fears, another
by his failures, another by his evil schemes, and still another by his hopes, his aspirations, the greatness of great
dreams. Whoever he is and whatever he is, the process of
living teaches a man a thing beyond psychology, ethics,

and logic. It teaches him what William James called "a more or less dumb sense of what life honestly and deeply means."

xi

Havelock Ellis tells a delightful little story:

For several mornings in succession I have been awakened just before dawn by a mouse gnawing on the farther side of the wainscot. In the deep silence the crunching of his incisors fills the air, and mighty jaws seem to be tearing away what sound like huge splinters. As I lie in the half-dreaming state listening to his tormenting activities, imagination involuntarily suggests to me gratifying pictures of the tortures which ought to be inflicted upon him.

Yet I sometimes wonder what may be the psychic state of my mouse who seeks so persistently and so fruitlessly to penetrate the mystery of his universe at that particular point. Surely his fellows must shake their heads and seek to persuade him, at all events by their own sagacious practical example, that probably nothing is there but Infinite Wood . . . And all the time there lurks in my mouse's mind the germ of the intuition that things are not what they seem; that something lies behind phenomena.

So I grow reconciled with my tormenting mouse, for I reflect that he is inaugurating that metaphysical attitude of mind which after long aeons becomes consciously and deliberately embodied in the philosophy of Kant.

Not much like the mind of a mouse, to be sure, but how thoroughly like a man's. In man's mind there does lurk "the germ of an intuition that things are not what they seem; that something lies behind phenomena." He must gnaw at the phenomenal wainscot with the sharp incisors of reason. He must get through to the reality on the other side. He must know, in the words of Heraclitus, "the thought by which all things are steered through all things."

One motive back of this persistent search—perhaps the deepest motive of all—is man's refusal to admit that he is made for defeat. Victory must be his, if not in this world, then in another. Does righteousness languish and wickedness flourish? It will be adjusted in the world to come. Do sickness and want shadow man's steps? Yonder there will be neither pain nor hunger. Does death cut short the promise of youth, does the decrepitude of age make life a burden? In the City of God there will be no dying and no growing old. If theology has lost its grip upon him, which in these days is more than probable, the chances are that he has picked up some ideas from religious philosophy, or perchance pseudo-philosophy, which enables him still to believe in victorious man. There are always exceptions, but men and women of every walk in life are driven by the frustration of desire to dream of a cosmic Utopia in which failure has no place.

A second motive back of the cosmic interpretation of life is man's proneness to believe that the far-off or obscure is of greater significance than the near at hand or clearly visible. Such exceptions as Edwin Markham only emphasize the rule. Says Mr. Markham:

> We men of earth have here the stuff
> Of Paradise—we have enough!
> We need no other thing to build
> The stairs into the unfulfilled—

Most human beings do not find earth to be enough. They do not find it enough that each man should play a worthy role in the drama of human design. Mankind must have the universe for stage and a God for playwright. They do not find it enough that human powers and the energies of nature be combined to produce an exhilarating performance all around. The drama must be cosmic, must be supercosmic, must echo through the universe and vibrate in harmony with universal being.

Perhaps after all this is less a natural human idiosyncrasy than an acquired feeling. These nineteen hundred years the Occident has been carefully schooled in the doctrine that real worth must be imported from some beyond. The doctrine has become embodied in customs and institutions, in religion, literature, art, and music. Contemporary teachers are not wanting to further the idea: the Christopher Dawsons, with their "absolute element in culture provided by a cosmic faith"; the Fosdicks, with their eternal fountains of serenity "that keep their freshness when all the superficial cisterns peter out"; the Thomists, with their *philosophia perennia*; the Santayanas, with their *templa serena* of metaphysics—not to mention any number of others, or the hordes of those who rely upon the argument of spirit rappings, astrological fakery, and primitive hocus-pocus.

It would be a situation difficult to explain if men and women as we find them did not show the effect of these ubiquitous, insinuating influences. The deeply felt need of cosmic support may go back to a reaction as natural as breathing, but the probabilities are that in the developed form we know it, it is socially conditioned. Let it be either or both. The impact of experience on men as they innately are, or as they are induced to become, causes them to reach out beyond the human environment for a conception of the cosmos which shall give superhuman worth to human effort. So true is this that thousands are easily taken in by any advertised solution of the riddle of existence, no matter how psychologically weird, intellectually obscure, and practically irrelevant it may be, providing it is cosmically pretentious.

xii

What have we learned since we met the man who was seated on a log at the edge of a lake? One thing we have not learned, for we knew it all along. Perhaps we needed to be put in mind of it, especially if certain speculative currents had drifted our way, but we knew without being told that people everywhere, educated and uneducated alike, do not worry about the actuality of the things they see and touch. They have problems to solve, many of them and of many kinds, but to establish the reality of their world of daily experience is not one of them. That world, as we found, they take entirely for granted. They would have to presuppose it in order to doubt it.

Philosophers refer to this way of taking the world as the stage of common sense. Strangely enough, the term is not intended to be complimentary. As philosophers use it, common sense does not mean good sense. It does not imply that the attitude is astute, sagacious, or rational. It means the acceptance of the experienced world at its face value, without inquiring into its metaphysical status. Among philosophers this is conclusive evidence of intellectual innocence, of naïveté, of a childlike or animallike trust in the senses which the slightest reflection would show to be ill-founded.

The common-sense level is nevertheless the level on which the business of living is conducted year in and year out. This is what our discussion has not taught us, because we knew it already, although it is just as certain that we did not always keep the fact in mind. If we had kept it in mind we would not be so easily tempted to wander off into airy conjectures. And we have by no means appreciated the far-reaching consequences of taking the visible world as the final testing ground of what we believe in and hope for.

Of what then shall we remind ourselves at the end of the chapter? Of this especially, that the common-sense plateau yields an abundance of home-grown theories of life. This is doubtless what Sir William Osler had in mind when he said: "Every man has a philosophy of life in thought, in word, or deed, worked out in himself unconsciously." It is what Mr. Justice Cardozo must have meant by a similar remark: "There is in each of us a stream of tendency, whether we call it a philosophy or not, which gives coherence and direction to our thought and action." Although this philosophy may, for all but a relative few, be too conventional, superficial, and loosely strung together to constitute mature wisdom of life, it does bring a degree of organization and rationality into behavior.

A critic has said that "in so far as the vast majority are

equipped with anything resembling an outlook upon life
and the world, it consists of a substratum of superstitions
about the supernatural, a smattering of social theory, a nest
of group prejudices, a few wise saws, a rumor or two from
science, and a number of slipshod observations of life." At
that he left out of account the utterly gross and mercenary
cravings which such theories all too often rationalize.

But we must guard against settling the question, as the
critic perhaps did, by arbitrary definition. It is unreason-
able to estimate the value of beliefs arising out of the
everyday world by standards of professional philosophers.
Judged from the inside, from the standpoint of the needs
they satisfy, very much can be said for these unprofes-
sional philosophies. They bear witness to man's idealizing
propensity, whether the idea and ideals which they gather
together are bred within the confines of necessity, or are
captured in the free spaces of speculation and domesticated. They are close to the life they serve, to its conflicts,
its defeats, its victories. They express its impulses, its
yearnings, its plans. They are attempts to make sense of
the human struggle and to win for the participants in it
the degree of self-respect without which existence is an
apology for living, rather than the eventful enterprise that
human beings crave.

Thus interpreted, lay philosophies are seen to emerge
from the universal desire for a life that has meaning which
can be contemplated with satisfaction. If an adequate philosophy can by no means stop where lay philosophies stop,
still less can it disregard them as of no consequence. The
problem is to carry these home-grown philosophies for-

ward in the direction they are already going. It is to
do consciously and with greater expertness what every
thoughtful person does semiconsciously in the course of
the years. It is to enlarge and deepen the understanding of
life in its natural and social setting.

xiii

Few people have to be convinced that their knowledge
is scanty, or that their philosophy is wanting in range and
depth. And they know all too well that they have not
learned how to choose unerringly from among desired
goods those that are most desirable. They are on the lookout, often pathetically on the lookout, for a better sum-
mary of what is to be known and a better criterion of what
is to be prized. Most of them experience those times when
it seems to a man that he has been busy about many
things and not about the one thing needful; when he
wants to be drawn out of himself and lifted above the
interests that ordinarily command his hours. Most of them
are acquainted with the feeling, half pain, half pleasure, of
the lack of something one cannot tell exactly what, and
with the hush of mystery which at odd moments pervades
a man's life, making all his projects seem trivial and all
his knowledge woefully inane. This feeling of their own
inadequacy and the conviction that life as they know it
falls far short of what it should be, sends men, despite repeated disappointment, to those who write or talk as if
they had solved the riddle.

It was Plato's opinion that people who do the work
of the world, "those who wander," as he put it, "in the

region of the many and variable," are doomed to be un-
philosophical, even though they may now and then "take
a leap out of their trades into philosophy." The reason
he gave was that they never penetrate to a changeless reality below the changing appearance of changeable things.
The philosopher, he believed, succeeded where the rest of
men failed. The philosopher was "able to grasp the eternal
and unchangeable."

Possibly Plato was mistaken. I think he was. He turned
away from the world of the senses which the ordinary
Athenian took for real, and he had good reasons for wanting to forget that world. It had done to death the noblest
human being he had ever known. I do not blame him if
he found it hard to believe in the reality of the world in
which this could happen. Nevertheless Plato did not lay
hold of an eternal and changeless reality. His philosophy
was a pattern of conceptions, and its changelessness was
a conceptual changelessness. It may have served Plato, but
it offered no help to those who had to remain in "the
region of the many and variable."

Spinoza, too, had reason for wanting to retire from the
world. Had it not persecuted him, excommunicated him
from the religion of his fathers, tried to assassinate him?
Who can blame him for wanting to escape from that world?
Who would deprive anyone in his position of the peace of
mind and the sense of being worthily occupied which he
needed, and which he was convinced could not be found
in the world about him with its unpredictable ups and
downs?

Spinoza turned to the study of nature, to Being in its

essence and totality, because in that realm of the infinite
and eternal there was no striving, no love or hate, no un-
satisfied desire, no conflict of purposes. For when life is
seen under the limitations of finite existence, when one
attaches oneself to objects of desire, always deceptive and
transitory, one can expect only agitation of spirit and
misery. So thought Spinoza. The solution seemed obvious.
Human ills vanish when all things are seen "under the
aspect of infinity." The "intellectual love of God," he
called it, amor Dei intellectualis, although there was
neither love nor God in it, only the quiet joy of metaphysical speculation.

Absorbed in the study of the supersensible, Spinoza
believed himself to have found the true way to wisdom
of life. He may have found it—for himself. I am satisfied that he did not find it for many others. Most men
will not, indeed cannot, play the austere game he played, a
game in which empirical objects and events are replaced
by intellectualized entities, and no player is allowed, under
the rules, to make a move called change.

xiv

What was true of Plato and Spinoza is true of us all.
We are all desirous of a satisfying existence, and the
search for it leads us to the formulation of a more or less
inclusive and coherent philosophy. Professional philosophers make a lifework of what other men are obliged to
do on the side, which of course makes a difference in
achievement, sometimes an enormous difference. Nevertheless every man is in his own way a philosopher, and the

professional philosopher is in spite of himself a man. Philosophy is not a superhuman product, even when it is the work of the greatest thinker. The temperament of the philosopher, the human frailty which he shares with other men of not being able to surmount the human standpoint, and the peculiar personal needs which drive him to philosophize, are present in all his work as contributing elements.

Since philosophy is the philosopher's lifework, as plumbing or farming is another man's, he naturally wants to advance in it, and esoteric philosophy or abstract wisdom may offer him the best opportunity to do so. But ideal as this may be for professional philosophers, it cannot be ideal for philosophic laymen who have other than philosophic work to do. What they need is a better quality of ideas and ideals, the enrichment and refinement of the philosophy with which they are already on intimate terms by virtue of having lived, rather than a formal introduction to a philosophy with which they can hope at best for no more than a speaking acquaintance.

It is not my intention to argue that no one is justified in trying to escape the realities that oppress him, or that no value should be attached to intellectual effort undertaken because of the personal satisfaction it brings. On the contrary, I wish that such escape and such satisfaction could be far more generally and freely enjoyed. And I know what it means to say out of the depths of suffering:

> Lass, o Welt, o lass mich sein!
> Locket nicht mit Liebesgaben,

Lasst dies Herz alleine haben
Seine Wonne, seine Pein!

Nor do I blame anyone, especially in these times, for wanting to run away from the world altogether. It does not seem to me admirable in the least to feel at home with the decivilizing forces so conspicuously active about us. But the trouble is that most people cannot run away without abdicating their manhood or womanhood. If they could run away, they would have no place to run to. They must stay where they are and take it. It is *their* need, the need of those who must try to make the best of life from within it, which deserves first consideration. The duty to provide a retreat for those who want ideal freedom for the exercise of their intellectual, literary, or artistic gifts must be put second to that primary duty.

Home-grown philosophies have the merit of remaining close to everyday needs, but they are deficient in range and depth of vision. Let us by all means seek to improve them by turning to professional philosophy for illumination, providing this does not entail loss of contact with the world for which the illumination is sought. It may be true —though I do not believe it—that genuine philosophy must keep itself unsullied from the world, in which case the chapters of this book are not philosophic in subject matter or method. Even so, they may broaden and deepen the common-sense outlook on things and thus contribute to the reader's philosophic maturity. This is what they are intended to do.

III

NEW TIMES—NEW IDEALS

i

We have been talking of a philosophy of life as if unaware of the times in which we live. And everyone agrees that our civilization is shaken to its depths. Something like it, to be sure, has happened before. Religions, philosophies, plans of temporal or eternal salvation, have flourished, then declined. It is in fact a recurrent phenomenon, a succession of seasons in the unfolding year of human history. A manner of living and a way of thinking about life may continue through centuries, organizing the activities of men into a design and supplying them with a rational ground for what they do, making them feel that their own lives and all lives together are united in a great, meaningful plan. Then with relative suddenness it may lose attractiveness and force.

The thing has happened before, but it has not happened before on the same scale and with the same depth of disturbance. Or does this only seem to be true because we were not actually involved in past struggles as we are in our own? Very likely. At any rate, one characteristic of our time is unmistakable. According to many observers it has become futile to discuss the rationality of anything. Institutions which until yesterday were regarded as inseparable from social decency and justice have been swept away. Ideals that for more than a thousand years were able to direct and discipline conduct have become mere words. And the regenerating sources—original creative thinking, free publication of ideas, growing social imagination— have been sought out in various parts of the world and suppressed by dictatorial power. With their eyes fixed upon the destruction going on, it looks to such observers as if a blind impulse to destroy had taken possession of mankind. They see nothing ahead but an age of intellectual darkness and ethical barbarism, in the course of which the noblest accomplishments of the past will be laid waste and man will take a long stride toward final extinction.

It is time that we take a look at this aspect of the situation and arrive at some understanding of it, if we can. What does it really signify when an inherited outlook on things disintegrates in this way? Must the answer be entirely discouraging or may there be an accent of hope in it? Are we on the verge of one of those cruel winters when aspiration passes into the tomb and there "awaits the requiem of winter's snows," or are we at the beginning of a spring when through uncertain and disagreeable weather we move on to pregnant June?

ii

As I recall similar instances in the past and contemplate what is taking place in our own day, I think of a black oak I have long admired. It rises seventy or eighty feet into the air, a thing of rugged beauty every day of the year and every hour of the day. Whether seen in the searching light of noon or in the mellow colors of sunset, whether barely visible as a dim mass on a dripping, sultry night or clearly etched against the sky at dawn—each recurring presence arouses a fresh sense of the oak tree's greatness as an achievement of life and intimates anew something of that unfathomable mystery we call nature, that complexity of being into which every living thing sends its roots.

But it is not the impressiveness of this oak which just now brings it to mind, not its strength or dignity or beauty. It is its behavior in autumn and winter—if a tree may be said to behave. Unlike the maples and hickories in the same grove, it refuses to give up its leaves. Rains, snows, winds have no effect. The tug of the elements is powerless to bring them down. They change from green to red, then to the color of the marshes when the winter's snows are first gone. They wrinkle, dry up, and rustle in the breeze, but do not release their grip. They linger through the winter as memories of departed days haunt the mind of a man whom a change of fortune has retired from active life.

Then comes spring. In March the leaves appear to be thinning out and before April ends they are gone. What rains, snows, winds, blustering from without, could not do, the quiet prod of life, working from within, does with ease. As the sun climbs higher in the Zodiac, and the responsive sap ascends the tree trunk and ramifies into branches and twigs, the clinging leaves drop away. For new leaves do not come because the old leaves have fallen; the old leaves fall because new leaves are coming; or, to speak more accurately, because the life cycle of the tree turns from sustaining old leaves to developing new ones. It is true of the oak and true of the Tree of Life. Everywhere the passing away of the old and the coming of the new are inseparable phases of a larger process active in both.

We may observe this on the vast scale of biological evolution. The reptiles are a good example. They gained in numbers as the amphibians declined until they flourished from Australia to the Arctic circle, ranging in size from small lizardlike creatures to the most colossal monsters that ever visited the earth. They ruled the land, they dominated the seas, they were masters of the air. And as they swarmed like an unconquerable army over the globe, non-reptilian animals pushed their way to the front—warm-blooded birds, premammals, true mammalia. The mammals advanced and the reptiles declined, slowly at first through many centuries, then rapidly, until finally they almost died out, leaving only scattered remnants of crocodiles, turtles, and serpents in the tropics and diminutive representatives in the warmer zones. The retreat of the reptiles and the advance of the mammals took place together.

A similar relation is disclosed in the succession of cultural epochs. The eclipse of the great Egyptian kingdoms was contemporaneous with the rise of new social classes to power. City-states, incomparable Athens and the rest, declined before the advance of World Empire. Paganism gave way to missionary Christianity. The Empire of the Caesars was pushed out of its administrative shell as the Holy Roman Empire slipped little by little into its place, until the secular State was gone, and the Church had taken charge of affairs. Other-worldliness seeped away as the interests of modernity grew with the growth of cities. Handicraft Economy was supplanted by Industrialized Business, and this in turn by the Scientific Industrialism under which we still live. In each of these and other instances an older culture retreated before an oncoming new culture. And in our own day, about which it is so easy to be confused, we can at least make sure that the same double process is operative in the same way.

iii

An analogy is of course not to be taken literally. A tree's annual change of leaves is not the same thing as periodic mutations in the strategy of man's search for happiness. Nevertheless there is a similarity between trees and people, between withered leaves and discredited ideals, which is interesting and instructive. We may profitably postpone noticing their un-likeness, although that too is important to understand, until we have made an effort to appreciate their likeness. We constantly talk, and especially write, as if ideals had a supermundane origin and history; as if they floated above the earth in an immaterial air, multiplied by a kind of spiritual cell division, and drifted to earth on an occasional auspicious breeze. The fact is that *ideals grow* out of the life of every day as leaves grow out of the life of the tree. I am not attempting to minimize the importance of ideals. They help to determine human destiny. They will serve that destiny better if they are seen to be what they are, expressions of the very life they aim to command, as truly expressions of it as leaves are of the tree's life. Evidence for this interpretation is not hard to find.

There was a time when our ancestors were snugly at home on a flat little earth securely fixed in the center of a glass ball, like a boat in a bottle. Their knowledge of the world, their theology and philosophy, their schemes of conquests and everyday ideals, were all adjusted to the crystal globe in which they were imprisoned. Their lives were not without force and dignity, certainly not without taste, and the echo of their lusty merriment can still be heard when the wind is in the right quarter.

Something happened. We today do not live on that flat little earth or in that cozy little universe. We need no Giordano Bruno to dissuade us from the notion of spheres in which the celestial bodies are "implanted, engraved, plastered, nailed, tied, glued, carved, or painted." Ours is an immeasurable cosmos of many universes which even Bruno, with his driving need of room for the speculative imagination, would find appalling in its proportions. The fossil remains of universes in which men once lived, the Egyptians, the Hebrews, the Greeks, are embedded in the accumulated drift of history. They proved to be too small for the play of man's spirit and were abandoned.

What was it that alienated our forefathers from that

neighborly cosmos of theirs? What enticed them out into those icy spaces where their descendants have tried in vain to feel at home?

Well, the Crusaders marched off "to wrest the Holy Sepulchre from the Infidel." As a result new trade routes were opened to the East. Spices, perfumes, silks, brocades, jewelry of new design and wonderful workmanship, the refinements of the more cultivated civilization of the East streamed into medieval Europe. Then Columbus sailed westward. He brought home a strange gift—a new earth. Galileo turned his telescope on Jupiter. Down came the crystalline universe on men's heads. Gutenberg carved the alphabet in wood, and ideas dipped their feet in ink and tramped through cities and towns.

What of those nearer to us in time, the American colonists? They moved their commonwealths farther and farther from the sea, and as they did, found themselves thinking of new rights and privileges. What of the westward-facing pioneers, climbing the Alleghenies, chopping their way through forests, gliding down the Ohio in flat boats, toiling overland with ox team and covered wagon? They opened up the country and through the clearing caught a vision of Jacksonian democracy. That is how only yesterday Bell, Edison, Ford, Marconi, the Wright brothers, and their kind, changed the modes of our daily living. The new modes of living gave birth to new ideals, whereupon the ideals of a former time, no longer vitalized by contact with what men were engaged in doing, lost their power to attract.

So it has been, so it is, so it will be. Men act, because

it is their nature to act, and their thoughts, carried on the tall shoulders of action, catch sight of new horizons.

iv

This is one side of the story, the similarity between leaves and ideals. There is the other side, the difference between them; or the differences, for there are at least three.

The first difference is that leaves are simply *had*, they are not *desired*. A tree feels no attachment for its leaves. It experiences no pangs when it loses them. It does not sigh to be in fashion or worry about the opinion of the forest. When its leaves fall a tree does not run around trying to pick them up and pin them back on the twigs, nor does it seek to restore lost glory by importing leaves from another climate, real or imaginary. If a tree were a philosopher, it would be a Stoic, and say in the words of Marcus Aurelius: "I now have what the universal nature wills me to have."

A tree, however, is not blessed or cursed with awareness. The falling of its leaves is an occurrence, as their coming was an occurrence, of which it takes no account. Each is an unconscious participation in a rhythm of nature which draws the tree into its swing. Summer after summer the oak puts forth the same pattern of leaf, completely oblivious of what it does, until its energies fail and its bare form stands for a time a memorial at its own grave.

Man and his ideals are more intimately and tenaciously related. Ideals are not mere occurrences. They belong. They are consciously owned. We recognize that the life of the tree is a profounder thing than the mission of the leaves of the season. When the leaves fall in autumn we know they have fulfilled their function. But when ideals weaken in their grip, it is hard to believe that they too have fulfilled their function. We do not sweep ideals together, set fire to them, meditate a moment on the passing of the years, then turn to new aims and purposes for the rejuvenation of life. We do not, and we cannot. We try to force obsolescent ideals back into the life-giving stream which was once their element but can be their element no longer.

For ideals, to say it once more, are not external incidents, passively accepted and passively surrendered. They are clasped to the heart. They are eager outreachings, aglow with anticipated good. Men of action fight to maintain the structure of society that promises to conserve what they prize. Men of letters seek to win immortality in the realm of literature for what they value most highly in the human spirit and in life. Mystics and persons who for one reason or another have no faith in the higher possibilities of the natural order, think to make their loss good in a supernal world not subject to decay. And those who can do no better than regret, sigh for the days when their idealism was congenial to the times. Poets, artists, laborers, business and professional men, communists, fascists, and adherents of democracy, reactionaries and progressives, militarists and pacifists, sinners and saints, the rich and the poor, the aged and the young—every one of them will hold, if he can, to the ideals he has learned to cherish.

There is not one of us who, if his innermost being could

be filmed and thrown on a screen, would not be depicted in a struggle to safeguard his ideals from the inroads of change.

v

A realistic idealist will not shut himself off from the truth that his aims are interwoven with other and larger aims. He will hold it before his eyes that he may understand his ideals in the context of his time, and those of his time in the context of other times. His idealism will move in the living current of human aspiration. It will be enriched and purified by the victories and defeats of the past. It will be quickened by the pulsing ardors of the present. He will recognize that to prevent new ideals from coming is beyond the power of the individual, but he will not conclude from this that it is entirely beyond his power to help determine what they shall be as they come. He will see himself standing on a watershed of alternatives. Life flows to the east and to the west. He can do something, if he will, to control its flow in his own life, and he can determine to some extent on which side he shall invest his energies. In a word, he can advance the human cause or set it back. If he will. In this uncertainty lies the hazard of our time. In it lies the promise of the puzzling, tempestuous days through which we are passing.

This seems to me incontestable. Men and women do, as a matter of fact, set their minds upon goals to be attained, some near at hand and easy to win, some far off and of a character to test the limits of man's powers, every one of them leaving its mark upon the world. If it is true, as Henry B. Brewster has said, that men "have two roles in the world; one as human beings, and the other as cosmic atoms, grains of dust filtering eternally through space," their uniqueness lies in their role as human beings. It is found in their conscious, deliberate endeavor to improve the circumstances of their lives through ideals of success, workmanship, and mutual dependability, and through loyalty to movements of civic, national, and international scope.

The ideals of men are negligible, it is true, from the standpoint of the universe. From the human standpoint they are extraordinary episodes in the story of our earth. So far as we know that story, man is the only creature capable of exercising purposive will in the making of himself and of his environment.

On what ground, moreover, can we ignore the idealists of heroic proportions, men like Wilson and Bowers and Scott, who lie buried in the Great Ice Barrier of the South Pole? They went quietly on "to keep the track to the end," in spite of every adversity and danger, until they died of hunger and cold. Not even the terrifying powers of nature in the Antarctic could overmaster their will to endure hardship, help one another, and meet death with fortitude. I do not see by what logic these data of experience are shown to be nonexistent, or how the most hardheaded can refuse to include them in the description of what the experienced world includes. It is as realists, not as dreamers or visionaries, that we have a right to say: *We can do something, if we will, to decide whether our ideals shall advance the human cause or set it back.*

vi

Ideals are espoused, leaves are not, this then is the first difference. A tree can make no mistakes in the choice of its leaves, a man can and does make mistakes in the choice of his ideals, this is the second difference. For ideals are choices. They are campaigns to win desired satisfaction from existence.

Men do not passively take what comes. In their own interest and in the interest of others they are lured by an imagined future. They make demands upon that future and work for the realization of those demands. Such demands are ideals, and, man being what he is, he can follow ideals to his ruin. He can choose destructive ideals as an individual; he can unite with his fellow men to choose them. Idealism is infectious, spreading from man to man, uniting the individual with others and making him capable of believing and doing what he never would have believed or dared alone. Ideals have brought men together in great material, moral, and aesthetic projects; they have attacked men like a virulent disease, sweeping multitudes of human beings and their most costly achievements to destruction. Ruinous ideals have contributed to the downfall of nations and peoples and may yet make an end of the human race. Fanatical commercialism and nationalism may succeed in carrying out their designs and the insects be the meek who inherit the earth.

A meditative person, sensible of the ugliness and misery which have resulted and may yet result from misguided ambitions, cannot help wondering with Mr. Tomlinson, "whether it would not have been better for us to have refused the gift of reason from which could be devised the edifying wonders of civilization, and have remained in the treetops instead, so ignorant that we were unaware that we were lucky." *Idealism is fire. It may warm and it may burn and it may consume.*

vii

A third dissimilarity is due to the different ways in which living processes occur in nature. Plants are fixed to a place; animals move about. One of the poetic passages in Spengler's best-known book touches upon this difference between the blind, dreamlike, earth-bound existence of plants and the searching, free-moving existence of animals. He asks the reader to imagine a landscape when the sun is going down:

The dumb forest, the silent meadows, this bush, that twig, do not stir themselves, it is the wind that plays with them. Only the little gnat is free—he dances still in the evening light, he moves whither he will. . . .

This midget swarm that dances on and on, that solitary bird still flying through the evening, the fox approaching furtively the nest—these are *little worlds of their own within another great world.* An animalcule in a drop of water, too tiny to be perceived by the human eye, though it lasts but a second and has but a corner of this drop as its field—nevertheless is *free and independent in the face of the universe.* The giant oak, upon one of whose leaves the droplet hangs, is not.

It is immaterial in this context whether we accept or reject Spengler's comment that the seeds of flowering plants tell in the early development of rootlets that they are destined irrevocably to become parts of a landscape, and that the fertilized eggs of mammals, in their early development of an enclosing sheath which shuts them off from the mother and the rest of the world, show that they are to define their own positions with respect to the surrounding All.

Let that be as it may. The oak tree in any case attaches itself firmly to the earth, and all its leaves are fed to the topmost twig by the roots underground. In times of special need, as during a drought, the roots reach deeper down, and every leaf realizes its possibilities by remaining in vital contact with this source of nourishment. The animal, on the other hand, goes in search of what it wants. And the man-animal has acquired a wander-thirst which sends him forth not only to all the corners of the world but over into the region of the supersensible. He sometimes wanders so far that he cuts himself off from his natural home and takes pride in his detachment.

In no way do ideals differ more profoundly from leaves than in their possible separation from the living unity out of which they came, and their segregation in the rarefied atmosphere of immateriality. A tree is never ashamed of its roots in the earth, a man often is. He can believe that his higher aspirations must rise above biological needs and natural desires, above his ambition to succeed in his life-work, indeed above all the ends and means to which he is devoted as a normal human being. He can bisect his interests into mutually exclusive kinds, those of the body and those of the mind or spirit. Every other form of life that we know anything about is a union of vital processes co-operating to further the survival and well-being of the whole. It is only man who can incite a civil war in his own being; only man who can split off a part of himself and set it to work against the remainder.

viii

We have affirmed that the ideals of a period grow out of the activities of the period, and so we are led to ask ourselves what turn of affairs it was that invalidated the ideals which we inherited as the highest orientation of life. The cause usually alleged is the spread among us of scientific views which had come off victorious in a battle with the theological views of our fathers. There was such a battle, and the victory for science had a pronounced effect. It cast discredit upon the theological conception of the world and of human nature and destiny, and so undermined the derived ideals of conduct.

There was, however, another cause. Had there not been, much of scientific knowledge would have fallen upon barren ground and withered away. And that other cause originated in the lively ferment of daily transactions. Traders, inventors, entrepreneurs, and scientists, working together, produced capitalistic, industrial, machine civilization. They contrived to set up a world between mankind and the natural environment. We reminded ourselves in an earlier chapter that this world, which owes its existence to human ingenuity, confronts men as an objective order whose laws must be obeyed.

So late as the early nineteenth century, people in general were still largely dependent, and felt themselves to be dependent, upon nature for the physical necessities of life and upon the God of nature for the needs of the spirit. In the course of that century this contact was broken. A revolutionary transfer of dependence took place. It proceeded with acceleration toward the end of the century, and during the first quarter of the twentieth century the transfer was practically complete. Needs of all sorts, of the body and of the mind, trivial and important, are now cared for by the world-wide unresting and impersonal machinery of production, transportation, and exchange. Millions of people of all ranks have become so directly dependent upon it for food, clothing, shelter, health, amusement, even culture, that their relation to this artificial world is analogous to the relation of their ancestors to the natural world and to God. It is their source of whatever makes them comfortable and secure, of whatever revives their spirits or adds to the refinement of their surroundings.

Now it cannot be remarkable that this shift in the *fact* of dependence should have produced a shift in the *feeling* of dependence. People who every day witness spectacular exemplifications of man's control over his material environment, who see him circumventing destructive forces of nature, taming others to do his will, putting up an encouraging fight against disease, loading his table with contributions from every quarter of the globe—people who witness all this and enjoy the benefits that flow from it, easily forget their relation to nature, to a wonder-working God and a world to come. They are fascinated by wonder-working Man and the good things of this present life. A revision of ideals was inevitable. Everyday interests and activities changed, new ideals came into view, old ideals dropped out of sight.

ix

It has long been known that something had gone wrong. Again and again defects were pointed out. Unnumbered sermons, speeches, articles, monographs, and books concentrated upon the theme and elaborated it. Many critics blamed blind industrial expansion. They laid bare the spiritual poverty often concealed under material display. They diagnosed what Tawney called "the sickness of acquisitive society," and warned us of the danger of collapse and widespread suffering. We were too infatuated to recognize the precariousness of our state. We refused to heed their diagnosis. "We want more!" continued to be our cry: "We want more!"

Then almost without warning the thing happened that could not be ignored. The great producing and distributing machinery slowed down and threatened to stop. Renowned engineers were called in. They were urged to locate the trouble, to repair the machinery, to set the great wheels revolving again with their old-time velocity. It could not be done. The wheels would not be accelerated; they continued to slow down. Gradually a suspicion took shape, gradually a furtive whisper spread from mouth to mouth, gradually it grew into an open and public declaration that mere repairs would not meet the need.

With startling rapidity new types of economic and social machinery were set up on the other side of the Atlantic, and we on this side entered upon radically devised economic and social experiments. The wheels began to gather speed. In our country some people stubbornly adhered to the idea that the old machinery was best. They insisted that all we needed was more repairs. Their protests were buried under an avalanche of ballots. As the wheels turned faster the faith revived that before long we should hear again the welcome hum of prosperity.

And now the dread has returned. What if these new machines prove worse than the old? The rumor persists that any day there may be a crash that will take us all down to ruin. And the question—the important question which outranks all others—is still this, whether the contemporary machine civilization is man's friend or enemy. On that question doubt grows in volume and in pointedness. An objective study printed in *Fortune* concludes with these words:

The sum and substance of the problem is this: from the purely productive point of view, a part of the human race is already obsolete and a further part is obsolescent. But from the consuming point of view, no human being is obsolete: on the contrary, an ever-increasing human consumption is not only desirable but necessary. These are the hard and pointed horns of the dilemma of our time.

We may differ as to the best make of machinery. We may disagree on the feasibility of the inventions which recent years have introduced. We all know that the institutions and ideals familiar to our fathers are passing away, and that in some form or other we face "the hard and pointed horns of the dilemma of our time."

x

Suppose we agree that periods like the present, when the moorings have given way and men feel themselves adrift, are periods when the common life of mankind is moving to a new orientation; it follows, does it not, that all who are interested in the quality of human living are challenged to put their faith to work?

What basic transformation in idealism does the present situation suggest and urge upon us? To answer this question, we must first ask another. What is it that human beings seek? What is it they really want?

The normal man or woman wants to be happy rather than miserable; to succeed rather than fail; to do right rather than wrong. These three wants have for most people become mutually contradictory. Each want is compelled to seek its fulfillment at the expense of the others. From early childhood we have been trained in a false philosophy. Home, church, school, and street have united to teach us that success in life is to be sought in the world of affairs, quality of living in a realm called spiritual, and happiness in more or less questionable byways. When school days are over or the congregation has stepped into the street, a sensible person is expected to take off his coat of ideals, roll up his ethical sleeves, and dig his hands into the mire. He is to be ethical when it does not interfere with business, and to be happy when not engaged in succeeding or being good. He is expected to be a cynical materialist, a soul without a body, and a lover of pleasure, depending upon the opportunity and the occasion. We are shocked when men and women made for something better seek relief from the emptiness of conventional success or the boredom of conventional goodness by throwing their lives away in self-indulgence.

In our franker moments, if we have them, we are forced to admit that many of us are kept from a similar recklessness by nothing more lofty than timidity. This is of course not true of everyone, or of anyone perfectly. Even perfect inconsistency is unattainable by fallible human beings. Lives of genuine excellence from every point of view, rising above the contradictory demands of convention, occur frequently enough to illustrate what can be done by noble and independent spirits. But it cannot be denied that counting us all together and the country over, our purposes are divided against each other within ourselves and within society. We are tempted into one unworthy and unworkable compromise after another. Practical occupation and natural enjoyments are water, idealism is oil.

A more rational and truly satisfying life is within man's power. It is not necessary that a man's life be divided into three segments of conflicting ambition. The happy, the ethical, and the successful man can be united in a personality at harmony with itself. Practical achievement, joy in living, adding something to the meaning of life, can be combined in a co-ordinated endeavor. The Greeks put that fact quite beyond doubt, and did it gloriously. I am not thinking of the illustrious Greeks whose names we remember, but of the men and women who produced the original texture of conduct which these writers and artists immortalized.

In our case, a theory of the good life which has come down to us by tradition, and a theory of success resulting from the circumstances under which we labored, stand in the way. As a phrase, we may some day be able to discard "the good life" because of its taboo implications; the thing itself we cannot discard and remain human. Whether or not we shall be able to invent a full-bodied term such as the Greeks had in *eudaimonia*, we can and must revive the thing which it symbolized: *a life of significance within the daily round, expressive of the complete man, and productive of happiness in the endeavor.*

xi

Here, then, is the problem. If we prove equal to solving it a new type of idealism will enlist the physical and intellectual energies of men. They will no longer look to a selected group, set aside from the rough and tumble of life for just that purpose, to redeem life, but will undertake the task of redemption together. The responsibility for formulating ideals, giving them the aspect of authenticity, and arousing an actualizing will in their behalf, will not be delegated to specialists in "higher values"; it will be the burden and the opportunity of all human beings alike, though in various forms and degrees. The work of the world and the art of living will be brought into mutually helpful relation.

Social wounds, like all other wounds, must heal from within. The world of everyday practice must be made self-redemptive or it will not be redeemed. We need the stimulating example of men and women who are not interested in economic success, men and women of wisdom and courage whose lives are dedicated in singleness of purpose to the highest individual and social ideals; we have never needed their example and their leadership more than we do today. But the conditions in which we of this complex modern world are placed cannot be mastered without the knowledge and collaboration of the people we call practical—those who produce and who buy and sell the commodities we consume, who move us from place to place, who manage our litigation, who attend us when we are sick, who make our laws and govern us, who gossip for us about the doings of the world. The farmer, the laborer, the businessman, the lawyer, the scientist, the doctor, the political leader, the journalist—all these must be enlisted with the clergyman, the teacher, the social worker, the philosopher, in the undertaking that concerns us all.

There is no reason why the dignity of any calling should suffer because the redemption of our common life is regarded as a common task. If it does, that is a price we must pay. The redefinition of success, happiness, morals, religion, which this entails must be undertaken, and the instruments must be invented to put the new ideals to work. This is the obligation laid on the conscience of our time. This is the business in hand with which no other compares in importance. This the practical thing to be done, in the profound not the shallow meaning of that useful word.

The change in mind and heart demanded of so-called practical people is enormous. I have no desire to minimize its revolutionary nature. Students of biology tell us that in all physical essentials there is less difference between a human brain and the brain of a gorilla, than between the brain of a gorilla and that of a lion. Well, there is more difference between the life aims of a Lowes Dickinson or a Graham Wallace, a Jane Addams or a George Norris, and the life aims of prominent persons one itches to name, than between the life aims of these prominent persons and the instinctive impulses of anthropoid apes. No generous emotion, no principle of justice, no dearly bought achievement of the human spirit, stands in the way of their ambition. There is nothing they will not sacrifice in their battle for power or prestige.

If these conspicuous materialists were as exceptional in their purposes as they are in the magnitude of their projects, the situation would be serious enough. They are not unique in their purposes. Countless numbers differ from them only in the small scale of their schemes and the meagerness of their success. The problem is not created by the materialistic ambitions of conspicuous individuals, alone. It is created by these and by the general pursuit of materialistic aims in their larger and smaller manifestations. Together they set the tone of contemporary life.

It would be foolish to underestimate the difficulty of going to the root of the evil and changing the ideals of the everyday world. Yet exactly that, and not something else, is what has to be done. If those who seek success in practical life insist on leaving the problem of a better world to the schools and churches while, in the pursuit of practical success, they continue to block the efforts which the schools and churches make, so that they constantly undermine the foundations upon which personal and public character are built, the outcome is not a matter of doubt. The eventual disaster will set a new record in human misery.

This drastic change in the attitude of "practical" men must be matched by an equally drastic change in the attitude of "idealists." They too must cure themselves of the error that man is constituted of two elements, one "lower," one "higher," differing in metaphysical essence. This dualistic view could hardly be better expressed than it was by W. G. Sibley, in speaking for both the "practical" and the "higher" life:

The duty of a minister is to preach the spiritual life. But he must confine himself to preaching the ideals, not to preaching on practical method for realizing those ideals.

Ministers of religion make a mistake if they turn their thoughts and their words from man's soul to considerations of his bread and butter, his cake, his pie, his clothes, his wages, his working hours. These considerations are ephemeral whereas the soul of man is a subject beyond time.

Proposals of this kind are sometimes made for the purpose of protecting the worst form of business practice. But there is no ground for assuming this to be so always. It is rarely the full explanation, and I take Mr. Sibley to have been perfectly sincere, as sincere as many others, in the conviction that a dual human nature, partly physical, partly spiritual, compels an intelligent person to adopt a dualistic view of life.

Unfortunately sincerity of intention does not insure a good outcome in action. Whether honestly or dishonestly

intended, the separation of man into outer desire and inner quality, into ephemeral hungers of the body and soul
hungers that are beyond time, *is* a betrayal of man's effort
to elevate the level of daily practice. It weakens the fiber
of moral character, and makes idealism apologetic exactly
where it needs to be bold.

One thing seems to me irrefutable. If the times unfolding before our eyes are to be managed in the human interest, ideals must be native to the practical world which
no one can escape except in appearance. They must thrive
in what men do and desire and are. The only promising
idealism is a hardy variety grown in the soil and climate of
daily relations, not a gardenia idealism developed under
glass.

xii

The theory of human nature which opposes man as
body to man as spirit has the unhappy effect of rendering
almost helpless two classes of persons in the community—
teachers and ministers of religion—who in a special sense
are expected to work for the realization of the best in mankind. It has been the hope, as Frankwood Williams said,
"that our children would somehow leaven the loaf and
gradually make life outside the school better and more in
accordance with life within the school"; yet "after one
hundred and fifty years, American education has left us
as vicious socially and as dishonest as we were before that
education began."

In so far as his description is true, the chief reason for it
is that we have separated the human spirit, exemplified in

the idealistic and beautiful life of the schoolroom, from the human body, exemplified in the materialistic and ugly life of the world outside. Even in school the division of the child into two absolutely distinct natures, one purely spiritual, the other purely carnal, forever at war with each other, has resulted in educational failure. It is this failure which has led to endless experimentation, to new schemes of discipline or doing away with discipline, and to radical changes in courses of study. Frequently the motive behind the reforms has had no relation to the trouble-causing dualism, thus leaving the problem unsolved.

Moreover, the child eventually leaves school. It is then that the dual conception of human nature is severely tested, often disastrously. So long as the driving forces in the world beyond school walls are expected necessarily to remain coarse-grained, aggressive desires, while the dominant purpose within the school must be to develop in the young a living interest in the higher things of the mind, the school teacher, broadly speaking, will be ineffectual as a contributor to social improvement. For it will be true of those who go from schools and colleges into the world, as Mr. Williams said, that "the finest, the most sensitive, probably the most capable of social contribution, are crushed or, after a terrific conflict, get 'wise' and start playing the game according to the rules used in the outside world."

xiii

The consequences are equally and even more manifestly serious for ministers of religion. In days when the belief in a world to come was central in man's outlook, or when it was at least a vigorous general belief, a minister of religion, as the earthly ambassador of that world, spoke as one having authority. Today, when life on earth has reasserted its original claim, other-worldly interests and other-worldly ideals have only a peripheral significance. They do not enter creatively into practical activities. Hope of immortality lives on, faith in it persists, but so much has been taken from its concrete representation, so much has been lost of the vivid anticipation of future reward or punishment which once lent immortality force, that it is no longer a regulating influence in practical matters.

But is it not true that energetic work is being done to put institutionalized supernaturalism back into the center of things? It is true indeed. One of the most militant ideals at the present time is that of rebuilding a universal spiritual authority strong enough to command every organized or unorganized effort in the community. To bring this about, certain church leaders are willing to make alliances with very unspiritual projects, perhaps hoping to take over the machinery and the power when the social structure based upon these projects falls as it must.

This effort to control man's actions and feelings may go far. It is, however, extremely doubtful that it will be able to re-establish the prescientific outlook. And unless this is done the return to supernaturalism will be only in outward form. The inner life of it will not be restored. There is no indication whatever that *applied* science is to have less of a place in the daily life of the future. All the evidence goes to show that it will have more of a place.

In that event, *theoretical* science, and the scientific interpretation of the world, will have more of a place, too. And
should this prediction prove to be wrong, should the light
of science be put out—which is a possibility, since desperate men will go to any length—the memory of its bright
flame will linger. It can never again be as dark as it once
was.

We have not begun to appreciate the equivocal status
assigned to clergymen in contemporary life. They have
been called "the professional tragedies of our generation."
Deprived of the right to interfere with everyday concerns,
they are nevertheless expected to save mankind from materialism and inhumanity. "As I stand aloof and look," said
Walt Whitman, "there is to me something profoundly
affecting in large masses of men following the lead of those
who do not believe in men." And there is to me something
profoundly affecting in large masses of men—thousands of
ministers of religion—following the lead of those who
have no esteem for them as persons and no respect for
their profession.

But a good word is to be said on the other side. People
of all ranks are deeply disturbed by the state of things.
Men and women close to the necessity of making a living
see with new clearness the damage done by giving a crassly
materialistic meaning to the activities called "practical."
Here and there ministers of religion are courageously attempting to bring the practical and the ideal into co-
operative union. They are injecting a realistic, hardheaded
quality into religion by refusing to give it a purely "spiritual" interpretation. It may be that the coming generation

will find additional ways of bringing religion into relation with secular interests.

In any case, a new brand of idealism is demanded of teachers, ministers, and the rest of us. Social dedication may descend upon a man suddenly, as a conviction of sin may overwhelm the sinner, or an experience of ecstasy may transport the saved. The practical application of this social dedication is another matter. Plato sometimes wished "that wisdom could be infused by touch out of the fuller into the emptier man, as water runs through wool out of a fuller cup into an emptier one." It could not be done in Plato's simpler day; who could imagine it to be done in ours? New ideals must be embodied in new habits and customs, in the reorganization of industry and business, in the redirection of all those processes which are the hands and feet of ideals. And in the contemporary world the good life, generally speaking, must actualize itself in and through huge machines and vast organizations.

So conceived, the task is obviously exacting. Again and again, however, idealism and a sense for the practical, working together, have accomplished splendid results. This chapter has discussed the desirability of making the union of the two a principle of conduct. Another angle of the subject—the relation of ideals to tested knowledge—will be studied in the chapter which follows. In Chapter V we will contrast three methods of realizing ideals. We shall then have before us, in outline, at least, what may be called realistic idealism. For the present the argument must rest where it has arrived.

xiv

We began this chapter talking of an oak tree. The other day it was cut down because it stood in the way of "real estate improvement." It will soon be forgotten, as the Winnebagoes are forgotten who often met in its shade. An oak tree can outlive by centuries the three score and ten years of those who talk about it, but it too must fall and turn to dust. Even the tumultuous age in which we live will shrink to documents and statistics. The great stream moves on and, as Emerson said, "Ages drop in it like rain." Finally, so we are assured, nothing will be left of life in all its forms but ruins and bones and tracings of leaves.

It is the thesis of this chapter that we are now in a spring not a winter of that progression; that this is why traditional customs and institutions are slipping from their places. New interest and aims are pushing them off. Men live on, though ideals drop away, as trees live on, though they lose their leaves. The rejected leaves, the rejected ideals, belong to seasons that are past. They enrich the soil for seasons to come.

We have seen that this picture is too simple. A man is not a tree, really; he is a man. And the life of mankind, as James Hart has said, "is more like that of an orange tree than an oak. All the processes are going on at the same time, budding, flowering, fruiting, an indescribable interweaving of rhythms." And a tree must needs realize the ends of its being, and those ends are its good, while men and women can sever their aspirational longings from their urgencies as natural creatures, and can choose ends that bring disaster upon them. Ideals intermingle with things, with ordinary and extraordinary things, with life-giving and death-dealing things. We pick them out of the life around us, often giving the place of honor to the instrument of our defeat. It may be that we are doing so now. Still, the times are in bud, the buds are swelling, the old leaves are falling, a new season is upon us. It is spring.

In spring we must expect some bad weather—storms and floods and washouts—the destruction of man's labors. Yet spring is the prelude to summer and harvest. What is the harvest to be? That will depend upon the skies and the laborers who work in the fields. And it is possible that the fields which have been tilled hitherto are to lie fallow and the harvest is henceforth to be gathered from new land never before under plow. We must adjust our hopes to this possibility. The destiny of mankind is not the destiny of a race or a nation, to say nothing of a social class or a generation.

Come what may, the world, seen in its larger contours, is astir with vast projects for good and for ill. No one knows whether future historians will write of our age in bright or somber words, but who can doubt that they will describe it as a season of expanding life? Meantime we must gather such joy of mind and heart as we can. If we are doomed, there is no better way to meet our doom. If doom can be averted, it will not be averted by our running away or waiting for the worst to happen.

❦ IV ❧

TRUTH AND IDEALS

i

Some time ago I happened to see an extract from a *Chronicle of an Ancient Monastery* dated 1432. It reported a lively dispute that lasted many days and that stirred up considerable feeling. The quarrel was over the number of teeth in the mouth of a horse. Learned books were brought out, ancient documents were consulted, erudition was shown the like of which had never been seen in that monastery or in the region round about—I only repeat what the old chronicler tells—but the problem could not be solved.

When the disputation had gone on for thirteen days with no end in sight, "a youthful friar of goodly bearing" asked his elders for permission to say a word. The permission being granted, he made a suggestion which would be regarded by us as a very sensible one. It was not so received by the brethren. It only gave them a fresh cause for anger.

"To the wonderment of the disputants," reads the

96

Chronicle, "whose profound wisdom he sore vexed, he
beseeched them to unbend in a manner unheard of, and
to look into the open mouth of a horse for an answer to
their questionings. At this, their dignity being grievously
hurt, they waxed exceeding wroth; and joining in a mighty
uproar, they flew upon him and smote him hip and thigh,
and cast him out forthwith." They excused their rough
treatment of the young friar, excused it to themselves and
to posterity, by adding: "Surely Satan hath tempted this
bold neophyte to declare unholy and unheard-of ways of
finding truth contrary to all the teachings of the fathers."

Having rid themselves of the traitor in their midst, or as
we might say, the radical in their midst, they resumed
their argument about the number of the horse's teeth. Finally they gave up the problem altogether, and the account ends with these words: "After many more days of
painful strife, the dove of peace sat on the assembly, and
they, as one man, declared the problem to be an everlasting mystery, owing to the dearth of historical and theological evidence thereof, and so ordered it writ down."

The story seems too grotesque to be true. Or if we believe it, we suspect that it is grossly exaggerated. But there
is no ground for such suspicion. The story illustrates the
intellectual method of the time. And those who used that
method were not weak-minded or unintelligent men.
Some of the best minds the human race has produced
were among them, and their devotion to truth was as
honest as it was intense. Why, then, did they adopt so
strange a mode of thinking? Why were they incensed
when the young friar proposed that they look into the

mouth of a horse to find out how many teeth a horse had? Why did they fly into a passion and throw him out on his head?

ii

One answer lies on the surface. They were in the habit of solving problems by looking up an established authority. All real knowledge was supposed to be on hand. The task was to locate it. The trick was to bring it to bear upon the question at issue. They were looking for that stored-up knowledge in the books and documents which they spread around them. Had they been able to find some writing of Aristotle or Thomas Aquinas covering the point they would have rejoiced in the discovery of the truth. The number of teeth in the mouth of a horse turned out to be "an everlasting mystery," as they put it, because there was a "dearth of historical and theological evidence thereof."

This explanation of their procedure is good so far as it goes; but there is a better one, related to it, deeper down. These monks and their intellectual contemporaries put no value on information that might be got from the examination of things in their particularity. The kind of knowledge now called relative would have seemed to them a contradiction in terms. Knowledge had to be absolute. It had to be true without regard to time or place or circumstance. They might have looked into the mouth of a horse to satisfy idle curiosity, but never to discover truth. For suppose you had counted the teeth of a particular horse, where was your proof, they would have asked with a kind of knockout finality, that the horse you examined had the

proper number of teeth? Obviously you would not know
that. And not knowing that, you might as well give up pre-
tending to know anything about the matter.

In short, they were not interested in finding out how
many teeth one horse had, or any number of horses had,
which you might single out in some farmer's pasture.
They wanted to know how many teeth HORSE had.
They wanted to determine once for all how many teeth
were necessarily included in essential *Horseness* or *Equinity*. And *Equinity* you would certainly never expect to find
roaming about in the world of the senses. If you knew
how to go about it and you were lucky you might find
Equinity grazing in the pasture of Reason, with other universals, but nowhere else. Therefore the first step you had
to take if you were in search of truth, as distinguished from
hearsay or opinion or probability, was to turn your back
upon the world of particulars, block off all the avenues of
the senses, and follow the lead of infallible reasoning.

If we keep these two facts in mind—that the test of
truth was believed to be conformity with the already
known, and that truth was looked upon as by its very nature absolute or unconditional—we can understand why
the kind of thinking we have just glanced at appealed to
thinkers then alive. In view of their presuppositions, their
manner of solving problems was not as fantastic as it
would otherwise seem. It was the rational way of going at
the job.

We shall appreciate this still more fully if we discriminate one further element in their situation. They had their
own motive for seeking to know. They wanted the truth

in order to possess it, not, as later came to be the case, to use it. The slogan, "Knowledge is power," meaning mechanical power, meaning power over the forces of nature, had not yet been heard. The ideal which it advertised had not yet gripped the imagination of men. Their slogan, had they had one, would have been, "Knowledge is insight," insight into the ultimately Real, into the quintessence of Metaphysical Being. And the proper attitude toward truth of that kind is one of beholding or contemplating. You want it to take home for inward illumination, not to do things with in the outer world.

iii

And here we are, five hundred years later, so accustomed to our world's vast spaciousness that we cannot creep back into their tiny world no matter how we try. Nor could we, even if we would, revive their disdain of the study of particulars. Why then talk about their intellectual method? Is it to amuse ourselves for a moment at their expense, or to admire ourselves for having advanced so far beyond them in mental maturity? No; for neither of these reasons; for a far better reason. It is that we may see how, and perhaps why, we fall back upon their kind of thinking when our problem is of a certain kind, the kind, incidentally, in which they were most interested, and for the sake of which they originally developed the method we have reviewed.

Suppose Thomas Aquinas were to visit our world. He would no doubt be dazed by our machine-rumbling environment. He would be startled by the naturalistic bias

which he would come upon in all walks of life. His amaze-
ment would increase as he entered our laboratories and
became acquainted with the technique perfected by men
of science to study physical nature. There is one kind of
experience, however, which would make him feel at home
in this bewildering world. He would know his way about
in our discussion of moral and religious ideals, indeed of
idealism in general. He would hear a number of strange
phrases, but the talk as a whole would have a familiar ring.
He could take up the discussion almost where he left it off
in 1274.

How shall we account for this curious anachronism?
Our age is noted for its "fact-finding" zeal, for its insist-
ence upon "practical results" and its hardheaded demand
for what can be weighed and measured. Even in education, aesthetics, and religion, where what we do is always
mixed with starry-eyed hopes for doing it, we are trying
to be "scientific." Do we forget all this when we turn
to ideals? Do we consult ancient books and documents,
or come with preconceived ideals derived from some superworldly order of being, which we hope to impress upon
the hopes, fears, loves, hates, ambitions, and aspirations of
men? Do we repudiate the practical world and physical
nature as a possible source of ethical or cultural opportunities?

iv

Well, call the roll of the people who by general consent are supposed to know the truth about the world in
which we live. Ask them regarding the higher interests of

life. They will answer, ten to one, yes, a hundred to one, that you must expect no help from the occupation in which they are engaged. Whatever their excuse may be, they leave the problem of ideals severely alone. They advise you to go to someone else if you are interested in that problem. In the language of the street, they "pass the buck." Take this outspoken statement from a newspaper office:

The press of America is giving its reading public just what is demanded in the way of news. . . . Reporters, editors, and circulation men must give that reading public just what it wants to stay in the procession, just as a merchant must stock his store with the merchandise that his buying public demands. No, it is not the fault of the newspapers. They are simply filling an order placed by the newspaper readers of America.

A director of film production, who objected to a criticism of motion picture morals, said the same thing:

The motion picture industry is a business concern. It must adjust its supply to the demand or go out of business. It is none of its affair to raise moral standards. The obligation of improving the public taste rests upon the churches and schools.

The president of a leading university, addressing members of his faculty who were agitated about educational ideals, said it once more:

The students are our customers and we must give them what they want.

These quotations may seem a little too pat. Here then is one that is not so pat. It says more than that we must give people what they want. It says indeed that we must give them what they do not want. Yet it, too, takes for granted the cultural sterility of everyday practice. This statement is by the president of another leading university:

I should insist that a university is concerned with thought and that the collection of information, historical or current, had no place in it except as such data may illustrate or confirm principles or assist in their development.

Here we have it with commendable clarity. Guiding principles have a status absolutely distinct from the life they are to guide. The world of action is sinful. Principles are holy. How can holy principles originate in a sinful world? We must get over the notion that wisdom, principles of conduct, and knowledge of causes may grow out of man's effort to make the best he can of living. They must be born by immaculate conception. We must adopt B. L. Taylor's ironical suggestion and revise the first chapter of Genesis to read: "In the beginning God created a set of principles and man was without form and void."

Do we fare better if we interrogate the scientists? Not much better. Here are two examples:

1. It is the job of scientists to develop their science without consideration of the social uses to which their work might be put.

2. One of the most refreshing things about the scientific worker is that he thinks nothing wrong and nothing right, save only the perpetual accumulation of verifiable knowledge, and the progressive formulation of scientific truth. It is not his fault if poison gases, explosives, etc., come

into being to oppress mankind; these things are thrown out by him, it is true, from Nature's storehouse, along with a lot of other miscellaneous luggage, and if evilly-disposed persons come past and carry them off, he cannot be held responsible, and is usually much too busy to notice that anything has happened.

Since the physical and biological scientists feel obliged to remain aloof from the problems of evaluation which they do so much to accentuate, how about the social scientists? A presidential address before the American Sociological Society offered this answer:

Sociology as a science is not interested in making the world a better place in which to live. The sociologist of the future will spend most of his time on doing hard, dull, tedious, and routine work in statistics and measurement. In this future state every one will be a statistician, that is, nearly every one . . . The individual workers will have plenty of machines, all of them electric. Indeed, there are likely to be more machines than thinkers. . . . The audience for sociological articles will be the scientific guild, and no attempt will be made to make these articles readable for shop girls or high school youth. . . . This specialization . . . does not mean that there will be any diminution in the popularization of science. There will be numerous articles and books by those who cannot be scientists or by the scientist's weaker self which will show the human significance of these discoveries and measurements—publications which will dramatize science, which will rewrite scientific results in terms of slang, which will put in them an ethical punch.

There it is again. We must have "ethical punch," but social science cannot furnish it. Social scientists are too

busy collecting facts to bother about the possible bearing
of those facts upon the humdrum lot of mankind. Let
someone else see to that. The aristocrats of the intellect
must accumulate their treasures and leave to a lower
order of intelligence the task of making life worth living
for shopgirls, high school youth, and the ignorant masses
in general.

What of the historians? They study the rise and fall
of ideas, customs, institutions, nations, peoples. Do they
suggest that historical events may be consulted in the interest of practical ideals? Some of them do. Curtis Nettels
is one of these. "History," he boldly declares, "is man's
guide to action in the present and future." Charles A.
Beard is another. He has consistently advised the study
of history with the view of discovering better social conditions for men and women in the future. Frederick Jack-
son Turner used to say: "Historical study has for its end
to let the community see itself in the light of the past,
to give it new thoughts and feelings, new aspirations and
energies."

But this view of the use of history is not orthodox. Most
of us never heard of it. The conception we acquired in
school or college, if we acquired any, is more likely to
have been the one expressed by another historian:

History has no social significance, as far as I can determine. In fact, the study of history is chiefly of importance as a mental and intellectual training. In itself the
study of history is of no value. It produces nothing, creates
nothing, has no commercial value, is of no aid to health,
wealth, or the comfort and convenience of man. The de-

light of the student of history is that his subject is far removed from the marketplace and is not in the least utilitarian. But as a factor in sharpening, strengthening, broadening, and liberalizing the human mind, it is beyond price. History is more than worth studying for its own sake. To inquire what it will do to guide you in life will get you nowhere.

But surely philosophers do not fall in line with this one-sided interest in knowledge. Alas they do. We have already had evidence of the fact. An additional quotation at this point will round out the argument. It appeared in the New York *Times*, reporting the remarks of a philosopher at a meeting of philosophers:

Philosophy . . . . etches no pattern of life upon the mundane sky. Some people study philosophy, as some study music or enjoy a sunset. "It is just a matter of temperament. Some like caviar, some like philosophy." At any rate, it is more profitable than such "silly diversions" as chess and bridge. While it "may be just as useless," the hypothetical interpretation of the unknown gives zest to life and stimulates the intellect.

These are of course selected quotations. They could be matched by others of an opposite import. They are, however, representative quotations, representative not only of individuals, but of schools of thought. And they differ from most of what one reads on the subject in forthrightness of expression alone. They say directly what many say by indirection or in association with related ideas that blunt the point. And what they say in one phraseology or another, is that ideals of life are not to be sought in the everyday world; that if there are such to be had they must be fetched from some realm apart, apart from this or that specific lifework, or apart from lifework altogether.

v

The divorce of knowledge from understanding has no more vigorous critic in America than the president of the University of Chicago. "The most characteristic feature of the modern world," he declares, "is bewilderment. Anybody who says he knows anything is at once suspected of affectation or falsehood. . . . We do not know where we are going, or why; we have almost given up the attempt to find out." This is not because we have been backward in collecting facts. We have been extremely busy collecting facts. Says President Hutchins:

Certainly we have more facts about the world, about ourselves, and the relations among ourselves than were available to any of our ancestors. . . . If, as we have been convinced since the Renaissance, the advance of the race is in direct proportion to the volume of information it possesses, we should by now have reached every imaginable human goal. We have more information, more means of getting more information, and more means of distributing information than at any time in history.

Nevertheless "we are bewildered." And the explanation given by him is that our vast collections of facts have little or no meaning beyond themselves. They bear no relation to guiding principles. "We are in despair," he thinks, "because the keys which were to open the gates of heaven have let us into a larger but more oppressive prison house."

The author of The Higher Learning in America has

heard of the claim that accumulating information has
yielded so little wisdom because we have not looked for
it there, have looked for it anywhere but there. The claim
has made no impression on his mind. Possibly he has seen
the book by Leonard White and Marshall Dimock, of the
University of Chicago, and John Gaus, of the University
of Wisconsin, a scholarly study of how principles are to
be lifted out of "the hurrying world of events." In this
study, *The Frontiers of Public Administration*, he may
have read these words:

> For the sake of clarity, may it again be said that, in our
> view, principle must be understood to mean a hypothesis
> so adequately tested by observation and/or experiment that
> it may intelligently be put forward as a guide to action, or
> as a means of understanding. The framing of hypotheses
> may be undertaken by anyone with a fertile imagination,
> but their relevance is affected by a sense of reality on the
> part of the inquirer. Therefore depth of insight in the
> formulation of hypotheses and understanding of the rele-
> vant data come from participation rather than from mere
> observation. Hence in recent social research the invention
> of the "participant-observer."

If he has read the paragraph it has not convinced him.
In one speech after another, in one article or book after
another, he has contended that only through rational,
analytical thinking can principles of order or direction be
found; indeed that the study of metaphysics alone, the
study of being as being, can illuminate factual material.
An example of his logic is stated in a series of propositions.
I assume that he intends the argument to be taken seriously.

The aim of higher education is wisdom. Wisdom is knowledge of principles and causes. Metaphysics deals with the highest principles and causes. Therefore metaphysics is the highest wisdom.

From the context we may supply two additional propositions: Metaphysics is gathered up in Aristotle. Therefore Aristotle is the fountainhead of higher education.

Back to the Greeks, then! Back to the leisure-group philosophy of the Greeks because medieval theology, which might be preferable, is ruled out by present legal restrictions and the general weakness of religious faith. At any rate—and this is where we come out—the requisite high principles cannot be discovered by looking to the kind of knowledge with which we are so abundantly supplied. Information gained from daily experience, from observation or experimental investigation, can yield no positive meaning as regards the higher interests of men. Principles of conduct and true insight must be sought in Revelation or Pure Reason. A true university must be conceived as a "stronghold of those who insist on the exercise of reason, who will not be moved by passion or buried by blizzards of data." We are up against an either-or alternative. Unless we hasten into the retreat provided by Aristotle, we shall be caught and overwhelmed in a trackless wasteland of meaningless facts.

In a word, this college president is a conspicuous and influential exponent of the dualism examined in this chapter. As an educator he unites with many others in our academic institutions who believe that wisdom must be dipped up from a spring deep within the castle of higher

learning. It may be carried over the drawbridge to the
thirsty on the outside, but it cannot be found outside and
brought in.

vi

What have we learned from these quotations from various fields? We have learned that our knowledge falls apart
into more and more bits, so that the farther we go in the
way of truth the farther we are from wisdom of life. We
collect data, work up statistics, draw graphs, make maps
and blueprints, heap up piles of factual wealth, and when
the most successful fact-gatherers are invited to a banquet
of those who know, to refresh their spirits and to discuss
plans for a more humanly significant use of what is known,
they all send regrets. One has bought property and must
needs have a look at it; another has acquired power and
must try it out; a third is married to a vested interest and
so cannot come. "I pray thee have me excused," they send
back word. That is why the master of the house—Life—
is saying today as in that other day: "Go out quickly into
the streets and lanes of the city, and bring in hither the
poor, and the maimed, and the halt, and the blind." The
salt of knowledge is good: "but if the salt have lost his
savour, wherewith shall it be seasoned. It is neither fit for
the land, nor yet for the dunghill; but men cast it out."

vii

This shirking of direct responsibility for the trend of
day-to-day affairs, by those who have or are reputed to have
superior knowledge, worldly or academic, is the most por-

tentous characteristic of our culture. Must intellectual
maturity necessarily have this effect? As a man grows in
experience must he learn that truth, beauty, good will,
ideals in general are to be looked upon as superworldly or
pure illusions?

The problem is a persistent one. It was acute during
the decline of the Greek and Roman world. At that time,
too, the study of the world as fact was making spectacular
progress and the external equipment of life was growing bigger and bigger. Business, government, military efficiency, the means of pleasure, all these were advancing
step by step. And step by step the shadow of ethical
skepticism was keeping pace with them. Outwardly, civilization was carrying on in impressive fashion. Inwardly, it
was dying at the heart. It was dying at the heart because
with all its getting it was unable to get social wisdom.

One circumstance of that epoch is especially apropos.
Theorists about life were numerous and never more lo-
quacious, but they had nothing to say about the direction
of the human venture. Above the medley of noises that
comes to us from the centuries immediately preceding and
following the birth of Jesus, we hear the voices of intellectuals crying down the worth of everyday effort. Stoic,
Epicurean, Cynic, Skeptic, Platonist, Aristotelian vied with
one another to prove that human beings engaged in their
daily occupations are necessarily debarred from participation in truth or goodness or beauty.

The economic and political setting of this spirit of disillusion becomes more intricate the more it is explored.
But we do know what it ended in. We know what the

prevailing "loss of moral nerve," as Gilbert Murray has called it, helped to bring about. The assumed ethical impotence of mankind and the assumed worthlessness of the earthly struggle were formulated into a social philosophy which became the foundation of a world empire. The lamp of the mind was put out. Intellectual darkness settled down upon the human scene for a thousand years.

viii

It may help us to deal with our own situation if we take a constructive hint from one who lived in the midst of that critical period and did his work in it with extraordinary ability and strength of purpose. We know nothing about him that cannot be deduced from his writings. No one has guessed so much as his name. We cannot tell why he preferred to remain anonymous. He appears to have been active in the Christian movement two generations or more after the crucifixion of its founder, and was one of the great religious thinkers not only of that time but of all history. The name that has been given to him is St. John, and he is spoken of as "that disciple whom Jesus loved."

This unknown writer speaks to us in one of the famous sayings which he attributed to Jesus. We have it as John viii, 32:

> And ye shall know the truth, and
> the truth shall make you free.

It is a puzzling saying, and it puzzled those who heard it. Does it mean that if you comprehend the truth, if you

take it in or lay hold upon it, you are no longer subject
to legal or moral restrictions; or that you are liberated
from the power of sin; or that you are lifted into a superior
status free from every entanglement with ordinary life?
These and still other meanings were read into the passage.

The fact of special interest to us is the position taken
by certain intellectuals contemporaneous with the religious
leader of whom we are speaking. Factions of these, known
as Gnostics, were coming to the front in the Christian
movement. They were attempting to transform it from a
way of life into a system of speculative ideas. To them
Christianity meant intellectual experience, not practical
performance. Their aim was to *behold* the truth, and
through this beholding to realize the highest human end.
How men and women might fare who had to do the work
of the world was a difficulty they left to someone else to
take care of. They strove to enter into the sacred realm of
pure knowledge, to attain to pure rationality, to woo truth
in detachment from the senseless earthly struggle to which
they thought men and women in general were doomed.

In the Second Epistle of John we come upon the hint
to which I have referred. "I rejoiced greatly," says the
writer of this letter, "that I found of thy children walking
in the truth." *Walking in the truth*—what an arresting
way of saying it! Intellectual exclusiveness and the ethical
complacency of the so-called worldly wise, seemed to St.
John the tragic negation of truth's essential function. Repeatedly he makes such statements as this: "Hereby we
know that we know him if we keep his commandments.
He that saith, I know him, and doeth not his command-

ments is a liar and the truth is not in him." Seven times
in the First Epistle he reiterates, "hereby we know"; but
it is not knowing the truth which seems to him to need
emphasizing; the important thing is truth's embodiment,
truth's ability to refashion men's lives. The three epistles
that bear his name resound with the admonition that the
test of truth is its ability to walk abroad in the world and,
like a good physician, to perform a healing function where-
ever it goes. "I have no greater joy," he writes in the Third
Epistle, "than to hear that my children walk in the truth."

ix

There is then a kind of knowing in which the object
known is universal and abstract, and the knowing process
is a form of intellectual grasping. When you have reached
truth in this way you have arrived at the end of a path.
You may stand there and look, or sit down there and
meditate, or kneel there and worship. Truth thus gained
brings with it a rare experience of intellectual expansion,
suffused with a spirit of humility if you are one sort of
person, or with a sweet feeling of intellectual superiority
if you are another sort. This truth at its best is to do its
work upon you personally. It is to win you the personal
salvation of your mind. Each individual is saved for himself, and the welfare of humanity hinges upon the intellectual salvation of larger and larger numbers of individuals. With it usually goes the doctrine that salvation,
in this case intellectual salvation, is reserved for the few
elect.

The other kind of knowing is radically different. In

it the object known retains its original concreteness, and
the process of knowing is the enrichment of that object
through the discovery of its interconnections in the wide-
spreading fabric of human experience. When you have
reached truth in this way you have not arrived at the end
of a path. You have set out to go places. You seek to
provide truth with a body; to give it feet, to give it hands,
to put it to work. You use it to turn on the light in some
dark corner of life, to bring understanding where there is
discord, to improve some particular or general situation.
It is a truth that is to accompany men wherever they feel
they must go, lest without its illuminating aid they lose
their way.

A critic may assert that this discrimination dodges the
issue. He may say that truth is after all truth; that what
you do with truth is another matter. And the critic would
have almost everyone on his side, because almost everyone takes it for granted that truth is something "out
there" which you have to accept, regardless of your pref-
erences. To speak of truth in the service of what men
want sounds suspiciously like saying that truth should be
made to order, should be measured to human desire. And
the criticism is valid, if rightly understood. Truth is not
a piece of cloth to be cut to anyone's liking. There is a
certain inevitability, a certain must be about truth which
no one but a skeptic will think of denying. The only question is what this inevitability or this must be really is.

The assumption that Truth, lofty, cold, changeless, exists
independently of man and out of his reach, is the common
assumption. It is a Mount Everest, crowned with eternal

snow, alluring, perilous, unconquerable. Generation after generation and century after century the human mind has strained and climbed, and still the foothills are shrouded in mist and the summit gleams far off as when the venture began. So it appears, and more than so; for mountain ranges are known to waste away, while Truth is believed to stand forever fast. Emily Dickinson has voiced a nearly universal faith in her poem, "Truth is as old as God." I quote it from *Letters of Emily Dickinson*, edited by Mabel Loomis Todd, which I understand to be the source book for subsequent writings about Emily Dickinson:

> Truth is as old as God,
> His twin identity—
> And will endure as long as He,
> A co-eternity,
> And perish on the day
> That he is borne away
> From mansions of the universe,
> A lifeless Deity.

As one reads and listens one gets the impression that although no one has climbed the fascinating peak, some men have reached, or at least mean to reach, a vantage ground from which the great mountain range is directly visible. They talk as if it were their one aim in life to gaze upon that eternal, inviolable, self-subsisting Truth, though it be from far off. Men of science, and rationalists who put supreme trust in Reason, are thought to be of this class. They often think so themselves. It is probably from these that the rest of us have picked up the mood, and something of the terminology.

"Science," says Max Wertheimer, for example, "is rooted in the will to truth. With the will to truth it stands or falls. Lower the standard even slightly and science becomes diseased at its core. Not only science, but man. The will to truth, pure and unadulterated, is among the essential conditions of his existence; if the standard is compromised he easily becomes a kind of tragic caricature of himself."

Etienne Gilson, speaking for rationalism, asserts that "though the various expressions of truth unavoidably bear the mark of their local origins, truth itself is universal in its own right." If we want more order in moral, social, and political life, if we hope to preserve what there is precious about liberty, we must find out the order there is in truth in itself and conform our lives to that order. "Humanly and naturally speaking," he declares, "there is no unifying force above reason. It could even be said that, absolutely speaking, it really is the only unifying force. What is rationally true is universally true, for the only thing that lies behind truth is reality itself, which is the same for all."

x

Now has a scientist ever *produced* any "pure and unadulterated" truth? Has a rationalist ever *demonstrated* that he had obtained even a glimpse of "truth in itself"? Have they not over and over shown up one another's failure to procure any such truth? The questions answer themselves. It is as if truth had decreed in the language of Exodus, "Thou canst not see my face: for there shall no man see me, and live." Neither the scientist nor the rationalist can disengage himself from his nervous system, not even from his senses, and still observe or think. No one can. It is difficult enough to avoid leaving a telltale fingerprint on truth; to avoid leaving a mindprint on it is altogether impossible. Every truth is in that sense somewhat impure, somewhat adulterated, and there is no hope of obtaining truth "universal in its own right." In the long history of thinking no man has yet caught sight of, or in any way established contact with, *Truth as such,* or else he has not been able to tell about the experience in a way to make possible a check up on his claim.

If truth must be thought of an autonomous, then we must conclude, as Hans Vaihinger did, that all so called truth is "merely the most expedient error." In that case we never have had or shall have any truth, and, what is more serious, no way of deciding which of our expedient errors are most nearly true. Or can a man pretend to know the way to Boston who, admittedly, knows only the most expedient way of going somewhere else?

The curious fact is that, in spite of the professed devotion to truth as truth, no one so much as tries for it. Some may *talk* as though they meant to draw as near as possible to an independently existing truth and have a square look at it, but they certainly do not *act* as though this were their intention. Take the scientist. Does he try to make his way to truth's abiding place? Does he walk right up to truth, or as close as he can get, throw a searchlight on it and illuminate its contour and structure? Surely not. He walks up to test tubes, microscopes, telescopes, galvanometers, statistics, pointer readings, mathematical functions, and the like. He puts some hypothesis to a test which is regarded as decisive in his technique, and if it stands up to that test he calls it true. Truth, so far as he is concerned, is the collection of such robust hypotheses.

The rationalist behaves in exactly the same manner, the difference being in the nature of his technique and the tests which he finds adequate. Reasoning is a less public performance than experimenting (which, incidentally, is one of its drawbacks), but its operating principle is the same. In reasoning, as in experimenting, a belief, idea, conjecture, hypothesis, is brought to a standard test, and if it meets this test successfully it is accepted as true.

This is the procedure wherever questions of true or false have to be settled. The historian goes to documents, the judge to the law, the businessman to sales, the farmer, laborer, or housewife to the various means of verification which have been developed in his or her occupation. For all of them "the proof of the pudding is in the eating." This is not to say that the eating *is* the pudding, but that it is the means of *placing* the pudding in the category of true or false. Such placing is what truth is known as, what it denotes in day-to-day practice.

People of course differ greatly in the tests they use and the care they take to use them. That is why emphasis upon "the will to truth" is needed. The emphasis is, however, misplaced if the will to truth is understood to mean crowding nearer and nearer to truth in the absolute or ultimate sense. The gaining of truth is certainly not made easier by venerating Truth in the abstract and showing only a casual interest in the means used to determine what is true in a given case. Carelessness in the use of truth-tools is in fact the surest way to get poor results, no matter what one's theory of truth may be.

Most people have progressed to the point of wanting accurate scales for weighing meat, groceries, coal, and such things. They insist upon exact units of measurement for milk, gasoline, cloth, boards, land, and other material quantities. They appreciate the necessity of having reliable tests for the purity of foods and drugs. It is only in realms which they profess to regard as higher than material things that they act as if scales and yardsticks were unimportant. In part, no doubt, this is due to the greater complexity and elusiveness of what has to be measured. A uniform standard is difficult to agree upon. But this fact makes it more, not less, desirable to have trustworthy truth-tools to work with, and the more necessary that we use those we have with skill and watchfulness.

There is then a "will to truth, pure and unadulterated" which must be insisted upon. It is *the determination to use only the best available tests of the true whatever the subject matter; the refusal to play fast and loose with these in response to extraneous demands; and the persistent endeavor to perfect the technique whereby the tenability of a proposed belief is decided.*

xi

We come back to the problem under discussion—the relation of tested knowledge to ideals of life. It cannot be necessary to argue that practical men and women in their

practical concerns insist upon *walking in the truth* rather
than upon *contemplating* it. No lawyer or banker or businessman, no doctor, no one in the public service or in a
newspaper office, recognizes anything to be true which he
cannot practice. That is what they mean when they speak
of anything as mere theory. *It will not walk with them.*
Farmers and laboring men behave in like manner. So do
housewives in kitchens and sailors on the high seas. Surely
this needs no demonstration.

Neither does it need demonstration that when the same
people turn their attention to moral or "spiritual" matters their common-sense realism is likely to melt away.
They do *not* insist upon a truth to walk with. They prefer
a truth which they can contemplate. If the problem happens to be one of religious, aesthetic, or ethical idealism,
the last thing lawyers, bankers, professional or businessmen, farmers or laborers, *then* think of is a workaday
truth. They either refuse to associate with ideals under
any circumstances whatsoever, taking no stock in them, or
they think it improper to approach ideals as they might
everyday ambitions. To mingle with ideals the self, they
think, must get itself ready; must take a bath or at least
change clothes and appear in its Sunday best.

The deplorable effect of thus dividing the world into
tangible things and intangible ideals has been discussed in
a number of connections in this book. The present question, the relation of truth to ideals, touches upon it again.
Severance of material knowledge and practical interests
from idealism is part of the same dualistic error, and the
effect of it is no less deplorable.

Granting for the moment that there are "spiritual" ideals, they are by no means our only ones, nor are they the most pervasive and influential. Ideals are the projections of wants. They envisage desirable possibilities seen in contrast with what exists or is had. They are therefore as various as our wants are. They may be as unsubstantial as the stuff of reverie, as removed from the day-to-day routine as the fleecy clouds that float over the earth on a sunny day; or they may have all the substance of silver and gold, houses and lands, physical satisfaction, any and every kind of object or thing met with in the world of the senses. They may aim at better business returns or better business relations, higher wages or an improved status for the laboring man as a human being, election to public office or a more just social order, greater reputation as an end in itself or personal attainment in intellectual or artistic facility, in moral personality, in religious experience.

This broader construction of idealism has often been advocated and defended. A concise description of its essential nature is found in an article by John R. Commons, published at a time when the State and the University of Wisconsin were singularly responsive to the challenge of social idealism in both the theoretical and the practical fields. Mr. Commons and those who were of a similar mind objected to idealism as "the yearning for perfection above and beyond the mere grind and bustle for necessities, luxuries and wealth." In contrast with this "spiritual" conception they offered what he called "utilitarian idealism." It was this brand of idealism which caused such epithets to be applied to the institution with which these utilitarian idealists were connected as "materialistic," "job-getter," "cow-college," "butter-fat university." "It may be," Mr. Commons confesses in his article, "that we have sacrificed a kind of idealism, but if so, we are part of a movement that is exalting another kind." This other kind, to which he had already given specific operational form in valuable economic and political measures, and to which he has added throughout his long and extraordinary serv-ice, is suggested in a quotation from this article:

I do not see why there is not as much idealism of its kind in breeding a perfect animal or a Wisconsin No. 7 ear of corn, or in devising an absolutely exact instrument for measuring a thousand cubic feet of gas, or for measur-ing exactly the amount of butter or casein in milk, as there is in chipping out a Venus de Milo or erecting a Parthenon. . . . Of course a cow is just a cow, and can never become a Winged Victory. But within her field of human endeavor she is capable of approaching an ideal. And, more than that, she is an ideal that every farmer and farmer's boy— the despised slaves and helots of Greece—can aspire to. But, most of all, this ideal of a perfect product is the only way of rendering a perfect service to others. . . . Utili-tarianism is the democracy of idealism. . . . It makes a science and an art out of what to the Greeks was degrading toil. It should make an ethics of service to others out of science, art, wealth, and toil.

Utilitarian idealism may of course be understood to exclude numerous important ideals, especially certain kinds of ideals. But there is nothing in the conception itself, nor in the conditions under which men live, to demand this restriction. The quality of being useful does not destroy the quality of being ideal. At bottom the question is simply whether, taking human hopes, plans, motivations, in their multifarious variety, we shall regard them as ideals only in so far as they supervene upon men from above them, or whether ideals may be thought of as indigenous to human activity of every kind.

Regardless of definition, such hopes, plans, and motivations, aiming to transform into actuality what is represented in the imagination as possible, virtually determine the destiny of men so far as human actions can. Communism, Fascism, Democracy, the New Deal, More Business in Government, Less Government in Business, The League of Nations, National Isolation—these and innumerable programs of every kind, small or large in scope, are so many forms of idealism, because they aim to draw upon the possible resources of the world and of human beings to give things hoped for the substance of sensuous existence. The remedial or devastating effect of these ideals which are intrinsic to practical living is beyond doubt. It is upon them, rather than upon the ideals characteristic of detachment from life, that attention must be centered by anyone who cares about his own life or about the course of events.

xii

The outcome of our discussion in this chapter, stated in intellectual terms, is that ideals are hypotheses in the undertaking which engages the interest of us all. We are all intent upon making our lives more livable, much or

little as that may envisage, much or little as we may be
able to carry out what we have in mind. Ideals may aim
at physical comfort, peace of mind, a higher level of intellectual, moral or aesthetic achievement, the exercise of
power as power, or something else; but ideals always reach
out to an imagined good state which is desired in place
of an existing and less satisfactory one. Since ideals are
hypotheses in the search for a more satisfying life experience, they must meet a double test. *They must prefigure
desirable changes, and these changes must be realizable in
fact.* The question is, are they *true* ideals: will they walk
with men and work with men in the endeavor to reach
the best that is attainable? Pierre Curie, who surely earned
the right to say it, summed up the double obligation in a
sentence: "One must make of life a dream, and of that
dream a reality."

Truth, ideals, and reality—the three are inseparable.
Something has now been said about the relation of truth
and ideals; something should be added about reality, for
reality at last conditions them both. This amplification
must wait until a later chapter. Here one concluding fact
may be taken to heart.

Ideals naturally make us think of the young, whose
ideals are still largely to be realized. It has always been
true that some of the young men and women who have
been interested in social improvement have devoted their
talents to the perpetuation of inherited ideals. Possibly
more of them are tempted to do this in a time of unusual
agitation and uncertainty like ours. Urged on, supported,

rewarded by their elders, they seek to keep traditional ideals alive and to protect them against the degrading effect of more modern conceptions.

But the vast majority of those who are now coming upon the field of action will try to improve their circumstances by looking about in the world they can see with their physical eyes. If they want to know the number of teeth in the mouth of a horse, they will catch horses and count their teeth. They will not gather about a motionless statue of Equinity in the formal garden of erudition and wait for a revelation of the absolute truth. If they want to know about love, decency, justice, honor, right, wrong, they will follow men and women into daily relations and transactions and there try to find better and worse meanings in operation. They will not gather about a sequestered oracle of wisdom and wait to be supplied with eternal principles.

Their efforts to make happiness more secure for more people, and to raise the ethical level of the satisfactions desired, may prove futile. Should this come to pass, the responsibility will lie heaviest upon those who have enjoyed educational advantages and those who have been schooled in practical life. Formal education and experience of life often produce the strongest resistance to change, especially as we grow older. Settled down into moral and religious apathy, we may think we are loyal to ethical and religious ideals when we are only stubborn in our adherence to what we are used to.

The young are sometimes wrong in choosing the new paths they do, but they are sometimes right. We are too ready to generalize that because they are young they are not interested in the number of the horse's teeth; that all they are after is to chase horses about, the wilder the better. We are too easily convinced that they are not interested in discovering virtues superior to those now exemplified in the world of their elders; that all they want is to throw off restraint, the more completely the better.

We end the chapter with an idea that has asked to be heard from the beginning of it. The most significant and effective relation between veterans of life and young recruits who are entering upon it, the most significant personally and effective socially, is comradeship in the working out of realistic ideals. It is for us who are older to show by precept and example to those who are still young, how to battle for more richly satisfying realities, and then as best we can, sometimes in pain and sometimes with tears of joy in our eyes, to watch them with sympathetic understanding as they march under their own banners.

❧ V ❧

REALISTIC IDEALISM

i

In the minds of most people realism and idealism will not mix. It would never occur to them to speak of realistic idealism. They would think it nonsense. In their vocabulary the word "real" stands for something solid—a rock, an animal body, a pocket full of money; the word "ideal" for the shadowy and dreamlike. That is because they have learned the words from books. And the words have grown into a theory that separates the facts or events as the words are separated. But life experience puts the real and the ideal together. And what life experience puts together let no theory put asunder.

Realism and idealism can be so defined as to make them incompatible. As attitudes toward the world, however, the two have always functioned and still function in inter-relation. Every man must be a realist at least in the sense that he cannot ignore bodily needs or refuse to notice the physical environment. He has wants which compel him to put forth practical effort even if he despises "the flesh"

and aspires to live only "in the spirit." Unless he belongs
to the "idle rich" and can shift the burden to other shoulders he must make a living, and must try to win a place
which makes the struggle endurable, and, if possible, enjoyable. In a hundred ways he must acknowledge as real
the conditions upon which he has to rely to make his life
as satisfactory as he can.

This practical *realism* is no more inevitable than practical *idealism*. "Man is born to idealize," as Mr. Justice
Holmes said, "because he is born to act." Everyone is
engaged in transforming the given real into something
else, something no less real but more satisfying. That is
to say, everyone is intent upon making desired actualities
out of imagined possibilities. And what are imagined possibilities which a man hopes to make into actualities but
realistic ideals?

It is this characteristic of human beings which sets
them off from all other creatures. For thousands of years
the environment has been worked upon to bring it into
better harmony with the desired. If there are departments
of life from which ideals seem to be excluded, or if in
these times it is hard to detect ideals at work below the
surface of what is going on, one reason is the error of
believing that all ideals are ideal. They are not—except
perhaps from the viewpoint of those whose ideals they
are, and when all other interests are in total eclipse. Men
strive to attain the not-yet-attained and willingly pay for
it with what they have. The ends aimed at may be good
or bad, material or spiritual, attainable or unattainable.
These distinctions touch the nature of the objects desired,

not the eagerness for the unrealized which runs through them all and is common to them all.

Practical and aspirational aims are thus naturally interdependent. Nor can this interdependence ever be altogether undone. There will always be some relation between a man's efforts to live and what he hopes to make of himself and his life. It can, however, be reduced to a minimum. A narrow workaday objective or a so-called higher interest may steal the show. Realism and idealism then move apart until they are regarded as opposing interests that cannot be reconciled. Let us for the present disregard this all too common outcome and concentrate upon what is after all the deeper manifestation—the living interdependence of action and aspiration.

ii

Man is by nature active, and he is aware of what he wants; not always and in every instance, yet frequently enough to become involved in the problem of deciding what he wants most. As the world is constituted wants are bound to come into conflict, one crowding out another. There are persons who find it relatively easy to choose between conflicting wants, or who act as if they did, and persons who find it so difficult to choose that they fall into the habit of letting the course of events determine the issue for them. In general, however, men and women recognize the desirability of making the best selection they can. They have learned the truth which William James stated so well:

The actually possible in this world is vastly narrower than all that is demanded; and there is always a *pinch* between the ideal and the actual which can only be got through by leaving part of the ideal behind. There is hardly a good which we can imagine except as competing for the possession of the same bit of space and time with some other imagined good. Every end of desire that presents itself appears exclusive of some other end of desire.

They have learned this truth, and they make an effort, often a praiseworthy one, to adopt some dependable rule of deciding which ends of desire are of most worth.

The problem of course extends beyond a man's own wants. Occasions arise when he has to choose between his own wants and the wants of others. Art Young, in a wistful cartoon, shows himself bewildered in the center of a path, a tall, white, persuasive angel tugging at one elbow, and a tall, white, stern angel tugging at the other elbow. The comment which accompanies the cartoon makes this confession, and he makes it for us all:

Hardly a day goes by that the problem of duty to myself —versus duty to others—does not arise. I confess having a well-developed ego—but am just as ready to admit that no one's ego is of much importance. But I am here. And when to forget self-interest and give way to the self-interest of someone else, has been one of my worries throughout a lifetime. The practice of a reasonable selfishness is just as much a duty as indulging in a "reasonable" altruism. But what is "reasonable"? When to loan money to a friend, when to help a world cause—this "me or thou" stands as one of the big problems of living.

The "me or thou" problem is not limited to the choice among duties. No man's interest in life is confined to the one aim of doing his duty. Even where the sense of ethical obligation is strong it does not cover the whole field of desire. The acutest "me or thou" conflict arises in the area beyond settled duties. Most of us must venture into that moral no-man's land where the drive of individual ambition and the conflicting diversity of wants give rise to the sharpest competition. While each person is acquainted with only the merest fraction of the people whose life aims and successes or failures affect his own, he is nevertheless affected by them in all sorts of ways. They impinge upon, and modify, frustrate, or advance his plans.

Interrelated as the lives of men are, some form of give and take is forced upon everyone. Indifferent individuals may let it go at that. Most people are not indifferent. They refuse to be satisfied with this externally enforced result. They try for something better than is attainable by the pushing and pulling of one interest against another, with such use of intelligence as shall make the pushing and pulling most effective. They make an effort to judge the relative merits of the ends aimed at, and try to secure a satisfactory adjustment of competing goods.

Human beings are not only so involved in each other's lives that they are compelled to respect each other's wants whether they like it or not; they not only examine competing wants with the intention of reaching a more acceptable result than can be brought about through sheer force; they happen to be interested in other people's interests. The scope of their imagination may be narrow, may be limited to a family, to a friend or lover, to blood relations, or it may be as broad as a group, a community, mankind. In any case, people are made happy or are depressed by ups and downs in the happiness of others. Desires of other people become identified with their own desires.

So true is this, that again and again it is deemed desirable to surrender self-regarding desires to other-regarding desires. "Long-headed selfishness," this has been called, and the argument is made that all action is self-centered and can only pretend to be otherwise. But this is not an adequate explanation. It must be admitted that everything a person does is expressive of himself, is an act of self-realization. To go farther and say that all self-realization is self-conscious, or self-inclusive, and that the interests of the other self or selves are never motivating causes of action, is not good psychology. The relevant facts have been correctly described, I believe, in these words:

Acts have a source and a termination. The source is always the acting self, but the termination may be either the acting self or another self. A father may bring home something to eat which suits his own taste but is liked by no other member of the family, or he may bring home something he does not himself care for but of which the other members of the family are especially fond. Whatever the ultimate psychological explanation may be, these two acts can not be reduced to the same category.

The reply may be made that in the latter case he does it after all because he likes to, and so to please himself. He does it because he likes to, but not necessarily to please himself. In rare instances the latter may be true; more often, however, the act is less sophisticated, being a direct response to the thought of the family. It is the anticipation of the pleased family, not the anticipation of the pleased self which impels to action.

The wants and needs of others, then, may induce a man to act without being translated into forms of self-interest. The prospective good or evil state of another person may directly stimulate behavior, just as one's own prospective good or evil may. And since other wants than those of the actor are productive of action, they must be added to the competitive complexity which creates the problem of choice for every thoughtful man or woman.

iii

Seen from a distance it looks as if a mob of desires, all crowding to get front seats in the theatre of life, were pushing and elbowing their way from one position of advantage to another, giving no thought to those that get poor seats or none at all. Closer observation shows the struggle to be less reckless. Desires overlap and intertwine, and there are desires to help the desires of others along. People differ greatly in the kind of life they desire for themselves, and in the extent to which the desires of others are imaginatively grasped and worked for. They differ in the tenacity of purpose with which desires are pursued. But the time never arrives for anyone when his own wants are so simple, and the wants he responds to beyond himself are so few and so harmonious with his own, that it is a simple matter to make a choice. The fact is that a good many give up the whole business as too difficult for them to cope with. They lose interest in the earthly performance and either become cynical pessimists or center their hopes on a front seat in heaven.

Out of this competition of wants have developed various theories of the good life. Standards of right and wrong presuppose it. It is responsible for the methods which have been invented to evaluate desires and to deal with conflicts among desires. The conditions of life, we were just saying, force an adjustment of a kind upon every one of us. Even lower animals give preference to some goods over others, although without comparing their actions and approving or disapproving them. There are human beings whose choices are scarcely less automatic.

We shall leave all such persons out of account. For everyone else Plato has spoken the truth: "The uncriticized life is not fit for human living." Havelock Ellis has spoken for them, too: "Life must always be a discipline; it is so dangerous that only by submitting to some sort of discipline can we become equipped to live in any true sense at all." The same thing has been said or implied by all the teachers of mankind, whether they were religious leaders, social reformers, or men of affairs.

In this as in every relation to the world no man starts with a clean slate or from scratch. Experience writes upon him before he is aware of it, crisscross, one impression upon another, like the pictures in the caves of his primitive ancestors. When it occurs to him to ponder which way to go he is already an irretraceable distance down the road. He could not give an unbiased answer if asked what is best to desire, how to balance one desire against another, whether to reflect upon conduct or simply drive ahead and take what he can for himself. The dice are loaded by habits formed before he knew he was forming any; by the customs which became authoritative without his planning it; by the whole complexity of associations and activities which were interwoven with his outgoing nature as he grew up in the community.

In one respect this is an advantage. The individual is not required to set himself up in the business of living entirely on his own. He can borrow from the accumulated wealth of human experience. He can draw upon the capital stock of knowledge, ideas, rules of procedure, amassed by those who preceded him. In another respect it is a disadvantage. He mortgages his freedom. He is constrained to carry on the established business, to guard against the loss of inherited resources and to add to their sum as he can. Counting up the profits and the losses, we can surely say that continuity of experience is a precondition of growth in civilization. But we can say with equal force that growth in civilization is contingent upon significant deviations from continuity of experience.

These items, severed from their vital togetherness so that they may be talked about, are of course subtler and richer in their context than any description can suggest. But even a cursory examination corroborates what has been said previously about the competition of wants. Some of these wants aim at things near at hand, others at possible satisfactions more or less remote. We see regulating devices and principles at work which have come down from the past, and new ones taking shape out of present struggles. Every man and woman is in search of happiness as defined by his peculiar nature and the environment in which he lives. There are people who think very little beyond what they immediately desire, but all in all they are controlled and guided not only by habits, customs, legal enactments, current fashions, but by more or less inclusive plans of life. Let us stand off far enough from details to see the pattern of these larger configurations.

iv

Since we mean to pass judgment upon these plans of life as methods of reaching the best result in dealing with conflicting aims, we must decide, at least in general terms, where we hope to come out, or what we shall set before us as the highest good. And I see no way of doing this, realistically, unless we begin with the desires of men and women as of primary importance. Anyone who denies this will be found to have adopted a theory of conduct which makes them secondary. In other words, we shall take our cue from universal human behavior and make this the goal: *the most livable life for all who have a life to live.*

Generalized in this way the statement might pass with most if not with all people. Not so if we add: *And each person to be the final judge of what "most livable" means for him.* Yet this is the specification which I should insist upon including. For if the good life is to be actually good it must be found good by him who lives it. True enough, we have only imperfect knowledge of what makes life most livable for anyone, to say nothing of everyone. But neither are we completely in ignorance. We do not need to be told by a philosopher, as Plato thought we did, whether it is better to be sick or well. We find it better to be well immediately. In the same direct way we are able to judge of any number of experiences. When there is doubt as to whether something is good or bad, in other words, whether it is to be desired or avoided, someone has to taste and find out. And everybody knows how reluctant, fortunately, most of us are to let another's tasting be substituted for our own.

Since the desires of the individual are primary and ultimate, a most livable life for everyone is out of the question unless there is a possibility of richly various satisfactions. Obviously this creates an additional difficulty. There must be adjustment of one to another. Here again we are at a disadvantage through ignorance. We do not know offhand how or to what extent unique livableness for each individual is attainable in harmony with all the other individuals who likewise are to be satisfied. Yet here too we do not proceed in total darkness. We have numerous examples of shared experience to guide us. We know that some courses of action take us toward, while some take us away from, a livable life in co-operative undertakings. Besides, desires are not mutually antagonistic throughout. Some desires support other desires, and all human beings have social desires which are as insistent as any. Consequently, variety of satisfaction, no matter how amply realized, does not involve a state of anarchy. It sets a problem which is frequently of great delicacy and, in its wider ramifications, always of great complexity, so that it cannot be solved easily, all at once, or in a short time. Nor is there any hope, as there is no need, that it will ever be solved finally. But it is possible to move step by step toward its solution if the men and women of average good will give their minds to organizing life as a whole so that the individuals who make up that whole have a fair chance to gain the richest quality of experience of which they are capable, and which the conditions of existence can be made to yield.

With this agreed upon as the goal, let us take a look at three outstanding philosophies of conduct: (1) The doctrine that might alone is and must be the arbiter. (2) The theory that a good outcome is necessarily dependent upon an alliance with a supernatural being or order. (3) The view that we have called Realistic Idealism. Which of these plans employs the best method of discovering and realizing the most livable life?

v

The method of dealing with conflicts of interests which is most obtrusive in the world today is the use of physical force. It is an old method. There have been times when it was even more universally relied upon than now, although it was never exemplified on so vast a scale or with such driving power as in the twentieth century. Still, its real character is not clearly perceived. The reason for this is that more often than not physical force is mixed with other forces. As a rule those who resort to it declare they do so for the accomplishment of ends which are not definable in terms of sheer might. They do not advocate might for might's sake, but for right's sake, for justice, honor, or something of the sort, all of which can have no meaning in a consistent might philosophy. Sometimes, to be sure, though not always, these added claims are hypocritical. We must get rid of this source of mystification, whatever its cause, if we are to appraise the philosophy of might as a desirable plan of life. What is this philosophy when reduced to what William James would have called its fighting weight?

The essential characteristic is *the deliberate ruling out of the other side as having any right to be considered.* A conspicuous historical example, now everywhere admitted to have been such, was the Versailles Treaty. In that settlement no weight was given to the interests of one side. Those upon whom the terms of the settlement were forced were denied a voice in deciding what the terms should be. Compare this ideal of conduct with the one set forth in the speech of Anthony Eden made at the outbreak of the new European war. The eventual peace arrangement may resemble the Versailles Treaty more than a promising basis for the new European civilization which Anthony Eden assured his hearers "will be built just the same," in spite of the appeal to arms; a new civilization in which "will be found liberty and opportunity and hope for all." A good many people are sure that the new treaty can be no better than the old one, and some want it to be much worse. They feel that the former settlement did not go far enough in crushing the opponent. Such matters are here not in point. No war gathers up in itself the totality of the "might makes right" attitude. It is merely its large-scale demonstration. What we are trying to do is to get a clearer idea of what it means to rely upon might as a way of resolving conflicts of aims. The contrast between the suggested proposal and the Versailles Treaty will help us do this. I quote the concluding words of the speech:

For some of us the challenge has come a second time in our generation. There must be no second mistake. Out of the welter of suffering to be endured we must fashion a new world that is something better than a stale reflection of the old, bled white.

It had been better could we have set ourselves to the task in a world at peace. Herr Hitler has decided otherwise. Nazism, however, is but a passing phase. Like all systems built upon force it cannot endure—in the long roll of history it will count but as a spasm of acute pain. The suffering will be bitter, the devastation wide. But what really matters is what follows after. Can we do better this time? Can we finally rid Europe of barriers of castes and creed and prejudice? Can frontiers and faiths, language and commerce serve to unite nations and not divide them? Can we create a true unity in Europe? Can we set before it a common aim of service? Can we inspire it with common ideals of freedom, toleration and mercy? This is what must be.

The differentiating thing then is not the use of power as such but the spirit and aim which permeate its use. Every plan of life must be able to exercise power, even physical power, to realize itself practically. In fact it will get no hearing unless it is backed up by power of some kind. This is important to keep in mind, especially for one who means to be realistic and at the same time to recognize the function of ideals.

The differentiating thing is not the use of power, neither

is it the manner of procedure. War between nations exemplifies the might ideal, but it may operate through the maneuvers of pressure groups arrayed against one another, or through the strategy of "spiritual" leaders intent upon suppressing "the carnal nature of man." It may dominate the technique of compromise and even the deliberations around a conference table. It is active in every case where there is a deliberate purpose to reach an objective without regard to the value of the goals that must fall by the way. Individuals or groups or nations act out the might philosophy, however they go about it, when they push others aside to take all they can for themselves.

Suppose this analysis is correct, perhaps it only proves that mutual considerateness is a purely sentimental ideal; that although appearances may seem to indicate the contrary, reality is always and forever expressive of might. Aspects of this subject have been touched upon in earlier chapters and we shall in later ones study specifically the nature of reality in its physical or material and in its human form. But whether might philosophy is or is not the one and only realistic attitude, it is incapable of furthering the most livable life. For it is its very genius to constrict, not to enlarge, appreciation of values. Wherever it rules it paralyzes social imagination, intensifies and spreads a destructive spirit, poisons the atmosphere with hatred and suspicion, and consequently is not directed toward but away from the attainment of the general welfare. Not only so, but it makes progress toward that goal more difficult in proportion to its prevalence.

vi

Might philosophy is familiar to practically everyone the world around, and it is widely respected and still more widely practiced, usually, as I have said, mixed with contrary influences. In the Occident a second plan of dealing with human desires is highly approved. The heart of it is reliance upon a Supreme Being or Power at work within or behind the world of the senses. The Christian church is its accredited representative, although there are numerous other organizations and movements that adhere to the same position. According to this view human beings are by nature wicked. If left to themselves they are incapable of making a proper choice among desires, and if they could, they have not the will to master their baser natures. Any respectable pattern of behavior must therefore be introduced from a supernatural region, which must also provide the power to live by it in preference to natural inclinations.

Much may be said for this conception. It stirs something deep in human nature, its provisions are easily understood, it has ethical authority. It sets a goal before men which offers to each one, from the humblest to the greatest, the opportunity of sharing in an enterprise vaster than any undertaking that man can devise. The trouble with all naturalistic plans of life, as seen by the supernaturalist, is their deficiency in just these respects. They have nothing but the life of desire to draw upon. It is difficult to see from this standpoint why one desire ought to be preferred to another, and, granting this to be done, where the energy is to come from to make the "ought to be" prevail. By what logic shall a man be persuaded that he does not want what he wants? What reason can be given why a man should not deprive another man of what he wants except that this other man does not want to be deprived? But the wants of another have no higher authority than one's own. Why surrender one's own, unless of course that is the better way to get what is wanted—which is not to surrender it after all. There are only two possibilities, the supernaturalist contends, and no more: either a plan of life "from on high" or a free-for-all among desires.

Supernaturalism has very definite things to say with regard to conflicts of desires. It defines right and wrong on the most unimpeachable authority, that is to say on divine authority, and indicates the good which is to follow right action and the evil consequences of doing wrong. Those who adopt this way of living are supplied with a card of right and wrong acts, which simplifies the whole problem of conduct, and they have access to various means of strengthening moral purpose when it weakens. That the true supernaturalist makes contact with something or other of extraordinary vitality is almost too obvious to mention. If evidence were needed beyond that of the daily lives of vast numbers who are dependent upon supernaturalism for faith in the worth of life, it is at hand in the heroism of the contemporary martyrs in concentration camps.

Superior to might philosophy as this view of things is

by virtue of the more critical vision and the more elevated devotion to human good which it calls out in
men, it nevertheless suffers from serious defects, one of
which in particular is relevant to the problem of bringing
about the best possible adjustment of competing desires.
Supernaturalistic programs turn away from man in his
full, natural manifestation. They concentrate on a piece of
him, on the piece called the soul or spirit, the theory being
that this is all that can be saved or is worth saving. Man
in his wholeness as a physical, intellectual, emotional,
practically ambitious yet aspiring creature is offered up to
an ostensible spiritual essence. An organized "higher life"
is developed within, but distinct from, the daily life of
the community, and a body of experts, who are under no
obligation to help in making the human venture a success,
except in so far as it bears on the welfare of the soul in a
world to come, are assigned the task of defining that higher
life, and of seeing that its provisions are carried out.

Supernaturalism therefore has the tragic tendency, already discussed in this book, of setting the business of
living and the art of life against each other as enemies.
But every man is composed of at least two pieces: the
"spiritual" piece which supernaturalism hopes to salvage,
and the "natural" piece, which depends for a happy destiny upon making good use of earthly opportunity. Each
can be thwarted and twisted but not killed. Schemes of
oversimplification at their best force mankind to get on,
more or less apologetically, in two areas of effort, the one
dominated by material ambition, the other by immaterial

ideals, and at their worst, only succeed in producing abnormal or pathologically exaggerated expressions of resistless impulse.

vii

We turn now to a radically different way of dealing with the urgency and diversity of men's wants. It too has long been in actual use. Instead of proposing that free rein be given to the most powerful individual or mass desires, without regard to what happens to the rest, or that certain desires be suppressed as "vanities of this world," again without regard to the goods thus sacrificed, this method undertakes to help men to extract all the happiness and worth they can from life. Naturally, this is a more elusive goal than one less generously conceived. But who can insist on a simple objective for people whose wants are far from simple, and who are coming more and more, as a great aviator has pointed out, to live together as it were in one room?

Yes, this third plan is more difficult to apply than the other two. This is not because of anything in the plan itself, but because it calls for an emotional and intellectual temper which we have not been sufficiently encouraged to develop—a willingness "to give the other fellow a break," and some degree of social imagination and co-operative intelligence. It requires the attribute which Mr. Justice Holmes valued most highly: "Faith in faith in effort." In view of what we hope to achieve these requirements are positive advantages.

Let us remind ourselves that we are proceeding on the

assumption that what people want from life, not only some
of them but all of them, is the primary authority. What
they *ought* to aim at can only be determined by observing
what they *do* aim at. Let us remind ourselves also of the
problems which this occasions: how to make sure which of
the individual's wants are preferred when a choice has to
be made, and how to prevent any person from losing out
because the wants of various persons interfere with one another. It is clear that these are practical problems demanding practical means for their solution, not merely theoretical problems to be solved by schematic generalizations.
And it is just as clear that we cannot expect a perfect outcome. We do not know enough, are not disciplined or good-
willed enough, to reach anything like perfection. All we
can hope for is the best result which our natures, conditioned by past and present circumstances, will permit us
to obtain; a better result than can be obtained otherwise.
The technique which enables us to secure in this sense
the most abundant and meaningful life puts us on the road
toward a progressively better solution.

Well, what is the specific nature of this promising technique? It is a procedure which enters into a situation where
desires block one another, and there tries to discover a line
of action that will be of advantage to all. A filling station
in a small town found that it was losing customers because
it was somewhat concealed from passing automobiles by
big elm trees. The owners of the filling station prepared
to have the elms cut down. Strong opposition arose from
residents who had admired the trees for many years, and
they were able to rally to their cause defenders of natural

beauty in the town and the surrounding county. The dispute grew hot. It was carried into the newspapers. One side insisted on business necessity, the other on aesthetic values. The two stood over against each other, refusing to budge. It seemed to be one of those cases where someone has to give in.

A young man became interested in the controversy who recognized the validity of both demands. He tried to think of a way out which would sacrifice neither one. The solution he arrived at was to unite in the expense of putting up a sign at the roadside calling attention to the filling station, thus taking care of justifiable business claims, while at the same time protecting the beauty of the surroundings by saving the trees. This young man was putting into practice the operating principle of the method under discussion.

This is a simple illustration, but it has in it all the elements of controversy. And its simplicity makes it easy to pick out the distinguishing marks of this way of going at things. These are (1) an honest attempt to appreciate as fully as possible the conflicting aims as they appear to the protagonists; (2) the intuition of a new aim through which the underlying purposes at issue can be achieved although a specific form of those purposes is surrendered; (3) the embodiment of the new aim in a practical program.

At first glance this may seem identical with what is known as compromise. The difference, however, is profound. In the procedure just outlined the situation is confronted as a whole; and while the participants are more keenly alive to some interests than to others, they intend that the eventual solution shall profit all who are involved. Activity therefore centers upon discovering a new end which, when discovered, will be seen to accomplish this result. In compromise proceedings interest in the situation is strictly one-sided. No responsibility is felt for the total eventualities and hence there is no seeking for a broader objective. The particular things desired at the beginning remain the same throughout. And what each participant ends with, and in most cases all he expected to end with, is "splitting the difference." Thereupon each intends to get more of what was originally wanted when an opportunity offers itself, giving up only what has to be given up for fear that otherwise more will be lost. There is always a novel step forward in the procedure under consideration which is lacking in compromise. And this difference is one of those vital differences which, as we say, makes all the difference in the world.

viii

An objection has no doubt popped up in the mind of the reader. Improvement upon compromise technique is all very well in theory, but is it in the range of practical possibility? Is it not rather pure wishful thinking, sheer romanticism, a sentimental avoidance of the plain facts? Can anything be more glaring than that those who have taken charge of affairs in the world have done so by being consistent and ruthless in the application of self-seeking strategy? Could they have succeeded as they did had they not carried out with more than ordinary rigor a disposition common to man? Is it not true that human beings show a stubborn disinclination to divide the goods of life with others? Are they not bent on getting everything they can for themselves and holding on to it? A proportion of mankind may be actuated by altruistic motives, but is it not a woefully small minority, and does it include the prosperous, the respected, the powerful?

No fair-minded observer will make light of this objection, or dismiss offhand the analysis of human nature which supports it. A plan will not work unless there is a will to work it, and this is true in a special sense of the one now before us. That a great many people do not care to make it work would be hard to dispute. They push their way from one vantage point to another, hunch up on every regulation adopted to make the going a little more equal, never observe the rules of the game unless some officer of the law has his eyes on them, and everywhere and always get away with everything they can. Gangster mentality abounds and by no means only in gangster circles. And there are well-disposed people, very many of them, too, who can only go along with any scheme of life which exerts pressure upon them. Besides this the charge may be leveled at all of us that we are creatures with hair-trigger feelings and highstrung nervous systems. We are shortsighted and easily frightened out of our wits. Occasions are therefore bound to arise when we will not stop to unravel difficulties, but will tear the threads and take the consequences. In other words, the practice of rational and humane living constantly breaks down here and there, and periodically it breaks down almost everywhere.

But is it intelligent to take these breakdowns as the

end of the matter? Shall we make the failure of a thing the criterion of its real nature? Would it be accurate to describe an automobile as a motor vehicle which turns turtle and kills its occupants? It is a fact that it does this; but this fact and all the other facts which belong on the debit side of the automobile's account with life, would, as everyone knows, if taken alone, give an utterly false notion of the automobile's usefulness.

Then how about people? Reckless ambition to get ahead of others, bursts of anger, blind passion, craftiness, vulgarity, all the wrecks of human nature, are part of the story. Taken alone, however, they give an utterly false notion of human motivation. We got a completer picture of the reality in the opening sections of this chapter, and the reader can get a still completer one by candidly observing what goes on about him. He will find more than enough co-operative spirit, more than enough practical ingenuity, and whatever else it takes to put realistic programs of mutual helpfulness to work.

And they have been put to work. They have been at work, as I have already said, for a long time. Not only inner personal conflicts, but the interests dividing generations, sexes, employers and employees, even nation and nation, have been explored for possibilities of better relationships, and better relationships have been brought about. Of course there is still plenty of room for improvement in our *modus vivendi*; there always will be room. It takes time to perfect so relatively simple a thing as a mechanical invention. It takes time to find the cause of a disease and cure it. Should it not take time to understand what we are up against as human beings, inside ourselves and outside ourselves, and to learn how to get on with each other? We have made progress in spite of tragic setbacks. There is no ground for doubting that we can learn to move forward with greater steadiness and security. We will do so as we become increasingly aware that only by living for a more inclusive ideal than the competitive struggle for survival shall we be able to live at all.

ix

Our discussion of three outstanding plans of life has been confined in the main to their operating principles. This was not done because the particulars of behavior are unimportant, but because principles of living are more basic than items of conduct, although the two are inseparable. Understanding the principles, one needs only slight experience of life to make a pretty good guess what acts will naturally flow from them and what rewards they hold out to the actors.

We have tried to enlarge our acquaintance with an idealism of a realistic type. There are idealisms so idealistic that they exclude all workable ideals, as there are realisms that take the reality out of everything experienced as real. There is not much to choose between them. The view presented in this chapter as realistic idealism sees in ideals the substance of projected desires, and sees in reality a stuff that is pervious to ideals. Whether this way of looking upon our world will spread among men, together with the humane, intellectually creative attitude which is its counterpart, remains to be seen. Everything depends upon the kind of men and women who succeed in giving life its predominant quality. And that is not entirely out of human control. "There is no inevitability in history," as Mr. Justice Frankfurter has said, "except as men make it."

We have reached a point where it becomes advisable to make up our minds regarding the nature of Reality, which after all is what we are compelled to rely on, and which sets the limit to what we can do. The so-called "practical man" is inclined to think such questions irrelevant. But they are not. Aldous Huxley has put it well: "It is in the light of our beliefs about the ultimate nature of reality that we formulate our conceptions of right and wrong; and it is in the light of our conceptions of right and wrong that we frame our conduct, not only in the relations of private life, but also in the sphere of politics and economics." Whether this leads to his conclusion that "metaphysical beliefs are the finally determining factor in our actions," or whether it is not quite as true that our actions determine our metaphysical beliefs, we should be in a better position to decide when we have finished the reading of the next chapter.

❧ VI ❧

REALITY

i

There are plebeian words and royal words. Among royal words there are at least three: right, truth, and reality. To these all other words must make obeisance. No doubt some people would elevate to an equal if not a superior status the words happiness, love, beauty. But none of these is self-dependent. Happiness must be *real* happiness; love must be true love; and beauty suffers from a like imperfection unless we say with Keats:

> Beauty is truth, truth beauty,—that is all
> Ye know on earth, and all ye need to know.

But in that event we leave the world of discourse altogether, and discussion has to wait until we return and can again engage in speech.

Even the word God, the most sacred of symbols, owes its prestige, does it not, to its association with right, truth, and reality? Compare the words "god" and "God." Take from the connotation of the latter the attributes of ethical perfection, finality as regards truth, the ultimate in the

way of reality, and what is there left of its august significance?

There remain then right, truth, reality, these three; but
the greatest of these is reality. Right unsupported by reality is illusion. Truth out of accord with reality is fiction.
It makes sense to ask whether right and truth have a place
in reality; to ask whether the real has a place in reality
makes nonsense. Reality is the most regal word of all. It is
the *ultima Thule* of language, the farthest out that a word
can reach.

The farthest out—and the deepest down. For who has
not thought of reality as the bottommost ground below all
surfaces, coverings, and shams? Said Henry Thoreau:

Let us settle ourselves, and work and wedge our feet
downward through the mud and slush of opinion, and
prejudice, and tradition, and delusion, and appearance, that
alluvion which covers the globe, through Paris and London,
through New York and Boston and Concord, through
Church and State, through poetry and philosophy and religion, till we come to a hard bottom and rocks in place,
which we can call *reality*, and say, This is, and no mistake.

Thoreau left Concord and neighbors to seek a "Real-
ometer" in the solitude of Walden Pond. He did not find
it. But seeking for it he put himself in illustrious company.
What a galaxy of first-magnitude stars shine in philosophy's
firmament to commemorate great searchers for the Real in
China, Persia, India, Greece, and the West! We need not
be ashamed to join in the search, although we purposely
remain in that larger company made up of those who

must look for reality while they earn their bread in the
sweat of their brow.

ii

Now what does this august word denote? To what does
it refer? We shall find that this is not an easy question to
answer. We began to answer it, each of us, in babyhood,
and the criteria we successively adopted early in life remain in principle the best criteria we have. Students of
child psychology tell us that when our first toys dropped
out of our hands they dropped as it were into nothingness.
Out of sight was not only out of mind but out of being. It
was quite a step in intellectual development when we
leaned over to see where they had gone, for we had learned
to believe that there is a place where things go and stay
when they drop out of our circle of vision or awareness. I
venture to suggest that this was the beginning of our idea
of reality.

But it was only the beginning. Like all other creatures
we made a distinction among experienced things by attending to some and paying no attention to others. In this
way we gave reality a selected content. Had we been philosophers we would have called the one kind real and the
other kind unreal, and announced it as a metaphysical
truth that the real is the interesting; that what is of no
interest does not exist. As we matured we added other
characteristics, especially two: that of being publicly rather
than only privately experienced, and that of being independent of or over against us, obdurate, objecting to our
doing as we please, or as we later come to say, "objective."

All this occurred when we were still children. Consequently we did not express our growing knowledge in literary form. We did, however, act on it. And doubtless we gave voice to our discoveries now and then, of which a few isolated memories, a few "bright sayings" may remain, as isolated fragments remain from the thoughts of the earliest philosophers. Meanwhile life has gone on, the life of the individual and of the race, adding to the difficulty of reaching a satisfactory answer to the question, "What does the word reality mean?"

iii

Judged by what one hears, the offhand common-sense reply would be that reality is a name for the way things really are. This is of course a pure tautology, a begging of the question. It throws no light on the problem at all. But it does suggest that in common usage the word is supposed to refer to the way things exist in their own right, as distinguished from the way they may be imagined. People who have given no special thought to the matter—which includes the vast majority of us—assume that the things we see, touch, hear, taste, and smell, exist as they are perceived and where they are perceived. Such things belong to "the real world." They have their own structural character, their own metaphysical habitat, and their own ways of coming and going. They do not change when they enter into human experience; it is the human experience into which they enter that changes. In their total togetherness these real things constitute "Nature," and they are governed by unvarying natural laws. Reality, in this way of taking it, is the outside, physical, autonomous whole of things. Something like this is the plain man's view, or, better, it is the view of all of us as plain men, which we are most of the time.

Something like this is the view, but the qualifying something cannot be left out. For the belief that reality is physical is no more universal, settled, or pronounced than the belief that the experience of the nonphysical lays hold upon reality too. Thoughts, feelings, and other mental phenomena are believed to be just as real as things reported by the senses. Here the problem grows a little troublesome, and assurance is mixed with doubt, yet the attitude remains straightforward and simple, even though inconsistent with the conception of reality as external and physical. Over against an outer world of things, there is an inner world of feelings and thoughts. The stuff of this inner world is conceded to be less substantial than physical stuff, but it is not conceded to be less real in its own way. Indeed, if it comes to that, if it is a question of one or the other, many people would take sides with Plato and Paul (to speak of no others), and flatly reject the physical world as the standard of reality.

Perhaps this statement makes the common-sense view appear more consciously held than it is. Common-sense people do not think of mental phenomena as constituting a distinct order of being. This is not, however, because they think the contrary to be true, but because they do not think that far. Their belief in a thought realm is vaguely, not clearly, in their minds. But though not expressly formulated, it influences them. That is one reason why the serving up of any half-baked theory of mentalism is welcomed by so many people with their mouths open and their eyes shut. It explains why even critical minds surrender so readily when they are confronted with Bishop Berkeley's view, that to *be*, is to be *perceived*; and why they half believe the view picturesqucly expressed by Schopenhauer:

Life and dreams are leaves of one and the same book. The systematic reading of this book is real life. But when the reading hour (that is, the day) is over, and the recreation time between the readings has come, we often continue idly paging the leaves, turning up now one, now another, without method or connection: frequently it is one we have already read, frequently it is one that is new to us, but always in the same book.

But even if a belief in mental phenomena as a distinct kind of reality is not admitted to be a common belief, there is the self to which these mental phenomena are present. The self, at any rate, is believed to be real in its own distinctive way. Its reality is regarded as the rock bottom of certainty. Skepticism may wear away one belief after another, but the skeptical self is left, as the igneous rock is left after its sedimentary covering has been eroded and carried down to the sea.

Probably no incident in the history of thought is so widely and favorably known as Descartes' confessed inability to include the doubting ego in his attempt to doubt absolutely everything. When he applied himself earnestly and freely to the general overthrow of all his beliefs, there was one he could not bring down. He could not doubt, he said, that he existed as the doubter. And his argument has appeared incontestable to many thousands of readers. It is in harmony with the practically universal conviction that everyone is aware of himself as existing; that everyone has a sense of personal identity and continuity.

We need not decide whether Descartes' argument is conclusive, nor whether the assurance of his readers is well founded. The point is that every man believes in himself as a reality distinct from, and other than, the world around him. He believes in a psychical reality, as he does in a physical reality. His first offhand answer may sound monistic, but his second word shows him to be a dualist. He talks of an external physical world, but also of an inner psychical world. He believes that the self or ego, with its experiences, moves about as one order of real being within another.

The average man would doubtless be puzzled were he called a dualist to his face, unless he had a sense of humor and were mildly amused. But the reason would be his unfamiliarity with the word or the concept, not his denial of the fact. He would surely feel worse were he called a monist, if thereby he understood himself to be accused of believing in the real existence of nothing but the things disclosed to his physical eyes.

iv

Take us then as we come, lettered and unlettered, we believe that the word reality refers to more than one kind of existence. It refers to more than two kinds; to at least three. We are neither monists nor dualists, but trioists—

if we may make a word to order. Some occurrences we
ascribe to a physical world outside us, and they have physical causes; some we believe take place in ourselves, and for
these we ourselves are responsible; and we feel that this
leaves much to be explained which must be referred to a
third kind of reality.

How this third kind might have been conceived, and
what it might have been called, had we not grown up in
our tradition, is impossible to say. Our common name for
it is the supernatural. Its exact characteristics and boundaries have never been determined, at least not as things are
determined in the other two realms of existence. It is
believed to be all that natural reality is not, especially in
being free from every defect and every tendency to decay.
The supernatural realm is where God dwells, or, in the
more intellectual view, it *is* God. Emerson stated the idea
with a forthrightness usually absent from the more technical presentations of it:

The Supreme Critic on the errors of the past and the
present, and the only prophet of that which must be, is
that great nature in which we rest as the earth lies in the
soft arms of the atmosphere; that Unity, that Over-Soul,
within which every man's particular being is contained and
made one with all other. . . .

This supernatural reality is causal in the sovereign sense.
"Beside all the small reasons we assign," says the same
author, "there is a great reason for the existence of every
extant fact; a reason which lies grand and immovable, often
unsuspected behind it in silence." Causes and effects in
the world of sense experience are auxiliary causes and ef-

fects, as muscles, eyes, sidewalks, and much else may be auxiliary causes of man's walking, which is directly caused by the mind.

Conceptions of this third reality differ enormously from one person or class of persons to another, but the recognition of its existence and its superior status in the hierarchy of being is practically universal. It overarches Main Street and Wall Street, Palm Beach and Scum Beach, the cotton fields of the South and the waterfront of San Francisco, Zion City and Harvard Yard. It reaches from coast to coast in America and the world around, and everywhere it has its say in what is thought and done. Perhaps no one has caught its essential meaning for men and women of all ranks better than Tennyson in these famous lines:

> One God, one law, one element,
> And the far-off divine event,
> To which the whole creation moves.

v

This triple nature of reality reflecting, as it does, three aspects of experience, creates a problem of consistent definition that is far from easy to solve. Matters are made worse by the fact that the results of philosophic speculations have seeped into the thought of mankind. No one knows who it was to whom the concept of reality first occurred, dividing that which appears from that which is. He must have had a mind of the first order. Still he could have no inkling of the troubles he prepared for the thoughtful among mankind. Age after age has added to our knowledge of the world, but all this knowledge, instead of making it easier to decide what reality is, has made it harder. H. M. Tomlinson is right: "A worthy definition of Reality, honestly attempted, would keep an intellectual critic so long brooding with a wet towel that we might despair of getting so much as a mumbled and indistinct reply from him." And perhaps Leopold Infeld, who speaks even more devastatingly in the name of science, is right: "The contents and intricacies of reality surpass the limits of our understanding."

One of the difficulties encountered in attempting a definition is the inclusiveness of the conception. "The character of the real," said F. H. Bradley, one of the keenest of philosophers, "is to possess everything phenomenal in a harmonious form." According to A. N. Whitehead, "Speculative Philosophy is the endeavor to frame a coherent, logical, necessary system of general ideas in terms of which every element of experience can be interpreted." By which he means "that everything of which we are conscious, as enjoyed, perceived, willed, or thought, shall have the character of a particular instance of the general scheme."

Thus the philosopher who goes after reality extensively. He cannot abide an exception. If there were ninety and nine items that safely lay in the shelter of his fold, but one was out on the hills away, far off from his philosophic system, he must bring it in. Alas, when he has found every one of them and locked them up, he cannot get people to believe that the sheep he has housed are real.

Others prefer to go after reality intensively instead of extensively. They do not try to collect every form and phase of it, only its essence. They, too, have been unable to reach the ultimately real. Someone has always extracted a finer essence. Consequently there are thinkers who have given up the attempt as futile. They have called reality the Unknown, even the Unknowable.

Rumors of these searchings and failures have reached the ears of thousands who have no acquaintance with the facts or the arguments involved. All they know, or think they know, is that the world we live in is somehow unreal. If they have a reason to fall back upon, it is probably that since the things that make up the world are forever altering and passing away, there must be something that lasts through the changes. Reality is that something. It is that something beyond or behind the ever-changing face of experience which endures, possibly in the eternal consciousness of God, possibly in the all-embracing life of an impersonal Absolute, or perhaps it persists forever the same intrinsically, by its very nature.

A smaller but still considerable number have a better reason than bare rumor for being of this persuasion. They limit the status of real existence to one type on evidence which seems to them indubitable. A strong simplifying bias may outweigh for them every other consideration. They may have experienced mystical states, or have studied some intellectualistic outlook, and so have learned to doubt the evidence of their senses, of their feelings, even of their minds. Moral or religious idealism, mysticism, physical science, or some metaphysical approach to the world, can blur or temporarily blot out the multiplicity of objects and events as they are come upon, and make it seem as clear as day that some one kind of experience alone opens the door to reality.

vi

A kind of idealism which occurs in many familiar varieties is vividly portrayed by Ellen Glasgow in her picture of Gabriel Pendleton:

He had never in his life seen things as they are because he had seen them always by the white flame of a soul on fire with righteousness. To reach his mind, impressions or objects had first to pass through a refining atmosphere in which all baser substances were eliminated, and no fact had ever penetrated this medium except in the flattering disguise of a sentiment. Having married at twenty an idealist only less ignorant of the world than himself, he had, inspired by her example, immediately directed his energies towards the whitewashing of the actuality. Both cherished the naïve conviction that to acknowledge an evil is in a manner to countenance its existence, and both clung fervently to the belief that a pretty sham has a more intimate relation to morality than has an ugly truth. Yet so unconscious were they of weaving this elaborate tissue of illusion around the world they inhabited that they called the mental process by which they distorted the reality, "taking a true view of life."

This moral or religious way of "taking a true view" is much better known than the mystic's, because the state of mind and feeling upon which mysticism is based is tenuous and transitory. Many persons have felt on occasion that all things are one with each other, and the self one with them all, but the feeling was so subtle and fleeting as scarcely to be noticed. Mystics themselves confess it to be an extremely fugitive state that declines to be arrested and examined. Even those who are gifted with unusual psychological and literary ability acknowledge their helplessness in attempting to put the experience into words. One thing the mystic is invariably sure of. He has been face to face with the One Reality. And the memory of that presence, although imperfect and essentially ineffable, proves to him that the things men busy themselves with from day to day are fraudulent contenders for the title of real. A quotation from P. D. Uspenskii's *Tertium Organum* describes an experience of the kind which mystics rely upon:

It was in the sea of Marmora, on a rainy day of winter, the far-off high and rocky shores were of a pronounced violet color of every shade, including the most tender, fading into gray and blending with the gray sky. The sea was the color of lead mixed with silver. I remember all these colors. The steamer was going north. I remained at the rail looking at the waves. The white crests of waves were running towards us. A wave would run at the ship, raised as if desiring to hurl its crest upon it, rushing up with a howl. The steamer heeled, shuddered, and slowly straightened back; then from afar a new wave came running. I watched this play of the waves with the ship, and felt them draw me to themselves. It was not at all that desire to jump down which one feels in the mountains but something infinitely more subtle. The waves were drawing my soul to themselves. And suddenly I felt that it went to them. It lasted an instant, perhaps less than an instant, but I entered into the waves, and with them rushed with a howl at the ship. And in that

instant *I became all.* The waves—they were myself: the
far violet mountains, the wind, the clouds hurrying from
the north, the great steamship, heeling and rushing irre-
sistibly forward—all were myself. I sensed the enormous
heavy body—*my body*—all its motions, shudderings, wa-
verings and vibrations, fire, pressure of steam and weight of
engines were *inside of me,* the unmerciful and unyielding
propelling screw which pushed and pushed me forward,
never for a moment releasing *me,* the rudder which determined all my motion—all this was myself; also two sailors and the black snake of smoke coming in clouds out of
the funnel . . . all.

But it is Science, not moral idealism, not mysticism,
which has done most to cast doubt on the world of the
senses. Fortunately an instinctive tendency to take everything as real to which life must be adjusted, and the sheer
impossibility of acting on any other basis, ordinarily saves
men and women from any attempt to conform their lives
to the outlook of physical science, saves them perhaps
from lunacy. The scientific outlook nevertheless hovers in
the fringes of their consciousness. Now and again it leaps
to the center of the stage and spoils the act.

Of late, qualifying words have been spoken by scientists;
it is noticeable that the confident tone of the earlier scientists no longer prevails. Here and there one of them
has frankly announced that the man of science is not concerned with reality at all. By implication, however, the
exact scientist still comes nearer to reality than anyone
else, and it is more true than ever that scientific reality bears
no resemblance to things met with elsewhere. Whatever

the scientific eye lights upon loses its empirically observed character, whether it is a star or a crystal, a dragonfly or a human being, or perchance

> . . . The Great God Pan,
> Down in the reeds, by the river.

Descriptions of this scientific transformation, as everyone knows, are common; but they are not often so pointedly and readably stated as they are in *New Pathways in Science*, by Sir Arthur Eddington:

> Our account of the external world (when purged of the inventions of the story teller in consciousness) must necessarily be a "Jabberwocky" of unknowable actors executing unknowable actions. How in these conditions can we arrive at any actions at all? We must seek a knowledge which is neither of actors nor of actions, but of which the actors and actions are a vehicle. The knowledge we can acquire is knowledge of a structure or pattern contained in the actions. . . .
> The working out of this connection is the province of the mathematician. . . .
> It does not trouble the mathematician that he has to deal with unknown things. At the outset in algebra he handles unknown quantities x and y. His quantities are unknown, but he subjects them to known operations—additions, multiplication, etc. Recalling Bertrand Russell's famous definition, the mathematician never knows what he is talking about, nor whether what he is saying is true; but, we are tempted to add, at least he does know what he is doing. The last limitation would almost seem to disqualify him for treating a universe which is the theatre of unknowable actions and operations. We need a super-

mathematics in which the operations are as unknown as the quantities they operate on, and a supermathematician who does not know what he is doing when he performs these operations.

vii

From the time of Plato, Protagoras has been the Judas of philosophy because of his doctrine that "Man is the measure of all things." When he taught that things are as they appear to men, he might as well have taught, so Socrates is reported to have said, that men have no better knowledge of things "than a pig or a dog-faced baboon or some other yet stranger monster." The discrimination which Protagoras made between opinions about things which prove to be reliable in the course of living, and those which do not meet this test, is rarely mentioned. It is brushed aside as irrelevant, on the assumption, probably, that opinions can after all go no deeper than the appearance of things, can never touch their reality.

The same highhanded method has been resorted to from that day to this. Every attempt to dignify the substantial content of daily life by accepting it as real has been ruled out in a pre-emptory manner. The Pragmatism of William James is a recent example. When he argued that the significance and truth of all our concepts and beliefs must be found in their experiential "cash-value," that is to say, in their immediate or promissory nature as specific observable occurrences, his view was persistently attacked as the rawest utilitarianism. What was he saying, the critics demanded, if not that every idea and ideal must be shown to have an exchange value in hard cash? No matter how much he objected and explained, the misinterpretation was adhered to.

John Dewey has encountered the same kind of difficulty in communicating his philosophy. In his effort "to trap and hold the slippery idea of experience," slippery because of its various and vague uses, he has run into the stubborn presupposition which certain types of philosophizing have made common intellectual property. As he himself says:

When the notion of experience is introduced, who is not familiar with the query, uttered with a crushingly triumphant tone, "Whose experience?" The implication is that experience is not only always somebody's, but that the peculiar nature of "somebody" infects experience so pervasively that experience is merely somebody's and hence of nobody and nothing else.

In vain has Mr. Dewey written that experience refers to "something as wide and deep and full as all history on this earth, a history which, since history does not occur in the void, includes the earth and the physical relatives of man"; that it denotes such things as "the field, the sun, and clouds and rain, seeds and harvest, and the man who labors, who plans, invents, uses, suffers, and enjoys." He is interpreted to say that experience is in a man's head and so belongs to a private subjective consciousness.

In a word, it is the firm conviction of almost all scholars and laymen, held to in spite of other convictions which contradict it, that anything which a person is aware of must be unreal for the very reason that he is aware of it. Reality is the ocean bed of being, and things experienced are the shells and seaweed tossed up along the beach.

viii

That is how we talk. That is what we believe we believe. What we actually believe is shown by what we do. The earlier part of this chapter and the opening chapter of this book directed attention to the fact that, tested by what we do, and by what we say when we are not trying to be intellectual, we believe in another kind of reality as well.

When a man rubs his hands and exclaims, "Now that's what I call a *real* porterhouse," or "This time we are going on a *real* vacation"; when a business man rejoices because "At last there are signs of *real* prosperity," or someone is made happy by a "*real* friendship"; in these and countless instances of a similar kind, the distinction between real and unreal turns on whether the thing referred to does or does not measure up to some standard applied within the common-sense world. There is no reference to an unconditioned, eternal, self-subsistent, ontological region superior to the experienceable.

One of the important lessons every child learns in the course of growing up, learns long before the idea of a reality *beyond* experience has dawned, is the lesson of differentiating between the real and the unreal *within* experience. And no single commitment has profounder bearings on the life history of any individual than his adoption in childhood and youth of the tests he thereafter relies upon to decide between reality and unreality in this intraexperiential sense.

We have arrived at this turn in the discussion: the world which is *spontaneously* taken to be real, if not *finally*, is the natural stage under our feet and the life around us. A person is a realist not when he turns away from this world, but when he turns toward it and seeks there good reasons for his behavior and his views. If we can decide what it is that men and women step out upon in that world with the assurance that it will bear them up, what they put their trust in or why they despair, this will offer a clue to what reality is known as and taken to be.

To follow this clue we must for the time being disregard a possible universal source behind all that happens and appears, knowable or unknowable, and examine the kind of reality which is depended upon by all of us from day to day.

Even so, the assignment is a large one. Dependability beckons to men under many guises and the taste for it varies from individual to individual and in the same individual in different periods of life, indeed in different areas of his life at relatively the same time. It is ever the reliable, the ultimate, the something that will stand fast when the surface of things slips and slithers away. But how variously that solidity is found!

To Democritus and Plato, for example, walking in the streets of Athens, the rock of the Acropolis under their feet, the marble temples rising above them, the busy wharves at Piraeus, the ships that came and went, all of it and all the rest of it was a dream world. Not a pleasant dream, either, but a nightmare. If we knew more about Democritus and Plato we might be able to say why it was that they could not trust what they saw and felt, but had to find Reality to be as different as thinking could make it. It was a shower of invisible, indestructible drops of material stuff, according to the former, driven hither and thither by the winds of Fate. The latter, going to opposite extreme, thought it to be a realm of immaterial forms, a heavenly hierarchy of pure intellectual essences, perfect and changeless, crowned by the supreme Idea, the Good.

And in the length and breadth of history did anything ever stand before men as a more solid embodiment of reality than the empire of Caesar Augustus? Yet there were those who staked their all on its unreality. "We look not on the things which are seen," they declared, "but on the things which are not seen; for the things which are seen are temporal; but the things which are not seen are eternal." Why did the early Christians choose as they did? We can try to guess; we can offer a few quotations as evidence; but we know little more than that they had lost faith in this earthly life and so reached out for the satisfaction promised in a world beyond.

There was a time when Augustine, in common with the lustier sort, took his chances of enjoyment in the odious Civitas Terrena. Later, disillusioned, he yearned for an inheritance in the resplendent Civitas Dei. His ambition to succeed was transferred from the one city to the other and reality followed his ambition. When he was young, Carthage and Rome were real. When he was old, no city was real but the Heavenly Jerusalem.

The thinkers of the Middle Ages had inordinate confidence in Reason, no confidence in what they could see. Consequently, genera and species were real, while individual plants and animals were not. Circularity was real; a circle drawn by hand was only an appearance. The streets of university towns were spattered with blood as rioting students broke each other's heads to settle the metaphysical status of universal conceptions. Some did battle for universals as *ante rem*, others as *post rem*. Some were sure that universals were *in re*, others that they were *in intellectu*, still others that they were merely *in nominibus*. This heady pursuit of intellectual abstractions must have amused or filled with wonder the common people who followed the warmer trail of desire to a less immaterial reality.

Then what a horde of new interests the Renaissance and the birth and growth of experimental science ushered in. The world in its physical structure and its wealth of living forms took fascinating hold upon men. They were on fire to know the innermost secrets of their new discovery, Nature; to master its forces, to explore and invent for "the relief of man's state on earth." Things, not concepts, ruled their lives. It might have been said of man after man, as Charles Williams has so well said of Francis Bacon: "The *thing* possessed him. The thing that *was*—fact—as distinct from words; the thing that *was to be*—knowledge—as distinct from fables; the thing that *was to say it*—truth—as distinct from argument." *Things* drew men to themselves as a magnet. A new ambition took the central place in human society, and Reality lost its resemblance to Reason and took on the character of the Thing.

These concentrations of interest and these realities which were their counterparts are in our tradition. They must be included in any generalized conception of reality. So, too, the present orientations of life and the resultant realities. We must count in the persons who listen to the marching feet of the proletariat or the tread of the fascist dictator and think they hear the rumbling advance of the cosmos. And who knows so well as the supersalesman how to "contact" reality? Nor can we leave out the types described in such books as *Ten Thousand Public Enemies, The Robber Barons, The Jack Roller, The Revolt Among the Share-croppers, Hollywood by Starlight, The Grapes of Wrath,* all of whom obey their own kinds of commanding reality.

x

Where a man's heart is, there will his reality be also. The result is that people live in different worlds. Beatrice Lillie and Bishop Manning may reside in the same city, conceivably may ride in the same subway, but who can believe that they live in the same world? Mr. Justice Mc-Reynolds and Mr. Justice Cardozo met in the same room and sat on the same bench, but who will claim that they looked upon the same human scene? So of all others wherever they are. Were this not true we could scarcely explain such conflicting documents as the one by a Governor of a New England state and the other by a depleted spirit in the Middle West. In a manner of speaking these men lived in the same country and faced the same economic depression; the deeper truth is that the second man was exiled from the world of the first. Said the Governor:

Standing together in the level gold of a late autumn sun flooding over the hilltops and giving here a tall steeple and the weathervane cock of an ample barn stored with harvest, and there some westward window, each its moments of glory, while the place of fulfillment, bearing under its heart the quick seed of renewal, falls upon seed and vineyard, we are moving once more to praise the Lord of life, our source and our stay through long generations.

I therefore appoint Thursday, the 28th of November, as a day of public thanksgiving to be observed in our churches with fitting rites and in our homes with feasting in the goodly way of our fathers.

Said the other:

Chief of Police
Madison, Wisconsin

Dear Sir:—

I destroyed myself because of my inability to support myself and my family. Please deliver the letter in my brief case to my wife, Mrs. — ——, —— ——, Madison. Also kindly ask the American Legion to assist her in every way possible to collect my army bonus insurance and to arrange my burial with as little expense as possible in order that there may remain for her all that can be salvaged. The car is hers. Turn it over to her immediately so that she can sell it for emergency purposes. Also all personal property in the car.

Signed ——

Do not drive the car until oil has been added. It is nearly out and the pump has an insufficient supply.

No one would think of denying that these two writings come from radically different life experiences, or that the sharp contrast which they illustrate is in principle a broad human fact. The question can only be whether the different combination of objects, events, and people which made up the environments of the writers shall be granted the status of reality. Is an assemblage or pattern of things staked off in the amplitude of existence to constitute a world? Must we not think of the real world as existing independently, with a character all its own, unmodified by human choices and reactions?

It might do to say so if the two worlds were entirely personal, which they are not. As one reads what these men wrote it is unmistakable that their personal experiences are bound up with objective circumstances. The success and failure of which they speak have the quality of finality about them which is the very test of the real, and the conditions to which they refer do not begin and end in their private wills. They are as external as the "ample barn stored with harvest" which caused the one man to anticipate "feasting in the goodly way of our fathers," and as obdurate as the unemployment which drove the other man to suicide.

There is then a sense in which one's real world is of this intimate, personal sort, as if reality were a great light and we the moths who circle about it closer and closer until we come to end in its consuming warmth. It is the axis around which doing and feeling and thinking revolve. It may be money, sex adventure, social standing, or the exercise of power; it may be a forty-acre farm or an empire, a small business or a huge corporation, a few meager aims or far-off goals inclusive of all mankind. Whatever it is that commands a man, to which he gives himself up, in which he invests his energies, and for which he fears and hopes, this is his reality. If there are other meanings, more comprehensive meanings, they cannot annul this near and vital meaning.

xi

We live in different worlds and try our luck with differing realities—there is a profound sense in which this is true, and there is a sense, perhaps even more profound, in which it is not. That is a paradox which has never been resolved. "I think that only is real," said Emerson, "which men love and rejoice in; not what they tolerate, but what they choose; what they embrace and avow, and not the things which chill, benumb, and terrify them." Big talk. The thing simply cannot be done. Each man lives in his own world with the reality he prefers, and he lives in a world which he must take whether he likes it or not. He must manage to get on with a reality that is given, even forced upon him.

No man creates reality like a God out of nothing. At best he selects as he can from the material accumulated and arranged by physical nature through aeons of time. He makes use of what innumerable lower creatures and his fellow men have produced before he came on the scene. When everything goes forward without serious hitch, opportunities chiming in with ambitions and plans, some men may talk as if the world were plastic stuff to work their wills upon. But how easily they are shocked into a

better understanding of their state! A few factories stop
running, a few banks close their doors, a few men establish
a new social order or threaten to, and all sense of mastery
vanishes. So delicate is the social body that a nervous chill
runs through it if a few people merely sit down.

And what of physical nature? A northeast wind piles up
tiny snowflakes, each of which would instantly melt on a
man's tongue, but the most powerful locomotives cannot
run through them, the streets of great cities are blocked,
and a hundred thousand shovels are needed to clear the
way. Krakatoa awakes, puffs out her flaming cheeks, and
human contrivances are flipped aside like the ashes of a
cigarette. What if nature should hurl a handful of stars?
Powerful as man has become, he goes his way today as he
did when his career began, at the mercy of a wider reach
of forces which, when it comes to a showdown, will stop
him in his tracks.

xii

So it is necessary to broaden the definition of reality, or,
rather, to recognize that it comes in a number of grades
and sizes. There is, first, the visible panorama which the
plain man will gather in the sweep of his arm and call "Nature." It is the world which has gone and still goes its way
without the admixture of anything human. Next, the animal kingdom, exclusive of man; for animals are *in* "Nature,"
dependent upon it, yet not strictly *of* it. Then the environment of cities, towns, farms, with their innumerable contrivances and machines, all the results of human effort.

Besides these, the intimately personal area, the world of things, animals, people, and ongoing affairs with which a man lives in closest give-and-take relation.

Every one of these strata of experience is authentic in its own terms and must be conceded to have a place in the sum of realities. They enter into the making of the individual's life and into the unfolding of the human story. One may prefer a private rendezvous with reality to a meeting in public, but the public realities will hang around. They will be accosted in the street; they will follow one into offices and homes; they will peer out of the eyes of men and women; they will approach from the institutional and natural environment and insist upon being recognized.

xiii

Sooner or later any serious discussion of reality will have to take notice of the fact that the experienced world has a way of adding to itself and of being added to. What accounts for the entrance of new elements? The coming and departing of ice ages and animal dynasties are striking examples of the innumerable ways in which physical nature passes from stage to stage, as the radio is a striking example of how inventors reach out beyond the boundaries of what we have and bring in things we did not have before. Where does nature go, where do inventors go for what they bring? If an impresario leads an operatic star before the footlights, there must have been one in the wings to be called. Is there a vast More of some kind, an exhaustless store of possibilities out of which the new actualities

come or are brought? Is it from thence that everything
has come that was in the past and is in the present, from
which man himself has come, and from which is yet to
come all that shall be in the future?

In some sense this must be so. But in what sense? The
imagination answers, with its incurable habit of pictorial
representation, by creating a *Somewhere* as the locality of
all possibles. The intellect, capable of abstract thinking,
makes over the Somewhere into a concept of Reality as
Reality, into pure Being, as yet unimprisoned in the wasting context of particularized existence. Then the experts
take a hand, presenting us with a "realm of essences," a
"supersensible order of being," an "eternally subsisting
abode of all that could exist," an "invisible world of to us
new and incomprehensible forces and relations." Eminent
philosophers like Mr. Whitehead, theological fundamental-
ists like Judge Rutherford, interpreters of mysticism like
Mr. Uspenskii, have tried to validate this view. Is this the
explanation we must adopt? Must we believe that exhaustless possibilities swim in a supersensible reservoir, ready
to escape down the sluiceway of time or to be caught on
the hook of genius?

Two reasons stand against the adoption of this explanation. One of them has already been considered. If reality
is placed *outside* experience, a distinction must still be
made between the real and the unreal *inside* experience. A
second reason, perhaps not so obvious, is equally incontestable. What may be spoken of as outside experience is
actually inside. We may follow any route we choose, and
go as far beyond the then known as we can, we no more

drop out of the world of experience than Columbus fell off the earth when he passed the known horizon. We always find, as he did, that the strange new landscape is continuous with the old familiar scene. Every invention, every discovery, every scientific or speculative advance, is the extension or elaboration of the known. It is a novel occurrence resulting from a newly established relationship between things or ideas within experience.

The possibilities which we speak of as though they had an abode in some metaphysical elsewhere are present actualities as yet unco-ordinated with other actualities in union with which they will show new characteristics and powers.

This problem of the possible, of which so much has been made, was flooded with the light of good sense by William James. A possible chicken, he said, "means: (1) that the idea of the chicken contains no essential self-contradiction; (2) that no boys, skunks, or other enemies are about; and (3) that at least an actual egg exists." In other words:

Possible chicken means actual egg plus actual setting hen, or incubator, or what not. As the actual conditions approach completeness the chicken becomes a better-and-better-grounded possibility. When the conditions are entirely complete, it ceases to be a possibility, and turns into an actual fact.

Follow this suggestion and you are rid of the notion—or the theory, if you have gone so far as to formulate it—that the possible is some hybrid kind of being inhabiting a mysterious realm between existence and nonexistence, ready, if its time arrives, to step out of its ghostly state and appear

embodied in tangible form. Concrete conditions will prove
to be sufficient. A possible invention is an actual human being in an actual situation working upon some actual concrete material to bring about some new contrivance. A
possibility in physical nature is some process now going
on which will arrive at an anticipated destination, providing other processes also going on, the influence of which
we do not know, do not interfere with the expected outcome.

In other words, all that happens is accounted for as well
as it can be without an appeal to reality as extraexperiential.
The so-called "realm of possibilities" is probably the echo
in our thought of the once current belief in a universe divided into layers, the highest of which was the *Ens Realis-
simum*, the self-causing cause of all causes, the pre-existing
source of everything that occurs. The fact which this idea,
or any idea substituted for it, is intended to explain is not
deniable. The world we see and touch spreads out into a
larger togetherness of things in space and in time. It is, however, deniable that this fact proves reality to be supersensible, or even that the experienced forms of it must be extended into a supersensible realm.

xiv

Now to return to reality in its experienced multiplicity
—to the physical environment, the animal world, the human community, and the miscellany of objects and activities upon which the individual's interests are centered. We
look again at these realms in order to make more explicit
the distinction previously touched upon between that which

exists and functions *without* human agency, and that which exists and functions *because* of human agency.

There was a time when man thought of everything after the analogy of himself. It was a nymph at work or play in the waterfall. When the sea rose in her might and wrecked the mariner in his ship, Neptune was to blame. In the seventeenth century, experts in spirit statistics tabulated 301,655,172 regiments of angels and nine great orders of devils to account for what happened. This humanizing of physical nature is no longer the fashion. The modern fashion is to dehumanize man. Our ancestors tried to read human nature into physical nature. We try to read physical nature into human nature. But then as now, purposive action was absent from the one and present in the other.

The humanly contrived world is solidly placed in the natural world, and the natural world undergoes changes because the humanly contrived world is set up within it. The processes of nature operate in both, but human purposes and plans are likewise operative. An orchard grows as a primeval forest grows, but "human nature" sets out the orchard, and "nature" the forest. Chicago, London, Paris, Calcutta, are dependent every moment upon "natural laws," as the Grand Canyon of the Colorado is; but man-made laws are causal agencies in the production of cities and not of Grand Canyons. Loves and hates are built into them. They are the materialized evidence of dreams and schemes and reasonings. All about us are such instances of the interoperation of natural forces, animal creatures, human plans, and personal ambitions. Everyone is acquainted with this fact. No one ignores it in practice.

The realms interpenetrate, but not invariably to mutual advantage. To some observers physical nature seems intent upon destroying man and his works, so that only by constant watchfulness and ever more ingenious counterattacks can the destruction be held off, as gardens are protected by incessant warfare on weeds and insect pests. Great civilizations, like that of Egypt, lie deep under desert sand, or like that of the Mayas, are overgrown by tropical forests. The universe is such as to have allowed man to evolve, for he is here; but it has not guaranteed him continuance. Stephen Crane has put it neatly:

> A man said to the universe:
>   "Sir, I exist!"
> "However," replied the universe,
> "The fact has not created in me
>   A sense of obligation!"

We know today, better than before, that nature has been blamed for catastrophes which were initiated by man himself. Great forests and vast areas of grassland have disappeared, millions of acres of fertile topsoil have been washed or blown away, animal and plant populations have been exterminated, mineral and water resources have been depleted, not because of natural processes, but because of human recklessness. "Man," as someone has said, "that greatest of all abraders of the earth's hide, more ingenious than sunlight, more persistent than frost, has learned . . . to destroy his planet with an amazingly increased dispatch." I know of no more profound study of Reality, realistically conceived, than Paul B. Sears' *Deserts on the March*, every page of which indicates the author's mastery of fact and his mature, critical judgment in appraising values. The following paragraphs are from this book:

Furthermore, man has not only become predominant, but as the price of his power, indeed of his survival, has assumed conscious, deliberate control. He has established a new order, with his own good as the criterion of it. He is attempting to rule the earth as a god might do, not only seeking what he needs, but manipulating all that is about him, supplying the conditions of life for the lower organisms which he uses, and combating those which are hostile with resources they do not have. He no longer accepts, as living creatures before him have done, the pattern in which he finds himself, but has destroyed that pattern, and from the wreck is attempting to create a new one. That of course is a cataclysmic revolution. . . .

It has been our task, by repeated and insistent emphasis, to show the unbalance which man has produced on this continent. And it should be clear by now that this situation is a very dangerous one. Unbalance creates further unbalance, and destruction of the means of subsistence proceeds at an accelerated pace. The picture we have seen is not one of utilization and adjustment, but rather one of exploitation and waste. We have seen how vast stretches of natural vegetation have been looked upon as obstacles of humanity, and destroyed, when in fact they are not only essential as a safeguard to the normal occupations of agriculture and industry, but could have been in themselves an unfailing source of steady, dependable wealth.

XV

We have just been talking about forests, prairie land, watersheds, dust storms, but it should not be difficult to perceive that it is just such things we should be talking about in this chapter. Our thinkers may make finer and finer intellectual distinctions until they have arrived at a concept of reality which makes it indestructible, but this will not save us if we continue to squander the substantial and veritable realities on which our very life depends. Investigators who have no desire but to report what they find are not too encouraging. C. K. Leith, an eminent geologist who has never been accused of being in the pay of Russia, has this to say:

The speed of our attack on mineral resources is indicated generally by the fact that the amount produced since the opening of the century far surpasses the total of all preceding history of the United States. In this respect we are literally digging ourselves into our natural environment on a scale which has no precedent in history.

In terms of years of measured reserves of present commercial grades the United States has supplies of oil, zinc, and lead for from 15 to 20 years. Its copper supply is good for about 40 years. The total for iron ore, including its lower grades, such as Alabama, is good for hundreds of years, but the known reserves of high-grade Mesabi ores now supplying about half of our requirements will last about 40 years, and for the rest of the Lake Superior region, supplying about 30 per cent of our requirements, the figure is less than 20 years. Coal reserves of all kinds, high and low grade, favorably and unfavorably located, will last 4,000 years, but the kinds we are now using in favorable location are measured in a century or two.

Further discovery and the use of lower grade resources will extend the life of most of these resources, but the range of possibilities is now pretty well understood, and with maximum allowance for such extensions, the figures are sufficiently small, when compared with what we hope to be the life of the nation, as to be matters of public concern.

Reports on the misuse of the soil are even more disquieting. Says Stuart Chase in *Rich Land, Poor Land:*

Kansas farms are blowing through Nebraska at an accelerating rate. In the spring of 1934, the farms of the Dust Bowl—which includes western Oklahoma, western Kansas, eastern Colorado, the Panhandle of Texas, and parts of Wyoming—blew clear out to the Atlantic Ocean, 2000 miles away. On a single day 300 million tons of rich soil was lifted from the Great Plains, never to return, and planted in places where it would spread the maximum of damage and discomfort—authentic desert sand dunes were laid down. People began to die of dust pneumonia. More than nine million acres of good land has been virtually destroyed by wind, erosion, and serious damage was reported in 80 million acres.

Morris L. Cooke does not write comforting words in his article, "Twenty Years of Grace":

The western dust storms are the swift dramatic result of our reckless land policies which permitted speculators to tear off the age-old sod covering millions of acres, in order to profit by war prices for grain. And eyewitnesses tell me red ribbons were tied on the plows which began the devastations.

Unless we can cope quickly and competently with soil erosion and its related water problems, our most prized national possessions will gradually lose their significance, our political institutions, our struggle for justice and equality of opportunity, even liberty itself. And so will pass also the opportunity for high undreamt-of adventure for which we have been laying the foundations in this country. As the yield of our soil goes down, the morale of the people will also ebb. And ours will follow the history of scores of civilizations which have arisen and flourished and disappeared. The acres—dead acres—will still be here as monuments of the folly of the "educated" man. There are twenty years to turn around.

These quotations speak for themselves. It would be immensely encouraging if the books and articles from which they are taken were being read and studied in schools and colleges from one end of the country to the other, and if ministers of churches were as sensitive to the defilement of the earth's body as of the human body. Moreover, the squandering of material resources is but one item in our prodigal spending. Perhaps just now we are even more wasteful of human lives, and of the natural curiosity, creativeness, and ardor of the young. And when has the trend of world affairs demanded so incredible a sacrifice of the physical and spiritual wealth represented by children?

Such realities condition achievement and joyous experience. The conservation of reality in this multiple form is therefore imperative. And it is a task of such magnitude that only by combining our abilities—scientists, educators, statesmen—leader and plain citizen—can we hope for success.

xvi

Whatever we do or do not do, reality will be in the doing. And the common opinion is that two characteristics must be ascribed to this reality: It is free from human admixture

and indestructible. But if our analysis has shown anything
it is that a definition of reality depends upon what we
choose to define. Reality is of course not at the beck and
call of man. No one can have just the reality he wants and
no other, and always he must rely on occurrences of it
which he has done nothing to produce. We know, too,
that when anything is destroyed it does not pass out of
existence in every respect; it changes the form of its existence, and in the new form continues to exist. Hence the
theory that the stuff of the world endures forever, is never
added to or decreased, and so is never destroyed. Some
people choose to restrict the term reality to that abstract
something which exists independently of man and forever.
We have seen reason to broaden the reference of the term.
We have included what reality is experienced to be, and
this has given us, among other realities, those which are
an interweaving of human and nonhuman elements, realities which are brought into being and pass away.

Is this a matter of mere words? Is the distinction a purely
verbal one? Doubtless there are critics who will say so.
There always are. Nevertheless it is not. A distinction is
never merely verbal if it enables the one who makes it to
see the situation in which he is better than he could have
seen it without making just that distinction. And this is an
instance of that kind. The broader conception of reality
is a clue that leads to deeper insight into life and its conditions. It improves a man's chances of finding his way
among life's facts and values.

For everything real has not the same significance. Abraham Lincoln was real when he was alive, his body was real

when it was dead, and the remains buried in Springfield were real. But the reality that was left after the fatal shot in Ford's Theatre did not write the Gettysburg Address or the Second Inaugural. And the reality that was taken away, could it have continued to be, would have altered the course of American history. I offer this as a simple and final illustration of the fact that realities are in the keeping of mankind, and can be thrown away or used with imaginative intelligence.

xvii

We have made something of a survey of the subject. We have walked around the outskirts of it, have climbed an elevation here and there to get a better view, and have taken a somewhat careful look at characteristic features of its central area. Much remains to be explored, very much indeed; yet we may claim to have made sure that reality is continuous with the substance of daily experience, and that it is nearer the truth to speak of realities than Reality. We have learned that the essential quality of the real is dependability, a thereness of some sort, whether an out there, a beyond there, an over there, or a there in the form of some commanding interest which organizes and directs a man's activities. We have learned that in a sense the real is dependent upon persons, it mirrors what they are and want, and is thus a phase of a biography; that in another sense it is independent of persons, it reflects quite impersonal processes and tendencies, and is a phase of natural history.

Reality implies the personal and the impersonal in working co-ordination. This is evident the moment the attempt is made to describe either one of them without reference to the other. Reality is neither "the bottomless cesspool which emits the stench of human experience," as it has been called, nor "the bottomless mystery from which arise the joyful and beautiful moments that redeem the vain and fleeting hours of life." It is that composite of things and forces, human and nonhuman, by means of which we live. Fortunately we may study the nature of the several realities in their interrelation and select from them, so far as that is possible, those combinations which lead to the best life we are capable of: best when judged by the satisfaction it brings, and best when judged by the quality of excellence attained through the release and investment of human potentialities and the potentialities of nature.

As we look out upon the world today there is no excuse for optimism and no reason for despair. We have gone far in the wrong direction. We have recklessly squandered the wealth of the earth and the wealth of human nature. But we are learning what we have done. In that knowledge is the possibility of a better performance. "There are twenty years to turn around"—in some cases more, in some cases less. How we turn around, to what we turn, what the realities are we put our trust in and raise to prominence, will decide what the human enterprise shall come to, for the individual and for the many, for the meagerly endowed and for the most highly gifted.

Reality is the most regal word of all. It is the *ultima Thule* of language, the farthest out and the deepest down that a word can go. But it refers to many, not to one. There they are, the realities, in the unimaginable wealth of concrete experience. It is possible so to choose among them that the result will be a new exuberance in the meaningless outpouring of life, the waste of the earth's bounty, the destruction of hard-won liberties, the betrayal of the nation's youth, the profanation of childhood. The realities are there on which we can rely if such is the course we are determined to follow. And the realities are there to rely upon if we set out for a life of as yet unattained variety and depth of satisfaction.

The choices made by our forefathers are built into our world, our physical, economic, moral, and religious world. It was not only assets they bequeathed to us, but the assets were considerable. We for our part may conserve and add to what we inherited, and hand on realities richer in promise for man's happiness. Our descendants may do so in their turn, raising the level of man's struggle and reward higher and higher, until the human venture is interrupted, if it is, through no fault of mankind, but because of a fatal change in "cosmic weather"; or, in Mr. Santayana's words:

> Until the patient earth, made dry and barren,
> Sheds all her herbage in a final winter,
> And the gods turn their eyes to some far distant
>   Bright constellation.

❦ VII ❧

MAN

i

We cannot well go farther in this book without thinking specifically about man. The human drama is contingent upon physical nature and also upon human nature. We must become a little better acquainted with the hero of the play. Or is he the villain? Hero or villain, he is incredibly elusive. It is of him that Stephen Benét has written in *John Brown's Body:*

> Swift runner, never captured or subdued,
> Seven-branched elk beside the mountain stream,
> That half a hundred hunters have pursued
> But never matched their bullets with the dream.

How shall we go about it to get a fair report? Spectacular individuals are not hard to pick out, but a conclusion based upon these alone would be worthless. A too limited survey can yield nothing of value, while an attempt at universality will end by mistaking a shadow for a solid object. Nor may we substitute an abstraction—human nature—for human beings in their endlessly varied particularity.

194

The business seems pretty nearly hopeless. How shall we bring under one category Confucius, the humanist; Buddha, the enlightened; and Jesus, the spiritually minded? Is there a formula that will do justice to Socrates, Plato, Aristotle, Pericles, Alcibiades—each unmatched in mind and personality? Can the prophets of Israel be brought into one pattern with the worldly kings against whom they thundered? The Pharaohs of Egypt were men; so were the Emperors of Rome, the Genghis Khans, Alexanders, and Napoleons, the Popes of the Church, the Luthers, Calvins, and Wesleys. Florence Nightingale must have a place by the side of Cleopatra. There must be room for Savanarola and Benvenuto Cellini, for St. Francis of Assisi and Cesare Borgia, for Gladstone and Huxley, for Clemenceau and Woodrow Wilson. The list is endless, even of conspicuous personages.

And if we look in another direction as we must, and try to bring together into one representation the middle classes, the underprivileged struggling many, the derelicts of humanity drifting about in the backwaters of civilization, the underworld of criminals and outcasts, and such bizarre worlds as Hollywood; if we remember Gertrude Stein's words: "I was then and ever since filled with the fact that there are so many millions always living and each one is his own self inside him"—that is, if we think of mankind, made up of individual human beings each following his own peculiar interests, each conditioned by his own peculiar talents and opportunities, we need not be told that a mathematically accurate description is unattainable.

It is not only because of their endless variety that men

are baffling. Each individual is baffling. How explain the gorgeous versatility of Shakespeare or Bach? Who can elucidate Abraham Lincoln? What key will unlock the inner secret of Victoria Woodhull or Mary Baker Eddy? Is there a net to capture the volatile spirit of Lawrence of Arabia? True, we feel little embarrassment in passing judgment on less gifted men and women. But the fault, excusable enough, is in our obtuseness. The puzzle is there. Every biography is a post-mortem performed upon a body that is dead. The poet has asked the unanswerable question which each of us in his own way has asked himself:

> You can weigh John Brown's body well enough,
> But how and in what balance weigh John Brown?

No, we cannot hope to reach a final answer. Much of the story will remain untold. It must be enough if the more obvious traits of human personality and the more pronounced currents of human striving are made a little more unmistakable.

ii

Man has speculated about himself, his origin, nature, and destiny, for at least four thousand years. Traces of such speculations are found in those early times, and there are hints that the problem was then already old in the culture of China, India, Crete, Babylonia, Egypt. Shocking characteristics were among the earliest to be discovered and published, and the fear has often been expressed that the human race would ultimately come to a bad end. The idea of salvaging the good in mankind by selecting a small minority of the best and rejecting the mass, has been advocated by men as far apart in time as King Gilgamesh and President Conant.

Today, cynicism about mankind has spread over a wider area and bitten deeper than before. It has spread beyond the borders of the *literati* and *intelligentsia* to the plain people upon whose healthy confidence in life we are dependent for ethical as for physical renewal. It has spread farther and bitten deeper still. It has found its way into the outlook of youth. This widespread cynicism, unrelieved as it is by any hope of an earthly Utopia or a heavenly City of God, has no parallel in history. P. S. Richards is correct when he declares that we have reached a pass where "The question is no longer whether we can believe in God, but whether and in what sense we can believe in man."

The hopelessness about himself into which contemporary man has fallen is reinforced by the belief in his animal ancestry. This is accepted today as uncritically as the belief in his divine origin was accepted a few generations ago. Carl Sandburg speaks the mind of the age in his poem "Wilderness":

There is a wolf in me . . . fangs pointed for tearing gashes . . .
a red tongue for raw meat . . . and the hot lapping of blood—
I keep the wolf because the wilderness gave it to me and the wilderness will not let it go.

There is a fox in me . . . a silver-grey fox. . . . I sniff and guess. . . .

I pick things out of the wind and air. . . . I nose in the
    dark night
and take sleepers and eat them and hide the feathers. . . .
    I circle
and loop and double-cross.

There is a baboon in me . . . clambering-clawed . . .
    dog-faced . . .
yaping a galoot's hunger . . . hairy under the armpits.
    . . . I keep the
baboon because the wilderness says so.

And not a wolf, a fox, and a baboon only, but a hog, a
fish, an eagle, a mocking bird, and much besides:

O, I got a zoo, I got a menagerie, inside my ribs, under my
bony head, under my red-valve heart: I am a pal of the
    world;
I came from the wilderness.

The poem, even in the mutilated form here given, stirs
something deep in the reader, something which he feels he
is, or has been taught to believe he is, and this feeling or
belief separates him intellectually from his grandfathers
more profoundly than oceans separate peoples. Just now
there is no alternative view. It is either special creation or
biological evolution. Of these, the latter is far superior as
a theory which harmonizes the known facts. We may hope
that in time some ingenious thinker will hit upon a new
interpretation, but until then the theory of evolution must
be conceded to hold the ground.

Evolution must be accepted, but every evolutionist is
not committed to the deductions which some evolutionists
draw from evolutionary premises. Many such deductions

are unfounded. Especially is this true of well-known por-
trayals of man. These are frequently poor likenesses. The
claim is made, for example, that in virtue of man's animal
inheritance, he is in essence identical with his next of kin
among living creatures; and this being so, that the best
solution for troublesome human problems is to be found
in the study of analogous problems as they occur in their
infrahuman form among the apes. A psychopathologist in
California is reported to this effect: "Men and women have
been trained by the demands of civilization to cover their
natural impulses with many layers of disguises till it is
very difficult to detect the real individual under the cloak."
Now "monkeys are human beings without their masks on."
Therefore "if we want to know how to behave, according
to the way nature made us, if we want to know what is good
for our instincts, we must study the monkeys." A colony
of thirty monkeys which he maintained enabled him to
discover human instincts in their natural form. From the
study of the sex life of apes he claimed he was able to pick
up useful clues to the natural sex needs of human beings,
and to study the various forms of misery resulting from the
conflict between the artificial limits imposed by civilized
society and impulses natural to human beings as simians,
which after all they are and can never cease to be.

iii

This ingenious theory, which is interesting on its own
account, is even more interesting as an illustration of how
a widely accepted type of explanation affects the study of
man. The genetic or historic method has accustomed us

to the idea that we come closest to explaining a thing when we have discovered how it came to be. From this we have passed to the belief that a thing's real nature is revealed in its primitive rather than in its developed form. Early religions were the outgrowth of fear; religion is therefore a form of terror. The earliest moral codes were folkways which the members of a tribe were compelled to observe by those in power; consequently right is a name for might. The acts of a baby are purely egocentric; hence every human deed is self-centered. The simplest psychic behavior is the stimulus-response reflex; it follows that human personality is an "easily understandable integration of stimulus-response behavior." Turning from religion, morality, behavior, personality as these actually occur in their complexity and variety, we try to find them in what they were before they had become what they are. We pick away the petals to discover the rose. According to this method man is what he was, and the proper study of mankind is monkeys.

Any comparison between men and apes strikes many persons as indecent. They will have nothing to do with it. For some reason they find it necessary to believe, or pretend to believe, that human nature must be beautiful. But their position is precarious. The rigid separation long made between animal and human psychology cannot be maintained. Such books as Wolfgang Koehler's *The Mentality of Apes*, Robert Yerkes' *Almost Human*, Mr. and Mrs. Yerkes' *The Great Apes*, and allied studies, report investigations which cannot legitimately be neglected by one who seeks information on the nature of man. The more the scientific student of the anthropoid apes learns about them, as Mr. Yerkes testifies, "the more helpful lessons for mankind he discovers in their relations to their world and to one another." It is perhaps a natural solicitude for human dignity, though certainly a mistaken one, which disdains to study the animals next below us as a means of enlarging and deepening knowledge of mental processes, social relations, and methods of learning. Why refuse to study complicated questions in simplified form?

To insist upon the propriety of studying monkeys does not turn them into men. There are advantages in dealing with problems in simplified form, provided we do not then mistake them for the complex problems which are to be solved. No doubt the study of the past throws light upon the present, but the present is not therefore the past. The creature that became man emerged as less than human in the evolution of the primates, and we have not escaped the influence of that fact. This does not prove that he never emerged at all, or that man is today what he was when he emerged. If he has not shaken off all traces of his long ascent, why must we conclude that he has not shaken off any?

Man is what he *is*, not what he *was*. No epoch or hour of history has greater authority than the present epoch and hour. The stage at which man has arrived is at least as authentic a revelation as any which may be selected from the ages left behind. That this shows him to be something very different from what we find in the brute is indisputable, unless we ascribe higher truth to methodological abstractions than to concrete realities. Man is capable of doing and suffering in a way that his animal brother is not.

He is tortured by fears and lured by hopes to which the ape is stranger. No ape brews the venom of human hatred nor does he transform passion into love. Apes speak no language, accumulate no tradition, never see the tragic or the funny side of things. They cannot invest their energies in schemes of conduct or sacrifice their lives for illusions.

Why is it that we cannot really understand ape psychology? Because we cannot return, even in imagination, to the simplicity of the ape's outlook and reactions. Is it for the same reason that we do not sound the bottom of human personality? It is not. It is because we are unable to master the complexity of man's interests and responses. Once gain a sense of man's enormous power and pathetic frailty, his resistless intelligence and clinging stupidity, his tender sympathy and refined cruelty, his possible nobility and coarseness—in a word, hold him before the mind in the bewildering actuality of his present being, and it is impossible to identify him with what he was before he had become what he is.

iv

The bewildering actuality of his present being—suppose we had a full comprehension of that. We would have made a good beginning in our knowledge of man, but only a beginning. For man is much more. If we are justified in rejecting the notion that a thing's "essence" is to be found in what it was in a past stage, we cannot claim that it is to be found in what it is now, neglecting what it has been. We must go at least as far as Aristotle felt it necessary to go. We must transcend a thing's local, transient occurrence and attain to an appreciation of its significance when viewed in the context of other examples of its kind.

What once was, what now is, did not explode into existence out of blank nothingness. It had a history. Things are events; deeds are rhythms; and "the lesson of life," as Emerson said, "is to believe what the years and the centuries say against the hours; to resist the usurpation of particulars; to penetrate to their catholic sense." Religion, for example, must be seen as it composes itself in historical perspective, viewed here and there, now and then, in primitive and developed form. As we go from one particularized type of religion to another we get a hint of something deep and urgent, something forever forming itself anew yet never coming to perfect expression. This growing something, very inadequately exhibited in any specific instance, but suggested when the several instances are studied in their temporal succession, is religion in the deeper sense, the *spirit* of religion, we sometimes call it.

So of every human project and institution. So of man himself. We cannot learn too much of how his career began, nor of the stages where he rested in the long journey down the centuries. Not that we may thereby hope to come upon an early phase of human nature more truly man than another—we have considered the futility of this attempt—but that we may attain to a standpoint superior to mere phases, and catch some meaning of the drama as a whole. The drama has a story to tell which no single act or episode discloses.

As we attempt to survey the human venture in perspective we can scarcely fail to detect significant characteristics

which may escape notice when attention is fixed on a
temporal cross section. We observe that from remotest antiquity man has refused passively to accept the world in
which he happened to occur. No organism passively accepts
the world, but the fact is conspicuous in the case of man.
When we first discover him in the dimness of prehistory
he is already busy trying to cajole or compel the mysterious
forces about him. His methods are crude, but they show
his bent. He intends to have a hand in his destiny. Beginning as a creature all but at the mercy of circumstances, he
slowly extends the area in which he is able to employ means
in the attainment of ends. At first his projects are simple,
his means weak and uncertain: simple weapons for hunting
and fighting, simple devices for catching fish, simple implements for tilling the ground. But the projects take on
greater and greater proportions, the means grow more and
more clever and powerful. In time he learns to bridle the
forces of nature, enters upon an era of spectacular inventions, plans to make himself master of the planet for ages
to come.

Who, walking abroad in any great city today, can picture
the landscape of only a few centuries ago? Who, looking
out upon the contemporary world with its amazing accumulation of mechanical power, its unbelievable multiplicity
of devices for material comfort, its countless organizations
and institutions, can stretch his thought to match the accomplishment? One may indeed question the high valua-
tion often put upon the transformation of the physical
environment and lament the sacrifice of precious goods

which it has cost; nevertheless considered purely as an accomplishment, no language is adequate to its majesty.

v

Few people have any true appreciation of these facts, but they would not object to them or deny their significance in a study of man's place in the animal kingdom. When they assent to the animal interpretation of man it is on the side of impulse, not on the side of intelligence. It is there, in what he wants and feels, that they believe man has made no progress beyond the animal or savage. Nevertheless in this realm also, which, until a better term is invented, we may designate the realm of the spirit, man has shown it to be his nature to recreate. He has gradually elevated the ethical level of his life and manners.

There are able people who deny this. They argue that man has made no moral progress whatever; that he has merely changed fashions in the garments under which he hides his fatal depravity. And it is not difficult to gather data which make the contention appear plausible. But if certain errors are guarded against these data are less telling. Slowly throughout the centuries, and very rapidly in recent times, the great mass of mankind has pushed its way to the front, demanding and obtaining active participation in affairs. This great mass is prominently in our minds when we think of contemporary human nature, whereas when we think of human nature in ancient times we disregard the mass then existing and remember only the illustrious few or a selected group.

No one in his senses would claim that men in the mass today live on a higher ethical plane than exceptional individuals or an exceptional group of people did in a selected period of the past. One may, however, be quite in his senses and claim that the general ethical consciousness is a finer thing the world round than it was in earlier times. There is still much of superstition, brutality, and aesthetic indifference, but the power of agreeable fiction is less tyrannical than it once was, fellow feeling is effective over a wider range, and interest in aesthetic experience is more pervasive and liberal. This is moral gain.

Nor is it true that man's ethical outlook has not changed because the basic wants summed up in the words food, shelter, sex, continue to be motivating forces of action. They are not the simple cravings they were. Each has been enriched by inclusion within a growing complexity of interests; each has been refined by a nicer perception of consequences and a greater sensitivity of feeling. This would be obvious were we not trained to approach experience through theory. We dip an intellectual net into fluid experience and mistake a catch of abstractions for quivering life. We disregard the differences between concrete behaviors, and are rewarded with the illusion of a quality common to them all. This we are pleased to regard as the *essential* character, although we never really come upon it, while the characteristics we do come upon we take to be *accidental*, hence negligible.

Well, it is just these neglected characteristics which enable us to distinguish the behavior of one man from that of another. To improve morally does not mean to

refashion an essence called human nature, or to cease to
be involved in the impulses and habits without which we
would not only cease to be human, but cease to be. It
means to bring impulses and habits under the influence
of criticism, so that the significance of right and wrong
may be better understood, so that sympathetic imagination may become more generous in its application, and
the satisfactions aimed at may be more abiding.

Are we to draw the conclusion from these facts that
human history shows an undeviating progress upward?
Scarcely. The picture is not so bright as that. There have
been losses and gains, now the one, now the other. We
have no way of telling whether, if other routes had been
chosen in place of those that were, mankind might not
today be in a far better state, physically and morally. The
contention is simply that in man a being has been achieved
who dissolves the world in his restless imagination and
precipitates it in dreams and schemes of betterment. It is
his genius to form purposes and invent the instruments of
their realization. He makes the power of natural forces and
the succession of natural events responsive to teleological
vision, and thus alters the world he inherits, the world in
its material and also in its moral aspects. Denied this opportunity in the realm of fact, he transfers it to the realm
of the imagination. Robbed of every compensating deflection, he sinks to the level of the animal, or, in Mr. Santayana's phrase, "folds up his heart and withers in a corner."

vi

If an adequate description of anything involves the consideration of its historic as well as its contemporary manifestations, what of possible developments still to come? Time has future as well as present and past dimension. Consider religion once more. Had we gathered together into one concept the qualities of all now existing religions and enlarged this by the inclusion of all the religions which from time to time have appealed to men, much would still be left out. Tendencies are alive in the world today which will make the religions of tomorrow something different from what they have so far been. And there will be tomorrows after tomorrow. This future aspect—what religion will become as men discover how to make new use of the propensities and experiences that are the sources of religion—must be taken into account.

Nothing of which we know differs in this respect from religion, least of all man. *Man's nature must be held to include what he may become.* Suppose Aristotle had given a perfect characterization of humanity as realized up to his day, would he have done justice to the theme? Did not men who came later show attainments and capacities which had not appeared up to that time? Yet the capacity necessary for this achievement must have been present even then. In other words, man was more than his present and his past disclosed. In some sense he *was* what he was still *to be.*

Now what of this man of the future? What can safely be

said of him? This is a subject, if there is no other, on which
we can agree. Of the man of the future we know nothing.
One may at best puzzle a little about him and hazard a
guess or two. Possibly all it comes to is a confession of one's
deepest hopes and aversions.

Let us then hazard the guess that a fruitful harmony will
be found between impulses which at present are in conflict. For a very long time man's animal ancestors were
united with other animals in a generalized mammalian
stock. Possibly the backward pull of this early relationship
is still influential in subtle and powerful ways. It may play
its part in a natural gregariousness, in a readiness to feel
and think as the crowd does. On the other hand, ages ago
man's ancestors started off on what turned out to be a human career. Something very urgent must have been operative in this venture. Possibly the potency of it is felt in
the desire for independence and individuality. Whatever
the explanation may be, men want to "team up" with
others, often to the degree of being completely lost in the
group, and they want to "go it alone," often showing an
unwillingness to be interfered with by anyone.

There have been times when these two needs—to be one
with others and to be oneself—could be reasonably satisfied in socially approved ways by everyone according to
his capacity. But a number of developments in the recent
past have produced conditions which make this more difficult than formerly. How is the individual to put trust in
feelings of social solidarity when practical affairs and public opinion, whose authority he cannot ignore, teach him

that all human beings are isolated units competing with one another for the most of what each of them wants? How shall individuality be attained under circumstances which make collective action increasingly necessary?

This double demand has made the realization of individuality a problem in every age. Genuine individuality, as John Dewey has pointed out in *Individualism Old and New*, is possible only if the individual is a sustained and a sustaining element in a social whole. Therefore when this social whole disintegrates or moves toward a new and perhaps increased centralization of power, so that the individual is displaced, the desire for individuality will feel itself to be menaced. It felt itself to be thus menaced in the past in Egypt, in Greece, in Rome, in Medieval Europe, in the Europe of the Industrial Revolution, and it feels itself thus menaced today.

Current outcries against encroachments upon individualism are not always prompted by a real concern for individuality. "Individuality for the many," says James Hart, "has long been little more than a joke. Try to imagine it for steel workers, for miners, for thousands in our large cities. As the flood creeps higher others are menaced, the so-called educated classes, for example, and they think it a present emergency." That is surely true. Persons who formerly acquiesced in the subversion of individuality because it did not touch their own, often oppose any step in social planning that interferes with their freedom of action. But it is not this class of persons only that is disturbed. The danger to individuality of any kind is widely recognized today and its preservation is regarded as a difficult problem.

vii

The curtailment of freedom which is so noticeable a phenomenon of our day endangers a most valuable attribute of human nature. Nevertheless some limitation has become unavoidable. Individualistic ambitions can no longer be permitted to have free play if larger and larger numbers of people are not to be deprived of a fair chance in life. There may have been a time when unrestrained individualism was necessary in order that the earth might be possessed and turned to human uses. I do not think so, but if there was, that time is gone. There is now no escape from society and no place for socially irresponsible action. "Personal liberty," "individual initiative," and the individualism called "rugged" were conceived in a wide-open world that waited for exploitation by individuals for their personal advantage. The possible consequences of such individualism in our world are too serious to be risked, once they are anticipated. That much at least has been demonstrated by what has happened. Even the ideal of "knowledge for its own sake" now institutionalized and organized as a profession, cannot with safety be allowed to set itself up as superior to social demands.

Unfortunately, every restriction of freedom carries with it the ill-chance of destroying something of inestimable worth. No single stage in the evolution of the human species was so significant as the emergence of the individual self, the occurrence in nature of centers of novel experience, novel ardors, novel ideas, novel achievements of a practical nature. It is deplorable that encroachments on freedom too often bear down hardest upon the best kind and permit the worst kind to escape.

If individuality is to be safeguarded, or preserved at all, a distinction will have to be made between its social and its antisocial forms. For individual potentialities will in the future be compelled to realize themselves along with, rather than over against, community of effort with others. It will take the hardest kind of hard thinking to make the change with a maximum of gain and a minimum of loss. Strong opposition will have to be met coming from those who do not know what it is all about and those who know only too well what it is all about. Interests and occupations will have to be reshaped in heretofore unheard-of ways.

This change may take more creativeness and courage than we possess. If we are wise and courageous enough, have time enough, and are favored by good luck, we may be able to institute a communal life in which the many will find new opportunity to enjoy novelty of experience in their personal tastes, in their relaxation, and in the work they do to make a living. If this co-operative form of individuality is out of the question, individuality for the many will vanish. It will be reserved for the few who prove to be powerful enough to seize and hold the privilege until their game too is up. The masses of us will take orders from those few. Individuality will either become communal, or in any liberal sense it will disappear, and with it will go the supreme quality of human nature.

viii

Possibly another problem will gradually be solved. Until recently the institutions and occupations concerned with the production and distribution of food, clothing, and shelter were based upon the needs to be served. In the words of the economist, demand regulated supply. It does so no longer. The machinery of production and distribution has attained such vast proportions, so much is involved in its regular functioning, that demand has to be created to meet the supply. What was once a phase of activity subservient to life has become an end in itself.

Perhaps not only *an* end, but *the* end. Year by year business institutions grow larger, absorbing smaller ones or crowding them to the wall. Experts are drawn in to deal with physical, chemical, economic, psychological problems. In the battle for markets the outposts are pushed farther afield, while the combat is intensified at home. With so much at stake it is natural that businessmen should devote themselves to something besides business; that they should seek to influence the enactment and administration of laws, national and international, and that they should try to control education and to supplant religion as the definer of ideals.

Large numbers of people, among them many who are engaged in business occupations, deplore the surrender of life to the enterprises necessary for making a living. It seems to them the result of forces which cannot be controlled. Let us hope they are wrong. They mistake the conditions they find existing for the ways things must necessarily be. It was once unthinkable that there should be religion without monopolistic priestcraft. It was formerly believed that political government must have its center in a royal personage. The unexpected has come to pass. Is it not possible that man will learn to conduct business without being dominated by Business? May not the future leadership in business undertakings belong to those whose vision is not limited to business success?

The present fashion, indeed the present necessity, may lead to an intensified concentration on the production and distribution of the things needed for the body. The fashion and the necessity may grow upon us. But this is not sure to happen. Human nature is not necessarily business nature. What man has done in the past and is doing now suggests other possibilities. The discovery may be made that the material wealth of society, instead of being the summit of human achievement, lays the foundation for its florescence.

ix

How much it is possible to do about these and similar matters depends at last upon the nature of mankind as a whole. If men and women do not have the stuff in them to make a higher type of civilization a realizable ideal, it is of course futile to aim at that ideal. That they do not have, is the outspoken conviction of numerous critics. "Man," says Oswald Spengler, "is a beast of prey. . . . He wills, and has ever willed since he existed, to be master. . . ." and "he lives by attacking and killing and destroying." Ortega ý Gasset divides people into two classes: the minority, "those who make great demands on themselves, piling up difficulties and duties," and the masses, "those who demand nothing special of themselves . . . mere buoys that float on the waves." Ralph Adams Cram urges his fellow countrymen to put aside the error that the people they see walking about in the streets are human beings. "The cruelty and meanness and the lust, the dullness of mind, the petty greed, the gross selfishness, that are characteristic of man at his lowest," give place, he finds, in the better part of the masses "to a type of childishness of very limited mental capacity, and to a tragic subservience to 'mob psychology' that pathetically limit the very real desire for beauty and righteousness, fighting ever against the grace of God that is always working patiently to overcome those limitations."

Mr. Cram hails with enthusiasm and almost worships the exceptional individual of heroic proportions, scattered very sparingly through history, the type which he calls "the flashing event of pattern men, geniuses, seers, creators, leaders." But "mankind," which has not changed in the thousands of years since the appearance of a distinct "human entity" and will not change in the future, this "mass-man," forever of Paleolithic grade, repels him and prompts him to exclaim: "Of all the moon-madness that from time to time engages the consciousness of man, none is more lunatic than his delusion of grandeur." There is but one service which this human mass can render. It can be the prolific matrix out of which the few individuals of ability and character may spring. The idea was eloquently set forth by Mr. Cram in the *American Mercury:*

What I mean is this, and it may be expressed by a parable. Some years ago I was on the island of Hawaii and in the great crater of Kilanea on the edge of the floating pit of Halemaumau. For once the pit was level full of molten lava that at one edge of this pit, at the iron edge of the old lava, rose swiftly from the lowest depths, then slid silently, a viscous field of lambent cherry color, along the length of the great pit, to plunge there and disappear as silently, only to return and rise again, when all was to happen once more. Indeterminate and homogeneous, it was an undifferentiated flood except for one thing. As it slid silkily onward it fountained incessantly. That is to say, from all over its surface leaped high in the air slim jets of golden lava, that caught the sun and opened into delicate fireworks of falling jewels, beautiful beyond imagination.

Such I conceive to be the pattern of human life. Millennium after millennium this endless flood of basic raw material sweeps on. It is the everlasting Neolithic Man, the same that it was in 10,000 B. C. It is the matrix of the human being, the stuff of which he is made. It arises from the unknown and it disappears in the unknown, to return again and again of itself. And always it fountains in fine personalities, eminent and of historic record, or obscure yet of equal nobility, and these are the human beings on whose personality, character and achievements we establish our standards. . . . In other words, the just line of demarcation should be drawn, not between Neolithic man and the anthropoid ape, but between the glorified and triumphant human being and the Neolithic mass which was, is now, and ever shall be.

A scientific companion piece is provided by E. A. Hooton, anthropologist of Harvard University, in his book, *Apes, Men, and Morons:*

When are we to realize that a great proportion of mankind continues to be as stupid, unteachable, bloodthirsty,
predatory, and savage as we are wont to imagine that
maligned and regrettably extinct precursor—Neanderthal
man? . . . I think it is because no little of the human germ
plasm is poisonous slime, and we have not had the intelligence and the courage to attempt to find out anything
about human heredity. We have imagined universal education, mutual understanding, and improvement of the social environment to be the ingredients with which we can
concoct the human millennium; we have mixed them up
and stirred them in, and turned out a horrible mess. There
must be something the matter with our basic element—
man himself. . . . The future of mankind does not depend upon political or economic theory, nor yet upon
measures of social amelioration, but upon the production
of better minds in sounder bodies.

x

How much truth is there in these estimates of mankind?
That there is some truth in them will be granted by anyone
who is not a complete sentimentalist. But is it true, as
Mr. Cram asserts, that the human being is an occasional
"glorified and triumphant product" and that "the mass of
homo sapiens" may be thrown together in a heap and
labeled subhuman? I think not. The pronouncement seems
to me one of those facile generalizations which the cul-
tured or socially privileged find it so easy to toss off.

Has it been demonstrated, as Professor Hooton claims,
"that modern man is selling his biological birthright for a
mess of morons; that the voice may be the voice of democracy, but the hands are the hands of apes"? It sounds

too smart to be true. And assuming it to be a fact that "a biological purge is the essential prerequisite for a social and spiritual salvation," the history of purges shows uniformly that those who conduct them have a very narrow conception of purity.

Men and women obviously differ greatly in native ability, in acquired intelligence, in care for the refinements of life. They differ in the extent to which conduct is influenced by reason and moral sensibility. And it is undeniable that improvement in these respects may be blocked by inborn defects. But it is well, for one thing, to remember that these defects are not limited to the so-called lower classes. Leonard Woolf has summarized the facts exactly:

In every community, even the most civilized, there are indeed a large number of persons, both in the minority and majority, whose psychology has remained mainly animal or savage. Civilization at the best is irksome to them; their instincts are thwarted by it; reason makes them uneasy and they dislike intelligence; humanism and humanitarianism are either ridiculous or disgusting to them, and all the "refinements" of civilized life, including the arts and culture, seem effeminate, wicked or useless. . . . But vast numbers of them—and the most dangerous to civilization—are to be found among the most respectable, pillars of church and state, aristocrats, generals and admirals, cabinet ministers, clergymen and schoolmasters, dons and professors, captains of industry and eminent bankers.

To complete the picture on the other side, Mr. Woolf might have added that in every community there are persons, in larger or smaller numbers, both in the minority and majority, whose psychology has passed beyond the animal or savage. Civilized life appeals to them; their instincts are offered up to it; they seek to be on good terms with reason and they want to be intelligent; humanism and humanitarianism they regard as essentials of character, and all the "refinements" of civilized life, including the arts and culture, seem to them the glory of personal and social achievement. And vast numbers of them—the most dedicated to civilization—are to be found among the least respectable, people without position in church or state, clerks, artisans, housewives, and unheralded toilers of every description.

The fact is, the mass-man is a myth, and the pattern-man is a myth. "We are all one wool," as the Scotchman put it, "mixed with more or with less shoddy." The grade of mixture is important, but it is infinitely various and the amount of inborn shoddy is extremely difficult to determine. Which suggests a second thing to be remembered. "Most people," said Henry Brewster, who was disturbed by what many overlook, "Most people have suffered far too much to have any active tendencies left at all, if the idea of some result to be attained is bound up therewith." They are "beaten by poverty, by disease, by weakness, by bad luck, by unrequited love, by drink, by vices, by dreams, and by ghosts. And yet they get on, and get on as well as the few whose pity for them is self-sufficiency and ignorance." Marie Dressler, too, has spoken an understanding word. "We are not so dumb," she said, "as a lot of folks find it convenient to think us. The sooner the producers, professors, and politicians wake up to the fact that the average citizen in this country has about ten times as much native intelligence and appreciation as they give them credit for, the better off they will be."

These quotations are not unanswerable proof of the intelligence and character of average human beings, but they do carry weight as the opinions of persons who are intimately acquainted with their fellow men. Anyone who cares to look about a little, and who has an eye for the capabilities flattened out under burdens too heavy to be borne, will easily find more evidence of the same sort. Many people are, in Horace Gregory's phrase, "but the partial fulfillment of a large design." A woman in *You Have Seen Their Faces*, says it in this way for innumerable others: "I've done the best I knew how all my life, but it didn't amount to much in the end." Though lost from view in "the masses," they stand up to the tests that have to be met, and manage to put sympathy and humor and beauty into life around them. Relatively few are reduced to the state described in de la Mare's poem:

> And he the cheated? Dust till morn,
> Insensate, even of hope forsook,
> He muttering squats, aloof, forlorn,
> Dangling a baitless hook.

xi

Excellence in any form, as everyone knows, is exceptional. Lives of excellence are not too plentiful in any group or class. Are they more exceptional among the many than among the privileged minority, unless the conception of excellence is inexcusably narrowed?

The gulf between the level of ordinary attainment and the heights reached by those who are in advance of their fellows is one which I would do nothing to keep out of sight. It does not, however, divide humanity into the worthless masses and the admirable few. According to an epigram of Oscar Wilde, "We are all of us lying in the gutter; but some of us are looking at the stars." A writer in England—perhaps it was Richard Sunne—discussing this epigram, remarked that many of Wilde's statements are more true when turned around. He thought it a better symbol of the condition of humanity to say, "Some of us are lying in the gutter, but all of us are looking at the stars." The amendment seems to me in accord with the reality.

The point just now is that the gutter crosses all class and group lines. It runs through wealthy suburbs and exclusive country houses, over college campuses, into the high places of politics and religion. As for the stars—the great fixed stars of generosity, sympathy, sense of workmanship, helpfulness in distress, devotion to causes of human betterment—who can truthfully say that these inspire deeper awe in the hearts of the "upper classes" than in the hearts of those who dwell lower down?

"The production of better minds in sounder bodies," by all means; but a sounder environment as well. For it should be commonplace knowledge by now that the environment is not merely the *setting* for the development of inborn human nature, but a *component* of human nature. Things and ongoing affairs are as essentially included as physiological and psychical powers. They are inseparable as the inside and outside of a bowl. This fact is too generally ignored by the learned specialists who sweep their roving eye over a world of facts and compress great areas of living experience into a cynical aphorism.

"Give a dog a bad name and hang him." John Dewey has suggested that human nature has long been the dog of professional theorizing, with consequences in accord with the proverb. There are many puzzling things in life, and one of the most curious is the psychological profundity of novelists. Novelists, "mere writers of fiction," seem to know men and women far better than our "thinkers" know them. Their people are not intellectual abstractions. They are living creatures responsive to forces which make or break them. It is therefore significant that novelists have a better opinion of people than the thinkers have. They seem rather to like them, not to dislike them, as the thinkers do.

At any rate we must conclude, I think, that it is unimaginative and unscientific to toss the majority aside as nonhuman. And it is rejecting the good with the bad indiscriminately, the promising and the hopeful human material along with that which is worthless and hopeless. One would have to be blind to see nothing but good in man or to see all men as equal in every respect, but one is just as blind not to see the good there is. Not until men in large numbers have freer access to the best fruits of civilization can we presume to say what they are capable of. Their spontaneous delight in being part of exciting projects with their fellows is one of their conspicuous characteristics. They endure hardship, they take pride in their work, they suffer and do not lose hope, they press on with no certainty that their effort will be rewarded. Something much better might be made of all this than has yet been attempted.

When those who influence men from above stop appealing to fear and envy as stimulants to advancement, and respected institutions stop perpetuating and exploiting ignorance and superstition for good ends and for bad ends —in a word, when such destructive influences are replaced by organized means to bring the best in human nature, whatever it is, to expression—we may be able to decide what men and women have it in them to become.

xii

Turning back over the route which this discussion has followed, the conclusion must be that man's nature cannot be exhausted in one stratum of existence. He is what he *is* in the complexity and contradictoriness of his present striving. He is what he *was* in those ages of which he is the ripening fruit. He is what he shall find the means of *becoming* in the generations to be while yet his race may last. Being so much, he presents the appearance of hopeless contradiction, denying what he expresses, expressing what he denies. In strictness indefinable, he defines himself every age and every hour. He escapes the neat formulas in which the unimaginative would capture him. He refuses to validate the graphs invented to picture his career. No work of reason or art has portrayed the depths to which he can sink or the heights to which he can rise. Helpless, without environmental opportunity, hard conditions have been unable to crush him, nor have favorable conditions lulled him to rest. He may come to naught in the end, but while the planet permits he will be, as Whitman said, "immense and interminable," like the great rivers; he will be the "god in ruins" of Emerson, the "not yet formed" of Browning, the "indescribable focus of the universe" of Hardy. So that, committing the aesthetic impiety of giving a turn to the Carl Sandburg poem, we may say:

O, I got a zoo, I got a menagerie, inside my ribs, under my bony head, under my red-valve heart:
I am a pal of the world.
And I got something else.
It drew me out of the wilderness, looking, looking. . . .
Wherever you meet me, you'll find me looking. . . .
You'll find me looking . . . looking . . . looking. . . .

❧ VIII ❧

SCIENCE AND MAN, I

i

Giordano Bruno is said to have remarked: "If the first button of a man's coat is wrongly buttoned all the rest will be crooked." It is surmised that he was thinking of the boyhood step whereby he surrendered his aspirational life into the hands of a monastic order. The remark is applicable to science which was young when he was. At the threshold of unfolding knowledge and power science relinquished the realm of ideals into the hands of church religion, and from that surrender crooked consequences have followed down to the present day.

We have already discussed the problem of how to bring what we know and do into harmony with what we aspire to be. The development of science has forced this problem upon us in its most serious and baffling form. Unless a better relationship between scientific progress and the interests of humanity can be worked out than was contemplated in the seventeenth century, or has been thought of since, the prospect is extremely unpromising. We may in that case look forward to the eventual downfall of the scientifically advanced races. Only those which are backward with regard to science can hope to survive—providing they can keep out of the way of their scientific neighbors.

What was it the early scientists did so that the first button of the coat was wrongly buttoned? What were the derangements that followed all down the line? To get an answer we must read a little history.

ii

In the summer of 1662 Henry Oldenburg, Secretary of the Royal Society newly founded in London, wrote a letter to Benedictus Spinoza. "Come, excellent Sir," he pled, "banish all fear of stirring up the pygmies of our times; too long have sacrifices been made to ignorance and absurdity; let us spread our sails to the wind of true knowledge and search out the innermost secrets of nature more thoroughly than has been done hitherto." It was as if the very spirit of the age had spoken, the great age that ushered in modern experimental science. Exuberant life was evident everywhere: in unprecedented commercial expansion, in violent political conflict, in vigorous social and religious ferment. Yet above all it was a time responsive to the exciting challenge echoed by Secretary Oldenburg: Let us spread our sails to the wind of true knowledge and search out the innermost secrets of nature.

Of the large numbers of men who ventured in the ships of the seventeenth century many never again saw land. Similar mishaps overtook those who embarked on the un-

charted sea of knowledge. Henry Oldenburg soon learned
to discipline his desire to see all sails spread in voyages of
intellectual discovery. In his early letters he implored Spinoza to publish his ideas in the teeth of malicious ignorance. "I adjure you," he wrote, "I adjure you by the bond
of our friendship, by every duty of multiplying and spreading abroad the truth, not to withhold from us your writings."
"I would by all means advise you," he wrote again, "not to
begrudge to scholars the results at which with your mental
sagacity and learning you have arrived both in Philosophical
and Theological matters; let them be published, however
much the Theological quacks may growl." It was the bold-
ness of inexperience. Experience tutored him to caution.

As the correspondence proceeded, Oldenburg grew appre-
hensive. Presently he greatly dreaded the publication of
some of Spinoza's views. In the end he sent this troubled
request: "Allow me, I pray, to advise you out of your sincere affection for me not to include anything which may
appear to undermine the practice of Religious virtue. Especially so since there is nothing for which this degenerate
and wicked age seeks more eagerly than the kind of doctrine
whose conclusions seem to give encouragement to flagrant
vices."

Intellectual backsliding was not singular at the time.
Many who were carried away by the intellectual *Wander-
lust* of the age, quickly found the open sea too rough for
their religious stomachs. A squall or two, and they sought
refuge in the nearest haven of tradition, never thereafter
to be tempted forth. Albert Burgh and Nicholas Steno were
conspicuous members of this company. They began their

careers as enthusiasts for the new learning, but made their reputations as uncompromising foes of science.

The first secretary of the Royal Society had special reasons for lapsing from his original impetuous devotion to the new enlightenment. War, the plague, a devastating fire, left the population of London nervous and suspicious, an easy prey to superstitious explanations. The Royal Society had to be circumspect in order to remain alive in this atmosphere. Moreover, Oldenburg was accused of disclosing political secrets in connection with his scientific correspondence. In consequence, he spent two months in the Tower. And he may have had fears for his own immortal soul as it became clear to him that the trend of science was materialistic.

But after all, no special explanation is needed to account for his deflection. Scientific diffidence with regard to "Religious virtue" was typical of the age. An avowed interest in the progress of knowledge seemed to endanger the spiritual interests of mankind. It was the normal behavior of the early scientists to stop short at the borders of revealed religion, and to exempt from scientific authority any belief or idea which could lay claim to religious sanction.

The root of the difficulty reached back to the medieval world, when analogous conditions brought about a similar bisection of knowledge. Thomas Aquinas, it is true, refused to separate the domains of reason and faith. He labored to bring together into one system the physical world, the world of divine grace, and the world of eternal glory. Henry Adams aptly said of him: "The hive of Saint Thomas sheltered God and man, mind and matter, the universe and the atom, the one and the multiple, within the walls of an harmonious home." This scheme accomplished two things. It protected the Church which had begun to suffer from philosophic speculation, and, by providing a place for the new knowledge which the revival of Aristotle gave rise to, it won a measure of freedom for speculative activity.

But the philosophic teachings of St. Thomas were not accepted by all thinkers. They were suspected of being hostile to the truths of faith. In fact the ingenious compromise of the Angelic Doctor hardly survived him. Duns Scotus, who was born probably in the year St. Thomas died, found it impossible for a critical intelligence to harmonize the deliverances of faith and reason. Church doctrines remained sacred and inviolable with him, but they were no longer included, together with what was known about the world of nature, in one rational system. The famous pupil of Duns Scotus, William of Occam, carried this tendency farther. He separated the two realms as by a chasm. Theological and philosophical truths were regarded by him as mutually contradictory.

No doubt this theory of dual truth was then and thereafter in some cases a disguise, conscious or unconscious, for a one-sided espousal now of religion and now of philosophy. Which it was in a specific instance it is impossible to decide without reading too much between the lines. What we know is that when an active spirit of critical investigation came to life in medieval scholasticism, the outcome was a division of knowledge into natural and supernatural, between which there could be no communication.

iii

The rise of modern science in the seventeenth century revived and intensified the antithesis. In Giordano Bruno's speculations the attempt was once more made to bring secular learning and the teachings of the church within an inclusive vision of truth. But Bruno's tormented career, long imprisonment, and tragic death show how intense the conflict had become. His martyrdom by burning in 1600 threw a warning glare over the opening decades of the century and every venturesome thinker was aware of the risk he ran. A dilemma was thus created, big with prospective danger to established religion, and with immediate danger to the scientific venture, which as yet had no intellectual or social prestige. Confronted by this dilemma, the early advocates of science either recalled the traditional irreconcilability of truths about physical nature and truths divinely revealed, or they invented it themselves.

Descartes, with whom modern philosophy begins, separated the material and the spiritual realms as the two poles of reality. He proposed to clear the ground by a thoroughgoing skepticism of all his beliefs, with the avowed intention of building up a view of things upon scientific evidence. But he refrained from extending his method of doubt to morality and religion. That there might be no misunderstanding of his intention, he explicitly announced his adherence to a moral and religious code the first maxim of which, in his own words, was "to obey the laws and customs of my country, adhering firmly to the faith in which, by the grace of God, I had been educated from my childhood, and regulating my conduct in every other matter according to the most moderate opinions, and the farthest removed from extremes, which should happen to be adopted in practice with the general consent of the most judicious of those among whom I might be living."

No one was more outspoken on this matter than Francis Bacon, who surely stretched the applicability of scientific inquiry as far as he believed it could be done. He, too, halted at what he called "sacred or inspired Theology." This, he insisted, should "be drawn up from the word and oracles of God, and not from the light of nature or the dictates of reason." His position is picturesquely stated in the concluding book of De Augmentis Scientarum:

Now excellent king, since my little boat, such as it is, has sailed completely round the world of knowledge, both old and new (with how favorable winds and piloting let posterity judge), what remains but that I should pay my vows, now that I have at last ended my journey? Of course there is left sacred or inspired Theology. However, if I am to treat of that, I must get out of the little boat of human reason and transfer myself into the great ship of the Church, which alone is able to direct its course by the aid of a divine nautical needle. For the stars of philosophy which so far have nobly served to guide me, will then no longer suffice.

Bacon took pains again and again to emphasize this division of knowledge into two incompatible kinds, the one arrived at by cross-examining nature, the other dependent upon divine revelation. He went so far as to declare that "the more discordant and incredible some divine mystery is, the more is God honored if it is believed, and the worthier is the victory of Faith." Probably he agreed with the opinion of his clever young friend, Thomas Hobbes, whose terse statement, flavored with a dash of his habitual cynicism, has been found very quotable:

The mysteries of religion are like the pills prescribed by physicians for the sick, which swallowed whole, have the virtue to cure; but chewed are for the most part cast up again without effect.

These provisos may indeed have been diplomatic gestures to appease those in power. The Church was now alive to the danger of a tolerant attitude toward science, and the Church had a long arm. Independent thinking had to be cautious and keep out of reach. Those who took a chance cannot be blamed if they considered it wise to have an anchor to the windward in case the storm should increase to violence. And yet if one reads Descartes, Bacon, Hobbes, Galileo, or any scientist of the period, with the hope of seeing the world somewhat as they saw it, one hesitates to conclude that when they separate revealed truth from natural truth they do it with tongue in cheek. It is more probable that these early scientists did not fully appreciate the implications of their method and did not foresee—how could they?—the rapid expansion of science into every field. They were thinking of the material half of the world, being quite frankly dualistic as regards the whole of experience.

Pierre Bayle is a test case. In Pierre Bayle a passion for clear and distinct reasoning was combined with fervent solicitude for the best fruits of the religious spirit. He would surely have attempted a unification of the two had this appeared to be in any way possible. But he could only

torture himself all his days elaborating sundry details of
the dividing chasm. We may safely conclude, I think, that
whatever motives of a peculiarly personal nature were influential in this or that individual case, the mind of the
first scientific century was in this matter divided against
itself. There appeared to be no way of harmonizing the
new and ever-growing knowledge of science with the truth
that was the same yesterday, and today, and forever.

iv

There is perhaps no better introduction to the meaning of science in our time than the study of the scientific
attitude of Francis Bacon. He is often said to have been of
no scientific significance. It is customary to think of him
as a cheerleader for science in the contest between science
and scholasticism. His writings stand against this low estimate. Although he was not himself a competent experi-
mentalist, nor even unusually well versed in the scientific
knowledge of his time, he was a scientist in the whole temper of his mind: in his conception of nature, his adoption
of objective experiment as the test of truth, and his vision
of the scientific task. He was a far truer scientist than some
whose laboratory genius has won them recognition as great
scientists in the twentieth century, yet who quickly return
to unscientific obscurantism when faced with ethical or religious problems. That he was almost utterly lacking in
ethical dependability has often been pointed out. He did
not hesitate to demean himself, to prostitute his talents or
to betray his friends, if this promised to secure him ad-

vancement. But there was one interest to which he remained constant. He never proved false to science. To the advancement of science he gave his best through all the ups and downs of his career. Science never asked him to give what he did not have.

It is very doubtful that a more unemotional human being ever existed than Francis Bacon. He was as nearly pure brains as it is possible for a man to be. "Intellect," as Lytton Strachey has said, "not feeling, was the material out of which his gorgeous and pregnant sentences were made. It was the common factor in all the variations of his spirit." Kuno Fisher has accurately characterized him: "If there were a thermometer to measure the intrinsic force of human passions, we should find, in the case of Bacon, that the degree of warmth belonging to his heart stood very close to zero."

This lack of emotional warmth, which was responsible for his most flagrant defects of character and for that conspicuous trait which David Hume described as his "extraordinary facility in helping himself," also made him the more perfect intellectual machine. It fitted him the better to take part in what he called the "disinterested observation of nature." He exemplified in his own person the ethical neutrality of science; the recoil of science from every consideration of the wished-for or the ought-to-be; the concentration of science upon the study of what is, has been, or is bound to come. He was, as it were, science itself.

There may have been other reasons, in fact there were, why Francis Bacon insisted that religion and morality, truly conceived, lie outside the reach of scientific investigation. But the deeper reason, the reason that could not be taken away and have left him Francis Bacon, was his lack of interest in the evaluation of human aims. He was temperamentally aloof from conflicts that arise out of antagonistic ideals. The moral disillusion often resulting from vast commercial and material expansion did not touch him. His coldly intellectual nature stood aside from the aspects of life which deeply affected warmer personalities. He saw it as his task to champion the mastery of the world in its material aspect, not to help decide what men ought to do or be. What men ought to do or be was a question he handed over to "sacred Theology." Possibly he did not expect "sacred Theology" to provide an answer; at any rate it would not clutter up his laboratory mind. He would be left free to study facts and to discover the principles or laws which they exemplify. This was his real interest. He was clear in his own mind, and he tried to make it clear to all who could understand him, that it was his mission to follow the way of objective science and no other. He proposed to engage in no investigation which could not be carried on by the use of natural human reason. Thus he said:

This holdeth not only of those points of faith which concern the great mysteries of the Deity, of the creation, of the redemption, but likewise those which concern the law moral truly interpreted: Love your enemies; do good to them that hate you; be like your heavenly Father that suffereth his rain to fall upon the just and the unjust. To this it ought to be applauded, "NEC VOX HOMINUM SONAT": it is a voice beyond the light of nature.

Francis Bacon epitomizes science in another respect. He thought of knowledge as power. He sought to know nature's innermost secrets in order to extend "human empire over all things possible." While he had no sympathy whatever with the demand for immediate practical applicability of every scientific discovery, he saw in *applied* science the ultimate justification of *theoretical* science. "Light-giving experiments," to use his own words, were valuable chiefly because they made possible "fruit-bearing experiments." Inspired as he was by such revolutionary inventions as printing, gunpowder, and the compass, which, as he said, had "changed the face and state of things in all the world," so that "no empire, no sect, no star seems to have exercised a greater command and influence over human affairs than have these mechanical discoveries," he believed that by the use of scientific method inventions and discoveries of all kinds might be made almost at will. Critically conducted experiments would disclose the laws of nature; knowledge of these would usher in an age of invention; invention of mechanical contrivances would enable mankind to win dominion on earth. "Man through the Fall," he declared, "lost both his state of innocence and his lordship over the created world. Both these can, even in this life, be partly repaired, the former by Religion, and Faith, the latter by the Arts and Sciences."

The idea in Bacon's mind was simple and clear. It was to domesticate the untamed forces of nature as wild horses had been domesticated; to put them into harness, hitch them to the human enterprise, invite mankind to climb in and ride away to wealth, health, and felicity. The vision of innumerable powerful horses champing at the bit was so entrancing that the question of driver and destination seemed hardly worth thinking about. "Only let man regain his right over Nature," he enthusiastically exclaimed, "let him be given the power: right reason and sound religion will teach him how to apply it." It did not occur to him that once hitched up, the horses might take the bit in their teeth and run away with the wagon, or that a reckless driver might seize the reins, tumble "right reason and sound religion" out on their heads, and gallop off to perdition.

v

One further circumstance must be considered if we are to get a fair picture of Francis Bacon as an embodiment of the scientific temper. It is the ambiguity of intention which disclaims, and at the same time asserts, supreme authority over the known. We have observed how sharp a line he drew between natural and revealed knowledge, and in what precise terms he excluded scientific method from questions of moral and religious evaluation. But this line of separation was then, and has been ever since, a convenient fiction, adopted either because scientific method was not yet prepared to study human beings in their entirety, or because organized religion would not permit men to be regarded as solely natural phenomena. The ultimate aim was nevertheless a complete naturalism. Everything was to be brought under "the light of nature." If the plan could be carried out, was the time not bound to come when nothing would seem to be known unless it was known scientifically? Was it not inevitable that science should little by little

invalidate conceptions derived from "sacred Theology"?
We in our day are aware that this has come to pass. And
it was the logical outcome of Bacon's scientific ideal. This
is shown in such paragraphs as this from his *Novum Organum:*

> Again: some one will doubt rather than object; whether
> we speak of perfecting by our method Natural Philosophy
> only, or the other sciences as well, Logic, Ethics, Politics.
> But we certainly understand that what we have said refers
> to all: and just as the common Logic which rules Things
> by means of Syllogisms pertains not only to natural Sci-
> ences, but to all; so ours too, which proceeds by Induction,
> embraces all things. For we construct a History and Tables
> of Discovery as much of Anger, Fear, Modesty, and the
> like: or of the examples of civil affairs; and no less of the
> mental emotions of Memory, of Composition and Divi-
> sion, Judgment and the rest, as of Cold and Heat, Light,
> or Vegetation, or the like.

The program of science, as Bacon sees it, is therefore a
sweeping one. Seeming qualifications and concessions are
to be understood in relation to its prior claim. Psychology
and sociology are to be scientific subjects; morality as found
actually existing among men is a natural phenomenon,
hence it too will be studied scientifically; even theology has
a "natural" side, which brings it in that respect under the
authority of science. Scientific method is to be extended
little by little over the entire field of knowledge.

Bacon was after all a lawyer. His client was scientific
method. Every step he took was calculated to win the case
for his side. He left it for the advocates of religion to protect the interests in their charge. That side was none of his

affair. There was only one door which, to the end of his life, he declared must remain shut against science. It was the door to an inner holy of holies where man as a pure spirit may meet with God and receive the impetus and power to rise above nature. "For certainly," says Bacon in his famous *Essays*, "man is of kin to the beasts by his body, and if he is not of kin to God by his spirit, he is a base and ignoble creature."

This may sound like a reservation of great importance in favor of religion, but it really amounts to very little when put to the test. It is a treaty exempting the citadel of the spirit from attack while the army is busily engaged elsewhere. And like the treaties between nations that are based upon considerations of self-interest, it will be regarded as mere paper when the march of conquest leads through the protected zone. This is all that scientific neutrality regarding religion has meant or can mean in practice. Anything "of kin to God" is a scientific mystery. The rights of this mystery will be respected so long as they do not lie in the path of scientific progress. When they do, the fortress of theology will be taken, the mysterious holy of holies will be blown to bits, and man's "spirit" will march among the prisoners of science.

vi

Francis Bacon died more than three centuries ago and the question therefore is whether his attitude of mind is characteristic of contemporary science.

One fact lies in the foreground. Science is no longer the new learning. It is not true today, as he complained it was in his time, that the best brains are drawn into "sacred Theology," or into "the quarrelsome and thorny Philosophy of Aristotle," because it is there that the honors and emoluments are to be had. Science has prospered, and scientific success, substantial and ubiquitous, is the distinguishing mark of the twentieth century. The marvels and wonders that swarmed half-formed in Bacon's excited imagination have been far surpassed by the marvels and wonders that are commonplace actualities to the present-day child. The technique which he thought of as the interrogation of nature, and which appealed so strongly to his lavishly gifted and intense, but narrowly concentrated, intellect, has been perfected by men of science and adapted to every field of inquiry.

It is as if Bacon's cold intellect, multiplied innumerable times, armed with instruments of astonishing precision and with engines of amazing power, had pushed aside every obstacle and captured the modern world; or as if the infant which he admired for its promise, had grown into a giant who is striding through the world exercising his muscle, as indifferent to ethical considerations as Bacon himself used to be.

Let us drop figures of speech and ask a matter-of-fact question. Are the ethical implications of contemporary science different from what they were in Bacon's mind?

As to scientific procedure there is only one answer. It is the merit of scientific investigation that it protects the investigator from extraneous influences. It is designed to lay bare the truth, no matter what it hurts, whom it hurts, or how it hurts. The deference paid to scientists is due in

part at least to their unconcern for the ethical, aesthetic, or
religious consequences of their experiments. This deliberate unconcern is rightly taken to be the negative side of a
positive interest which is today what it has always been, the
mastery of the world of fact.

It is this positive side, this determined, never-ending
search in every nook and corner for knowledge of the way
things really are and operate, which the informed layman
looks upon as the innermost purpose of scientific activity.
Of course the knowledge thus gained cannot but have a
profound effect upon the beliefs and attitudes of those outside the scientific field, but this is a consideration which
the scientist leaves out of account in his scientific work.
He has, and is expected to have, one ideal, scientific progress, and one loyalty, to be true to scientific method. A scientific Polonius would say:

> This above all: to thine own science be true
> And it must follow, as the night the day
> Thou canst not then be false to any man.

Science is ethically neutral in its processes but not in its
results. It does things to man's world and his outlook. One
of the things it does is to deprive the natural order of the
kind of meaning which has long been deemed necessary
to sustain an ethical or a religious spirit. This is, I know,
not the universal opinion. Scientists and religious leaders
can easily be found who deny the charge. Even so eminent
a scientist as Max Planck declares: "Wherever and however far we look, we nowhere find a conflict between religion and natural science, but on the contrary complete

agreement, and especially at the most decisive points." Another eminent scientist, H. Poincaré, said it in words of which all of us have heard at least the echo: "Ethics and science have their own domains, which touch but do not interpenetrate. The one shows us to what goal we should aspire, the other, given the goal, teaches us how to attain it. So they can never conflict since they can never meet." Poincaré believed truth alone to be beautiful and the search for it the sole end worthy of a man's activities. L. P. Jacks, an outstanding religious leader of Great Britain, expects the *seeming* conflict to be brought to end "*by each side resolutely going on with its own work*, the one of affirming truth against error, the other of affirming good against evil, making no attempt to force a verbal reconciliation, but confident that the deeper they get into their business the nearer they will approach one another, until finally they meet at the same point and discover that all along they have been serving the same cause and obeying the same master."

These optimistic views are offset by what is perhaps a more contemporary, and certainly a better supported, conviction. "The scientific mind," says Joseph Needham, a biochemist, "when it does face at last the meaning of the universe as a whole, can but assert that it has no meaning." A. N. Whitehead, a philosopher-mathematician, describes the world which physical science portrays, as "soundless, scentless, colourless; merely the hurrying of material, endlessly, meaninglessly." Julian Huxley, a biologist, calls it "A universe of appalling vastness, appalling age, and appalling meaninglessness." Sir Arthur Eddington, a physicist, finds it to be a perpetually evolving complexity of fiery globes, in which the appearance of man was an unfortunate accident, "a trifling hitch in the machinery," a "bit of star dust gone wrong."

vii

We need not undertake to decide which of these descriptions is nearer the truth for scientists. There can be no doubt which it is in the mind of the public. The public mind is pretty well made up that from the standpoint of science the world is without meaning, not only the far-flung world of the astronomer and the physicist, but the nearer world of the geologist, biologist, and the rest. The steady pushing back of man's origin into the unimaginable past; the brutish nature of the struggle by which he is shown to have supplanted lower forms of life and his own kind; the purely physical-chemical stuff, or, at best, physiological stuff, of which everything human is said to be composed; all of this increases the difficulty of harmonizing the teachings of science with the customary ethical and religious beliefs.

The situation which has thus been brought about for men and women who, living in the modern world, feel that they owe allegiance to science and to ethical and religious ideals, is astutely pictured in Mr. Needham's stimulating book, *The Great Amphibium:*

In short, for the scientific worker ethical neutrality is an indispensable aim, and he must at all costs strive to attain it, but for the whole man it is by no means an unmixed good. It is as if the house of the spirit, which was previously inhabited by the genius of religion, always pre-occupied about God, Man, the Good, the Holy, the Right, were thoroughly spring-cleaned, swept, and garnished leaving nothing but the empty rooms and bare walls of scientific ethical neutrality, whereupon seven other demons, all worse than the first, including war and pestilence, enter in and take up a permanent residence there.

Scientists seem to be about as nervous as anyone in these "empty rooms and bare walls of scientific ethical neutrality." Apparently it would comfort them to have at least the old religious mottos still in their places. The growing heedlessness of behavior noticeable in the world makes them even more uneasy. They have done their best to popularize science and the propaganda has been enormously successful. It has destroyed the prescientific innocence beyond repair. Of course no one intended that scientifically adolescent mankind should indulge in sowing wild oats, but that is the most generous construction to be put upon what has happened. Scientists, I say, seem to be as much disturbed by this unhappy outcome as anyone.

But they cannot be very deeply disturbed, not as a rule. If they were they could not be satisfied to make a superficial examination of the situation. Let the reader study what the scientists say. Let him take the best examples, some discussion of the problem like Max Planck's in his lecture, *Religion und Naturwissenschaft*. Its solemn tone and abundant learning will not escape him, nor the broad outlook and the civilized spirit of the lecturer; but I do not see how he can be impressed, even moderately, by the solution which is finally offered. For according to Dr. Planck the answer is simply this. The *Unknown* which the various religions try to bring nearer by means of visible symbols is the very same *Unknown* which the natural sciences approach through their analyses of the objects of sense. Religion and science are therefore allies in a common battle, the battle against skepticism and dogmatism, against atheism and superstition, and their joint battle cry must always be, as it has always been, "Forward to God!"

For my part, I say frankly that this seems to me plain hocus-pocus. No one could be deceived by it for a moment if the problem and the solution were transferred to everyday life and translated into everyday terms. How would it sound if put in this way? No one can tell where your road leads to; no one can tell where my road leads to; which proves that they both lead to the same place. You and I are fellow travelers who refuse to stop anywhere but in the city the whereabouts of which are unknown. Hence our slogan must be, as it has always been, "Step on the gas!"

Mr. Needham's proposal seems to me in this respect much to be preferred. It at least sets forth with inescapable clearness the alternatives to which he believes man is reduced:

We shall do better to follow each road out to its farthest end, and to accept the Lucretian estimate of the world in the laboratory as well as that of St. Augustine or St. Teresa at other moments and in other places. All are alike partially false, none means exactly what it says, save only that of philosophy, which, unfortunately, can say practically nothing.

This much of our answer, then, we can make to our matter-of-fact question. The meaningful whole of things, in which formerly the life of mankind had a meaningful place, has gone to pieces under the impact of scientific advance. Not only has this happened, but the very hope of finding a meaning of that kind now appears to be irrational.

Science has exerted another influence which, although it has scarcely received any attention, is probably the most profound as it is the most subtle, of those which have weakened ethical and religious aspiration. Thousands of capable men and women are engaged in scientific occupations that demand the utmost possible degree of ethical neutrality. Their work is made known to the young in schools and colleges, and through every means we have of informing adults, and they are honored for the work in which they are engaged. There can be no question that in this way "scientific ethical neutrality" has had at least a double effect. Even in the popular mind it has freed from the authority of moral judgment an extensive area of experience which required such freedom, and its influence has spread to areas where ethical distinctions are in some sense imperative, and there has tended to blur or eradicate all distinction between right and wrong conduct.

This much of the answer we have. It shows the resistless destruction of the foundations of traditional religion. Yet we are asked to reaffirm in our day the treaty between science and religion which guarantees to each a complete autonomy in its own sphere, as if history could teach us nothing. This is one of those superficial compromises which only postpones the day of reckoning.

viii

If *theoretical* science has reshaped man's conception of the world, of himself, and of human destiny, *applied* science has been even more influential. Applied science comes home to everyone no matter what his stage of intellectual development. It is applied science, too, that is recognized to be the possible instrument of incalculable evil. This possibility has received a good deal of attention especially since the application of science to warfare has reached its present diabolical efficiency.

When some years ago Frederick Soddy pointed out that science might deliver terrific power for destruction into morally irresponsible hands, and said, "Surely it will not need this last actual demonstration to convince the world that it is doomed, if it fools with the achievements of science as it has fooled too long in the past," his fears were treated by many persons as too pessimistic and theoretical to be worthy of notice. They hardly listened when he asked: "Physical force, the slave of science, is it to be the master or the servant of men?" Or when he answered, "The cold logic of science shows, without the possibility of escape, that this question if not faced now can have only one miserable end."

Today, however, there is nothing incredible or even conjectural in such statements as Julian Huxley recently made:

The problem of what man will do with the enormous possibilities of power which science has put into his hands is probably the most vital and the most alarming problem of modern times. At the moment, humanity is rather like an irresponsible and mischievous child who has been presented with a set of machine tools, a box of matches, and a supply of dynamite.

Perhaps there should be encouragement in the fact that the problem has intruded itself upon the meetings of the British and the American Association for the Advancement of Science. Presidential addresses before both associations have considered the social implications of scientific development. In these addresses, as in those delivered before great religious bodies, thoughtful men have asked, almost in the words used by Edwin Grant Conklin in his address as retiring president of the American association: "Will science, which has so largely made our modern civilization, end in destroying it? Has it not placed powers in the hands of ignorant and selfish men which may wreck the whole progress of the race?"

At the latest meeting of the British association, before a brilliant audience which, according to newspaper accounts, suggested a first night at the opera, and which not only packed a modernistic motion picture theatre but overflowed it so that arrangements had to be made that the address might be heard by hundreds in a near-by hall, Lord Rayleigh absolved science of all blame for its abuses. On Sunday some 1,500 members of the association, many in vividly colored academic robes, attended services at Great Saint Mary's Church to hear the Bishop of Winchester. The bishop declared modern civilization to be largely a failure, but he thought it illogical and unjust to attribute this deplorable fact to science. He ascribed it to lack of character in those who made use of science. "Man as he is at present," he said, "is incapable of using wisely some of the best gifts of science, as a child is incapable of using a sharp knife."

The constant recurrence of this idea is not reassuring. It demonstrates, I fear, that no practical solution is to be looked for from these otherwise commendable efforts. For it is not bad men or bad impulses that have made or now make scientific achievement potentially dangerous to humanity; it is the warp and woof of modern life in which we are all implicated, with our goodness and badness and indifference, our ambition for worldly success and our idealisms. It is scientific civilization that we have to manage in the human interest, not this or that individual or group that happens to have run amuck.

To see the problem in these more difficult proportions seems to me a first step toward its solution, if indeed there is a solution. A truer appreciation of our state than is shown in the usual declarations of great scientists and great religionists I find in E. B. White's "Hymn to the Dark," printed in *The New Yorker*:

This is the prelude to darkness, this great time
Of light and war and youths who follow Hate
Shaped like a swastika, sadist economies,
The dominance of steel and the sword stainless,
The dissenting tongues cleft at the root and bleeding,
Singers with their throats cut, trying
(While yet there's time) to point out where the venom is,
Ink never drying
On the insatiable presses,
Science triumphant, soy beans more than edible,

And the stud chemist, with his lusty pestle,
Serving the broodmares of hysteria,
Getting the gasses and the incredible
Sharp substances of our enlightened dying.

.   .   .   .   .

This is the light that failed. Oh Christ,
Make us an end of light if this be light,
Make us an end of sound if this ethereal
Babble, caught in the glowing tubes, translated into waves,
Be sound. If darkness comes, let the dark be
Velvet and cool . . . kind to the eyes, to the hands
Opened to the dust, and to the heart pressed
To the rediscovered earth, the heart reclaimed
For the millionth time by the slow sanity
Of the recurring tides.

Yes, I find in these verses a sense of where we are and what we face that I miss in learned disquisitions which as a rule show strong attachment to a vested interest but are not touched by human tragedy. Without this sense of dread or horror to begin with, no improvement of the situation is conceivable. Nevertheless, bitterness of spirit is not enough. Turning away in disillusionment will not help us out, if help is to be had. We must seek for a more positive way of meeting the difficulty.

Francis Bacon and the early scientists, as we saw, aimed "to extend more widely the limits of the power and the greatness of man." They were thinking primarily of mechanical power, which they lacked and which we have in abundance. If we, too, need to extend more widely the power and greatness of man, it is in order that the very success of their venture shall not contribute to our ruin.

❧ IX ❧

SCIENCE AND MAN, II

i

The social problems resulting from the wide dissemination of scientific knowledge are problems of peculiar difficulty. Possible solutions are not easy to think of and harder to put into effect. They are problems of such importance, however, that every opportunity to see them more clearly must be taken advantage of.

It would help us all, in the first place, to clarify our conception of science by doing away with a number of vital errors. One of these is a confusion between science as it actually is, and the aura of myth and legend which envelops it. Popular science is not science as conceived by the scientist. It has a good deal of magic and the miraculous about it, and very little of the scientific temper. Belief in science may even be a form of superstition. For superstition is a frame of mind. It is a manner of believing, far more than it is this or that belief. The attitude of many people toward institutionalized science is not unlike the

251

superstitious credulity of the average medieval man or woman toward institutionalized religion. They believe in Science and in what scientists tell them, very much as their ancestors believed in the Church and what they were told by their priests.

There is abundant reason why this should be so. A man cannot read a newspaper or listen to a radio without being told of ideas emanating from science which he can only accept on faith. His mind is bombarded by half-understood scientific pronouncements which are advertised to have the profoundest bearing on his life, the truth of which he is unable to determine. "Freud Explores Unconscious Mind and Finds Only Sex Impulse," "Pavlov's Dog Proves Mind Is Matter," "Sodium Amytal Cures Insanity," "Napoleon's Career Explained by Abnormal Pituitary Glands" —such are the things he reads and hears. Science has discovered ballistics; science has invented the lie-detector; science has produced the unbeatable G-man; so on and on. Commercial institutions assure the public that after years of scientific research, at enormous expense, they have produced a perfect article. Men of science are drawn into the advertising game. They feel they must give the outcome of their research to the public in spectacular form. Leading scientists write hair-raising mystery stories about the cosmos. Religionists join the hue and cry on behalf of a scientific religion.

It must be remembered too that, seen from the outside, science has its sacred buildings, its mysteries, its esoteric language, its priests and acolytes, even its incantations and mummeries. To get on the inside takes years of preparation, a ceremony of initiation, disciplined training, and adherence to a conception of things in which much is sacrificed that is dear to ordinary mortals. To the layman, the whole business is beyond comprehension; something for the mind, if not the knees, to bow down to. This superstitious awe unquestionably interferes with an intelligent appreciation of science.

Another false notion could be dissipated with profit. Much trouble might have been saved had the noun "science" never come into use, had everyone learned to use instead a verb like sciencing or scienced. We are all in the habit of believing that a thing must somehow exist corresponding to every noun in the language. When people speak of science, or hear it spoken of, they do not think, except incidentally, of busy scientists and their science-making and science-preserving activities. They think of something above and beyond all this, a huge entity which has an independent existence of its own. Science is a kind of metaphysical mother, wooed by men of science and giving birth to a mighty progeny of atoms, molecules, chemical elements, and laws of nature, not to speak of vitamins, electric light bulbs, radio tubes, yeast cakes, breakfast foods, and cosmetics.

Now in this sense science has no existence outside the mind of its fabricator. What we actually have are laboratories and organizations, instruments and apparatus, a systematic technique of investigation, an army of workers, and an accumulation of tested knowledge. One may think of these in their interrelation and refer to them as a whole. In fact it would be awkward not to be able to do so. But there is always the danger that a generalization of particulars will take on substantial form. This is exactly what has happened for most of us in respect to the particulars of science. Science has become a thing, a superhuman thing, a deity or devil, depending upon who the person is and what he is most interested in doing.

It would put us a considerable distance forward if the word science spontaneously and naturally called to mind men and women engaged in certain kinds of investigation, using a special kind of method to achieve a special kind of result.

ii

This much of the task is surely not insuperable. The distorting mists of fabulous science can be blown away, leaving a clearer view of scientific method and scientific knowledge. We are capable of realizing that science is a company of investigators, able, highly trained, and well equipped, but still human beings, tempted in all points like as we are, yet without emotional sin.

Let us assume this much to be done. Several tasks of greater difficulty remain, one of which is liberation from the notion that science is limited to a specific type of subject matter. Or, to state the error in another form, that the more abstract the subject matter is with which an investigator deals the nearer he approaches to ultimate reality. A number of serious consequences follow from this misinterpretation. It impels the scientifically-minded investigator to believe that no matter what he is investigating, if he wants authentic results he must reduce his material as nearly as possible to the basis of mathematical physics. It discourages the development of a rigorous experimental technique which is applicable to processes in their concretely experienced form. It casts suspicion upon the reality of the world in which every man and woman must live, the world he sees and touches, and in relation to which he will succeed or fail.

For a long time the discoveries of physical science, shocking though they were to certain beliefs in the supernatural, did not ruffle the world's substance. Solid bodies, however small, acting on each other according to fixed laws of causation, remained the substratum of things. Recently this firm materiality has fallen to dust in the hands of the physicists. To less than dust, as General Smuts has described this scientific revolution:

With the coming of the twentieth century, fundamental changes began to set in. The new point of departure was reached when physical science ceased to confine its attention to the things that are observed. It dug down to a deeper level, and below the things that appear to the senses, it found, or invented, at the base of the world, so-called scientific entities, not capable of direct observation, but which are necessary to account for the facts of observation. Thus below molecules and atoms still more ultimate entities appeared; radiations, electrons, and protons emerged as elements which underlie and form our world of matter. Matter itself, the time-honored mother of all, practically disappeared into electrical energy.

"The cloud-capp'd towers, the gorgeous palaces,
   The solemn temples, the great globe itself:"
Yea, all the material forms of earth and sky and sea were dissolved and spirited away into the blue of energy.

And there is always Sir James Jeans to quote: He is responsible for the statement that physical science is rapidly "moving toward a hypothesis which will cover all known facts with complete accuracy—if indeed it has not already attained such a goal," and when this feat is accomplished, physical substance will have been dissolved into pure thought. Assuming that the books written by Sir James to popularize his ideas were not only bought but read, many thousands of people are aware that according to this advertised "last word in contemporary physics," the content of experience is stripped of all material covering, and naked reality is seen through a thin veil of mathematical symbols.

Sir Arthur Eddington's view is more cautiously stated. According to him the scientific observer has dispensed with the sense of smell, hearing, and touch. He has only one eye, since he has no need for stereoscopic vision. From his one eye all of the retina but a small patch has been removed, so that he can no longer recognize form, size, gradations of light and shade, and can see in but one direction at a time. He can determine whether an opaque object is in a certain position or not, and whether two objects are in apparent coincidence or not, and this happens to be enough for the purpose of studying the physicist's reality. "The point is," says Sir Arthur, "that all our knowledge of the external world as it is conceived today in physics can be demonstrated to him. If we cannot convince *him* we have no right to assert it." The rest of our kaleidoscopic world is pure fiction, due to the inveterate storyteller in man's brain. It is of no interest to the physical scientist.

Spokesmen for science, to be sure, rarely stand by their impoverishment of reality to the bitter end. They only remove the *foundation* of the common-sense world view; the superstructure is to remain and, so far as they are concerned, may be mistaken for reality by the uninformed. The "spiritual" demands of men are to be satisfied too. Scientists are among the most conservative defenders of traditional religious symbols and practices. There is nothing in the least unusual in General Smuts's position when, having indicated how science has dissolved "all the material forms of earth and sky and sea," and spirited them away "into the blue of energy," he says: "The world consists not only of electrons and radiations, but also of souls and aspirations. Beauty and holiness are as much aspects of nature as energy and entropy. An adequate world view would find them all in their proper context in the framework of the whole."

Everything depends upon how this is to be taken. General Smuts means it to be taken radically, in a way that modifies even the interpretation of the world by physical science. As a rule, however, it simply means that you may believe anything else you please, providing you accept the world view of physical science as supreme. And this is to sell all other views down the river. No such compromise, whether the scientist needs it for himself as a man, or thinks it is needed to restrain the brutishness of the multitude, will stand the strain put upon it in the contemporary world.

It would be silly for the man in the street to dispute these interpretations of reality in the realm of physics; but in his own realm, the world of daily experience and practice, he has a right to speak. And it is significant that to speak with authority there where he is at home he must forget what the physicist tells him. Moreover, shall we not remember that when the physicist works in his laboratory he has the good solid floor under his feet, and that it is still under his feet if he goes to the window and becomes absorbed in what goes on outside? Well, in the same way he has the good solid floor of the observable world under him when he dares to lean far out over the parapet of the senses.

It is rumored that the most revolutionizing concept of physical science, which does away entirely with stufflike entities, reducing them all to configurations in space-time, could never have been reached without reliance upon ordinary pencil and paper. I am not trying to be funny, nor do I mean to imitate Macaulay who believed that by kicking a stone he had disposed of Berkeley's doctrine that so-called matter is idea. I am repeating what was said in earlier chapters. The kaleidoscopic, teeming, visible, and tangible world is pre-eminently the form which reality takes for us all, and the man in the street is well advised if he holds to his natural conviction that he has every right to this standpoint.

When an artist paints a winter landscape, we do not admire it as a proof of the unreality of spring. Neither does he. He is satisfied if his picture stirs in the beholder a lively sense of winter. When a woman gathers beach plums in autumn, lets them simmer on the stove, presses out the juice and makes it into jelly, we do not accept the jelly, to say nothing of the pulp she has left, as evidence that the wild fruit on the branches was an illusion. Neither does she. She is pleased if her conserve adds a piquant accent to the roast. Why then should we surrender our common sense and believe that the intellectual product which the physical scientist extracts from life's fullness is more real than the living fullness from which he extracted it?

iii

If the differentiating mark of science is not to be found in a peculiar subject matter, in what is it to be found? In method or technique. Taken comprehensively science denotes scientific workers, the institutions and organizations engaged in furthering scientific work, and the technique of observation and demonstration usually referred to as scientific method. It is this technique or method which may be regarded as most representative. All other aspects of science take their character from this methodological side. Workers, apparatus, organizations, accumulated results are scientific insofar as they are involved in the scientific technique and for no other reason.

It is sometimes maintained that science requires that the subject matter of investigation permit of a strictly quantitative examination. If this characterization is adhered to, scientific method is restricted to one type of subject matter only. It is excluded from all investigations where qualitative distinctions must be dealt with, from all studies of life phenomena, sense experiences, ideas, feelings, purposes, evaluations, and the like. The permissibility of limiting the definition of science in this way is very questionable. At any rate, we shall assume that science may be more fairly and at the same time more intelligently defined in broader terms. So defined, the indispensable characteristic, as we have seen, is not to be found in *the peculiarity of the material or subject matter* under investigation, but in the *particular way the material or subject matter is dealt with* whatever it may be.

What then is scientific method? Stated in the fewest possible words, it is a way of investigation which relies, and relies solely, on disciplined empirical observation and rigorously exact proof. Its aim is objective verification. And by objective verification is meant, first, that the investigator's wishes and wants, his aesthetic, moral, or religious predilections, his faith in or desire for a particular conclusion, have been carefully eliminated as determining factors; and, second, that proof extends beyond inner or personal conviction, to outer or public demonstration. The extent to which this can be done depends upon the matter to be investigated. But whatever the problem may be, it is possible to devise a technique which assures the highest attainable degree of objectivity as just defined; and whenever this is honestly attempted the investigation is scientific in the comprehensive meaning of the term. The significance of objectivity sought in terms of method instead of subject matter is obviously far-reaching. Its relevancy to the problem of a socially responsive and a socially responsible science need not be pointed out.

iv

This brings us up squarely to the most deeply embedded misunderstanding of the scientific venture. Unless something can be done to correct this error we may as well give up. I refer to the belief that science consists in the "selfless

pursuit of truth." It seems to be agreed on all hands that
the truth about the world in which we live must be sought
no matter what happens to mankind, and that science is
the one perfected method of seeking it. In a passage already
quoted and discussed, Max Wertheimer said: "Science is
rooted in the will to truth. With the will to truth it stands
or falls. Lower the standard even slightly and science becomes diseased at the core . . . The will to truth, pure
and unadulterated, is among the essential conditions of its
existence." Thinking people accept this statement without
qualification. But it has to be qualified, or, rather, it has
to be taken in one sense and not in another, or it is false.

In the discussion of Mr. Wertheimer's affirmation
(Chapter IV, pp. 117–120), it was pointed out that its ac-
ceptableness depends upon what is meant by "The will to
truth, pure and unadulterated." If the meaning intended is
that the scientist must will to reach the truth *as such*, as it exists in and of itself, the criticism was and is that, judged by
his behavior, no scientist ever seeks truth of this kind. If,
however, the meaning is that scientists are committed to
the use of the most highly developed method of investigation and the most rigorous test of what is true with regard
to given data, and that the scientific worker must exercise
the utmost care not to allow feelings or desires, his own
or those coming from anywhere, to have the slightest influence in determining the conclusion at which he arrives
—if this is what is meant, there can be no question that
science stands or falls with "the will to truth."

The antagonism reported to be shown by Nazi leaders—
Dr. Joseph Goebbels, Alfred Rosenberg, Bernard Rust—

toward the alleged "Jewish" physics of Einstein, Heisenberg, von Laue, Planck, or Schrödinger, and the substitution in its place of the "German" physics of Willi Menzel, Johannes Stark, Philipp Lenard, on the ground that science "is conditioned by race and blood" would, if carried through, make an end of scientific investigation from top to bottom. If we are correctly informed that in Russia certain fields of research are "officially neglected," this, too, endangers science. So does the granting of funds, as is sometimes done in America, for the specific purpose of coming to a predetermined conclusion. We may go farther and say with H. Levy, there must be "an 'unplanned zone' in every field, to give scope to human originality and initiative." Science requires, among other things, free play for intellectual curiosity, the privilege of learning all one can about anything one happens to be interested in, without feeling obliged to arrive at any set conclusion whatever, to say nothing of any prescribed conclusion.

Loyalty to exact method is the absolute minimum. But this exactness of method is not a "selfless pursuit of truth." It is not even necessarily a *disinterested* pursuit of truth, free from all purposes other than its own pure continuance. One reason why it is not was presented in the chapter just mentioned. Here we take note of another reason. We watch investigations as they are conducted. Do they lose their scientific character the moment they are initiated by the desire for an answer to a particular question? Obviously not. Scientifically trained youths by the hundreds are annually absorbed into industry, and are employed on industrial research projects, without ceasing to be scientists in spirit or workmanship. Scientific experiments are continually undertaken to discover more effective poison gases, more powerful explosives, improved means of protection in warfare. Scientific medical studies have for many years been directed toward securing better physical and mental health. In fact, unless science is defined with extreme narrowness, the association of strict scientific procedure with human and social programs is an outstanding characteristic of our age.

Furthermore, are all scientists moved by only the highest motives? Are there not scientists, who knows how many, whose predominant ideal is something less noble than the disinterested search for truth? They do assigned research jobs or they follow a trail they have hit upon, with no higher thought than to advance in their profession. Not that professional ambition is in itself disgraceful, but it is no more lofty as a motive in a scientist than in anyone else. As a class, scientists show a very superior "will to truth," an unsually strong determination to explore the unknown, and the most delicate sense of honesty in reporting what has been found true and what not true. But this far from saying that science is a vast beehive, and all scientists are worker bees, roving far and wide to provide man with the honey of pure truth.

v

Scientific activity is influenced by subtler forces. Erwin Schrödinger has written of these in *Science and the Human Temperament*. I know of no one better qualified to speak on this difficult theme. The upshot of his study is that a hard and fast line cannot be drawn between subjective ways of apprehending reality in painting, literature, music, social and political ideas, and the objective way of apprehending reality which we have in the body of truth furnished by the sciences. Every one of them is in some manner molded by the human temperament.

This temperamental interference with objectivity is of course most obvious in the humanistic sciences. The historian, for example, must go beyond the discovery and narrative of bald fact. It is his task to weave historical events into a meaningful pattern. As Mr. Schrödinger points out: "It is here that scientific history begins, while the work of the conscientious chronicler is looked upon as merely furnishing the raw material." And "the selection which he makes from the raw material at his disposal, his formulation of it, and his final presentation must necessarily be influenced by his whole personality." This is true of all humanistic sciences. There is always the ideal of maintaining the greatest degree of objectivity, and always the intrusion of the subjective element of human creativeness.

But does the same observation hold of the nonhumanistic sciences? Are there subjective elements in physics, the exactest of the sciences? Yes, there are. Let us see how they enter. "From all physical research," says Mr. Schrödinger, "the subjective intrusion of the researcher is vigorously barred so that the purely objective truth about inanimate nature may be arrived at. Once this truth is finally stated it can be put to the test of experiment by anybody and everybody all the world over, and always with the same result." Human subjectivity, then, does not enter into a properly conducted experiment when this has been set up.

Well, when does it enter, if not into the scientific experiment? It enters into the setting up of the experiment. This always takes place within the general structure which the science has assumed up to that time. The data which are accepted as working materials are furnished by previous experiments. The number of such experiments, Mr. Schrödinger admits, is undoubtedly very large, but "it is infinitesimal when compared with the number of experiments that might have been carried out, but never actually have been." The data worked with are therefore selected data. These "data represent results that have been achieved by former researches. These results are the outcome of selections formerly made. Those selections were due to a certain train of thought working on the mass of experimental data then at hand. And so if we go back through an infinite series of stages of scientific advance, we shall finally come to the first conscious attempt of primitive man to understand and form a logical mental picture of events observed in the world around him." Such facts cause this eminent physicist to say: "All this leads to the inevitable conclusion that we cannot close the door to the entry of subjective factors in determining our scientific policy and in giving a definite direction to our line of further advance."

This general statement is amply supported by facts. For instance: Grimaldi, who was a boy when Francis Bacon championed inductive science before the world, anticipated some of the latest theories in Quantum mechanics. Heisenberg's experiments, in our time, were attended to and followed up; Grimaldi's, in his time, were not. Mr. Schrödinger explains why this happened:

They were regarded as pointing to a phenomenon which had no general interest for science as such, and for the following one hundred and fifty years no similar experiments were carried out, though this could have been done with the simplest and cheapest material. The reason for this was that, of the two theories of light which soon afterward were put forward, Newton's corpuscular theory gained general acceptance against the wave theory of Huygens, and thus the general interest was directed along a different path.

To these subjective interests which are internal to science are to be added the influences of the cultural trends in the world at large. The most impressive chapters in *Science and the Human Temperament* are those which discuss the question "how far the picture of the physical universe as presented to us by modern science has been outlined under the influence of certain contemporary trends which are not peculiar to science at all." Impressionism, simplicity of design, freedom from the control of rigid law, relativity, endless change, these are some of the trends that dominate our arts and crafts, our politics, and our industrial and social organizations. According to Mr. Schrödinger, similar influences are definitely felt in contemporary physics. And he should know. Scientists, he contends, "are children of their age." The scientist "cannot shuffle off his mortal coil when he enters his laboratory or ascends the rostrum in his lecture hall."

The argument must be read in its completeness to be fully appreciated. I am acquainted with no book which the student of the subject in hand can so ill afford to leave unread as this one by Mr. Schrödinger, published by W. W. Norton and Company. Those who read it will, I believe, find the statement arresting with which we must leave the subject of science as the "selfless pursuit of truth":

From all this it follows that the engaging of one's interest in a certain subject and in certain directions must necessarily be influenced by the environment, or what may be called the cultural milieu or the spirit of the age in which one lives. In all branches of our civilization there is one general world outlook dominant and there are numerous lines of activity which are attractive because they are the fashion of our age, whether in politics or in art or in science. These also make themselves felt in the "exact" science of physics.

vi

Einstein is said to have approved as a brief definition of relativity the sentence: "There is no hitching post in the universe—so far as we know." That may be true of the universe as conceived by the mathematical physicist. But there are hitching posts in the world of daily experience, and it is important that we tie up to the right ones. Why should the most objective thinking we are capable of not help us to determine which these are? Some of us like to believe that General Smuts is right in promising that this is what the science of the future will do by broadening its vision of the facts that can be scientifically studied:

Our scientific world-picture will draw its material from all the sciences. Among these, physical science will—in view of its revolutionary discoveries in recent years—be a most important source. But no less important will be the contribution of the biological sciences with their clear revelation of organic structure and functions as well as of organic evolution. And last, not least, the social and mental sciences will not only supply valuable material, but especially methods of interpretation, insights into meanings and values, without which the perspectives of our world-picture would be hopelessly wrong.

It is gratifying to have J. S. Haldane, without apology to anyone, declare: "Neither biology or philosophy can afford to cringe before the physically interpreted or mathematically formulated universe"; and H. S. Jennings, with equal frankness: "It is important to realize, what is often forgotten, that such limitations of the field of science must make the picture of reality that science attempts to give incomplete and therefore misleading. Whoever excludes from science any class of data of experience thereby proclaims that science cannot present an adequate picture of reality." Julian Huxley takes us even farther in his *Scientific Research and Social Needs:*

Personally, I know that looking at science in its relation to social needs, as I have had to do for this survey, has cleared my own mind a great deal; and if the scientific movement in this country can do this and become conscious of itself, and of its limitations, and of its relation to the economic driving forces of society, that will be a very valuable step. The chief moral of this book, it seems to me, is that science is not the disembodied sort of activity that some people would make out, engaged on the abstract task of pursuing universal truth, but a social function intimately linked up with human history and human destiny. And the sooner scientists as a body realize this and organize their activities on that basis, the better both for science and for society.

These remarks, which I have quoted because they were made by scientists, suggest that the sciences are specialized types of activity; that they are the outcome of varying degrees of methodological selectivity and intensity; and that they belong, singly and collectively, within the circle of that larger whole of experience to which human beings respond. In other words, the sciences are potential means in the service of human life, the most extraordinary means yet invented; they are not ends to which man's life must, for some unaccountable reason, be offered up.

Why talk as if truth were God? If we must exclaim with Job, "Though he slay me, yet will I trust in him," let us remember the rest of the verse, "but I will maintain my own ways before him." The desire to know is one among a number. It is no more final than another. Indeed our primary desire is to make what we can of life. That is why we want truth. We believe it will help us. And it will, providing it is the kind that can. It will help us providing it is truth related to our need, or better said, *truths* related to our needs. We do not know too well what these needs are, consequently it would be ruinous to look for only the truths that promise to advance the desires which at any time we happen to have. We are unavoidably pushed into the semidarkness where our needs are only dimly seen, and into the dark where they are not visible at all. It is precisely there that we stumble because we lack the light of knowledge—which proves the importance of knowing what we are about, and proves no less, the primacy of the desire to make what we can of life.

Some among us can afford to seek truth for the fun of it. Mankind can well afford to accumulate some kinds of knowledge without reference to its utility. But if this is to be the ideal toward which all of us must strive; if we must seek to know only for the sake of knowing, letting the consequences be what they may; then a poet unknown to me has said the last word:

Truth is a rope.
It runs from the straining hands of man
Up over a beam in the foundations of infinity,
And binds its other end around his neck,
Making of him as he stubbornly climbs from the earth
His own inescapable hangman.

vii

From these considerations of science as method and of the world picture it leaves upon the mind, we revert once more to applied science. Take a single aspect of the problem, the effect on society of the results of industrial research. It is reported that $235,000,000 were set aside by industry for scientific research in the United States in one year and that this was after the depression had started. The "producer bias in research," as it has been called, has developed rapidly since 1914. Julian Huxley has well said: "There ought to be much more research organized for the consumption end—directed towards the needs of the individual citizen as an individual and as a citizen." There ought to be "a replacement of the present socially irresponsible financial control by socially responsible planning bodies."

The question was discussed by Sir Josiah Stamp as president of the British Association for the Advancement of Science. The results of research, he reminded his hearers, "these scientific infants, duly born and left on the doorstep of society, get taken in and variously cared for, but on no known principle, and with no directions from the progenitors. . . . These things just 'happen' generally under the urge of profit, and of consumers' desire, in free competition, regardless of the worthiness of new desires against old, or of the shifts of production and, therefore, employment, with their social consequences."

No excuse is necessary for quoting three paragraphs from his trenchant presidential address, "The Impact of Science upon Society."

In some ways we are so obsessed with the delight and advantage of discovery of new things that we have no proportionate regard for the problems of arrangement and absorption of the things discovered. We are like a contractor who has too many men bringing materials on to the site, and not enough men to erect the buildings with them. In other words, if a wise central direction were properly allocating research workers to the greatest marginal advantage, it would make some important transfers. There is not too much being devoted to research in physics and chemistry, as modifying industry, but there is too much relatively to the research upon the things they affect, in physiology, psychology, economics, sociology. We have not begun to secure an optimum balance. . . .

Apart from the superior tone sometimes adopted by "pure science" towards its own applications, scientific snobbery extends to poor relations. Many of the hard-boiled experimental scientists in the older and so productive fields, look askance at the newer borderline sciences of genetics, eugenics and human heredity, psychology, education, and sociology, the terrain of so much serious work but also the happy hunting ground of "viewy" cranks and faddists. Here the academic soloist is still essential, and he has no great context of concerted work into which to fit his own. But unless progress is made in these fields which is comparable with the golden ages of discovery in physics and chemistry, we are producing progressively more problems for society than we are solving.

What we have learnt concerning the proper impact of science upon society in the past century is trifling, compared with what we have yet to discover and apply. We have spent much and long upon the science of matter, and the greater our success the greater must be our failure, unless we turn also at long last to an equal advance in the science of man.

It would be unjustifiably optimistic to conclude that these are the sentiments of the majority. Most scientists are still on the other side. They do not feel any obligation to help toward a better co-ordination between scientific and social progress. They demand perfect freedom of research, and "the public be damned." As if it were the chief end of man to glorify the scientist and enjoy him forever.

Do they not know to what harmful uses science may be

put? They do. But they blame any bad outcome on "men of evil will," on the "military intelligence," on "the forces of disunion, envy, hatred, and malice, which are always walking up and down the world," and which find in certain scientific discoveries "a little corner admirably adapted for them to lay their eggs in."

Joseph Needham, who wrote the words just quoted in defense of science, wrote something that seems to me to go much deeper, so much deeper indeed that I know of no way to bring the two ideas into harmony:

The best man is the man who is friendly to, even if he cannot himself enter into, each one of the great forms of human experience, and the worst man is the man who is willing and desirous of throwing all but one form of experience on the scrap heap.

Willing and desirous of throwing all but one form of experience on the scrap heap—there are scientists, as there are businessmen, college professors, ministers of religion, not to mention those who have nothing to do but try to have a good time, whose scheme of life comes to no more than that. Nevertheless the number of scientists who are ready to share in the responsibility of preventing the discoveries of the scientific worker from oppressing mankind is larger than it used to be. I have quoted from addresses which speak for this tendency, and here add a paragraph of peculiar forthrightness from the most recent publication on the subject which I have seen. It is from a paper, "Science, Religion and Social Ethics," by Sir Richard Gregory, Bart., the retiring editor of Nature:

The view that the sole function of science is the discovery and study of natural facts and principles without regard to the social implications of the knowledge gained can no longer be maintained. It is being widely realized that science cannot be divorced from ethics or rightly absolve itself from human responsibilities in the application of its discoveries to destructive purposes in war or economic disturbances in times of peace. Men of science can no longer stand aside from the social and political questions involved in the structure which has been built up from the materials provided by them, and which their discoveries may be used to destroy. It is their duty to assist in the establishment of a rational and harmonious social order out of the welter of human conflict into which the world has been thrown through the release of uncontrolled sources of industrial production and of lethal weapons.

viii

Ethical neutrality throughout the whole range of science was harmless in Francis Bacon's day because science was relatively powerless. It is not harmless in our day because science is powerful. The means now placed in men's hands by scientific discoveries, if employed without ethical supervision, threaten to make an end of everything worth striving for. The present separation of scientific interests from wider social interests has, as we have seen, a history behind it. Respected institutions exist to keep the separation in force, and we are almost entirely without organized means for bridging the gap. Yet nothing is more obvious than our need of bringing about an intelligently working relationship between loyalty to scientific method and ideas of social change.

In certain fields where formerly we knew of no better way to adjust clashes of interest than to let them fight it out, we are learning the art of collective bargaining. Its value as a means of obtaining the best results which the circumstances then and there permit is well recognized. Collective bargaining was not the invention of some isolated specialist who handed it over as a finished thing to groups lined up against each other. It grew out of the interplay of opposing forces, out of efforts made to reach an adjustment which would permit an interrupted process to go on again. And we may, I think, be sure that it is still in the early stages of its development. There is every reason to anticipate that as a social principle collective bargaining will be extended to conflicts from which it is at present excluded. Its technique will be improved, the range of values included in its survey will be extended, and the claims which these values make on civilized people will get a more appreciative hearing.

The significance of this development for the problem which has been before us in this and the preceding chapter should be apparent. We are to learn how to apply the art of collective bargaining to the impact of science on human happiness. Representatives of science, ethics, religion, law, politics, business, labor, education, are to be brought together to formulate experimental programs to enrich the satisfactoriness of individual and social living.

The phrase "collective bargaining" as here used is not intended to denote the process in its most artificial form. It does not refer to the kind of compromise in which you "give a sprat to catch a herring," but to the method of resolving conflicts discussed as Realistic Idealism in Chapter V, the one feasible way of realizing the largest measure of good for all concerned. Intelligently and imaginatively employed it brings together, as we saw, two aims which reinforce each other: the aim to secure a hearing for competing values, and the aim to bring to birth, out of the very travail of conflict, a newly discovered and mutually satisfying plan of action. Every social advance, every forward step in politics, morality, or religion has come about in this manner. A new idea has been born out of a confusing and discordant situation because some trained, dedicated person, or some resourceful, interested group, refusing to accept the discord as final, has searched for and found a constructive idea which served to adjust the difficulty.

Of course this may be a vain hope. We may continue to go on as we have already gone too far. Russell Lord's words, in his deeply disturbing book, *Behold Our Land*, may describe not only what has been and is, but will continue to be true:

Without calling names, consider for a moment the sites of some of our great universities and colleges. Here is one of the oldest in the South. It has been there nearly two hundred years. The country of its situation has, in the past two hundred years, washed out, over at least three-quarters of its area, down close to the raw red subsoil. Some of its finest old historic places have fallen to ruin, with scant stands of broom-sedge and jack-pine trying to keep a foothold in hideous gullies. The flora of the region has changed in character; the land has run down in appearance until most of it is desolate and depressing; living standards have

visibly lowered throughout that country and all adjoining.
All this is undeniable; the facts are written large upon the
hills. It all went on under the eye of a scientific teaching
and research staff of considerable distinction; yet it all was,
and is, by them completely ignored. They go right on
teaching their geology, their botany, their zoology, their
chemistry and physics, their archaeology, Greek and Latin
and English, with no thought or mention of the tragic
transformation of the good green country roundabout.

ix

Science has spread its roots into all we do and think and
feel. We cannot tear them out, and if we try to tear them
out we will only endanger the flowering of our civilization.
The insights and facilities which we owe to science are
invaluable. They have won a measure of freedom for the
human mind and a degree of control over physical forces
not approached in all prescientific time. But life is an art,
the great art, greater than any specialized interest or occupation. We too easily forget that men lived magnificently before science haunted their dreams, magnificently
in aspiration, in thought, in action. If we care what happens
to mankind, the task confronting us is to bring science
within this older and profounder art. Science must be em-
braced in the free creative activity shown conspicuously
by men and women of genius, and in less exciting, though
equally authentic form, by countless thousands of incon-
spicuous men and women who take the materials at hand,
often meager and unpromising, and make impressive lives
out of them.

It is not certain—let us think of it again—that this will

be done. Too many scientists may continue to insist upon absolute freedom in their profession, including freedom from the slightest responsibility for the social consequences of their work, leaving it to religious leaders, for whom meantime they make the task more and more impossible, to take care of these consequences. Popular leaders may succumb increasingly to the blandishment of mechanical power, so that greater and greater numbers will be mentally enslaved and spiritually dispossessed. Aldous Huxley may have spoken prophetically: "One day, perhaps, the earth will have been turned into one vast featherbed, with man's body dozing on top of it and his mind underneath, like Desdemona, smothered."

But science cannot long remain free in a society of slaves. If technological science must continue to throw men out of work and there is no remedy, the day must come when science itself will go on relief. If the meaninglessness which theoretical science has read into the universe must, as science advances, be read into the human scene in its entirety, the scientific spirit cannot survive. "Concern for man himself and his fate," as Einstein has said, "must always form the chief interest of all technical endeavors, concern for the great unsolved problems of the organization of labor and the distribution of goods—in order that the creations of our mind shall be a blessing and not a curse to mankind." The dispossessed have never accepted their fate as final. And when they have thrown off the yoke that oppressed them they have destroyed the good with the bad.

We face a critical dilemma. One horn is the destruction of man by science; the other the destruction of science by man; and a third possibility, a path of escape between the horns, is untrammeled study of fact in union with the hunt for the most promising means of general happiness.

Have we the wisdom and the courage to choose this path and to broaden it into a highway?

✑ X ✎

THE TWO ATHEISMS

One reason why the harmful side of scientific development has failed to receive adequate attention was referred to in Chapter VIII. Traditionally it has been a marked tendency to hand over the problem of human purposes to theistic religion, with little or no regard for what this might mean in a thoroughly scientific age. At the same time atheism has seemed so reprehensible a position for anyone to take that it has received remarkably little objective study, although a strong drift in that direction was clearly perceptible. I submit that from the viewpoint of human welfare this is suicidal. It has become not only desirable, but absolutely necessary, that we examine this unpopular subject in the hope of throwing light on the situation which modern men and women face. The present chapter undertakes that task.

i

In the last quarter of the nineteenth century Charles Peirce fired the first gun on behalf of what later came to be known as Pragmatism. At the time it was scarcely noticed. Near the opening of the present century William James constituted himself an amplifier for Peirce's gun, and the resounding shot was heard on both sides of the Atlantic and as far off as China.

The original shot was an article in the *Popular Science Monthly* setting forth the doctrine that the *meaning* of an idea is the *conduct* which it designates. If there is no such designation the idea has no meaning, and if different ideas specify the same kind of behavior they mean the same thing. In other words, ideas are rules of action: to develop their meaning you have to determine what kind of doing or undergoing they are calculated to eventuate in. That, and that alone, is their significance. William James, endorsing the position of Peirce, summarized it in this manner: "The tangible fact at the root of all our thought-distinctions, however subtle, is that there is no one of them so fine as to consist in anything but a possible difference in practice."

Although the doctrine was formulated as a philosophic principle so recently, it had been incorporated long ago in a practical maxim, "Actions speak louder than words." Before the invention of language all meanings were embodied in behavior, as they still are for animals. You knew what a man intended by watching what he did. But when our remote ancestors had learned to talk, some of the watchfulness was transferred to the talking. This gave rise in time to the belief that meanings are an inherent property of words. At some period down the line, however, the discovery was made which Emerson repeated in his own way:

"What you do thunders so loudly in my ears that I cannot hear what you say."

The desirability of conduct formulation is excellently stated in an early document that happily has escaped destruction. It dates from a time when certain ideas and beliefs, then considered important, showed a strong tendency to separate themselves from practice and develop into pure abstract form or meaningless terminology. The idea is credited to the brother of Jesus:

What doth it profit, my brethren, though a man say he hath faith, and have not works? can faith save him?

If a brother or sister be naked, and destitute of daily food,

And if one of you say unto them, Depart in peace, be ye warmed and filled: not withstanding ye give them not those things which are needful for the body; what doth it profit?

Even so faith, if it hath not works, is dead, being alone.

Yea, a man may say, Thou hast faith, and I have works: Shew me thy faith without thy works, and I will shew thee my faith by my works.

Thou believest that there is one God; thou doest well; the devils also believe, and tremble.

But wilt thou know, O vain man, that faith without works is dead?

The pragmatic principle announced by Charles Peirce and William James is a philosophic generalization of this insight. What could be more sensible? The function of words is the communication of ideas, and the meaning of ideas is to be found in what they specify in practice. Neglect of this conduct significance has most unfortunate results. Phrases are released on the world without regard to the

propriety or justice, or even the intelligence, of the results
they may lead to. It is difficult to imagine the extent to
which words and ideas may thus act as pushbuttons, turning off the current of thought and turning on the current
of feeling.

A few years ago the world suffered from an epidemic of
such words. Hun, hyphenated-American, slacker, whipped
up a blind war fervor which had all sorts of unanticipated
aftereffects. Phrases which one must now apologize for
mentioning, such as "Making the world safe for Democracy" and "Doing your bit," powerfully stimulated behavior, without suggesting what was implied in concrete
performance. Irresponsible and reprehensible things were
therefore done under their verbal protection. If at that
time one asked to have the meaning of these and similar
ideas made sufficiently precise for enlightened action, one
was accused of being a "pro-German." I need not add that
we are in danger of seeing the whole thing repeated.

Today we have analogous examples in emotive words
like communist, fascist, red, brain-truster. Many words in
our daily moral vocabulary belong in the same category.
They sometimes refer to specific conduct, still oftener they
are expressions of offhand likes or dislikes. Such words are
not true words, but pseudo words. They are what the
psychologists call signal reflexes. They stimulate action not
through the communication of meaningful ideas, not by
indicating with at least reasonable precision the nature and
consequences of the intended action, but by exciting suspicion, hatred, envy, fear, animosity, and kindred passions
which can only explode in blind behavior. Feelings cannot

of course be utterly discarded, and if they could they should not be, for they are needed to lift and gladden experience; but the refusal to designate the meaning of ideas in terms of practice gives to the feelings a disproportionate if not a tyrannical power.

ii

Ideas play *emotional* tricks on us when they are left undefined as to the acts or experiences they designate, and they play *intellectual* tricks on us as well. They make us believe that we know what they denote when all we know is how to use them in discourse. To use a word in speaking or writing without a hitch is no evidence whatever that it has a meaning. Many words, especially key words in sentences which are supposed to carry a heavy burden of meaning, never tie up with any actualities. They do not refer to any context in experience, only to other words in a series of words.

It may be a good thing that we can do this occasionally. It is restful and saves energy. But like coasting downhill with the clutch out, it is always risky. And, anyway, you cannot rely upon coasting to go places.

Nor can you rely upon free verbal association to arrive at meaning. If because of laziness, ignorance, fear, or some other reason, we refuse to connect words with conduct, the same word will come to stand for diametrically opposite practices, and different words for identical practices. Abraham Lincoln, in a speech delivered in Baltimore toward the end of the war between the states, gave an instance of such ambiguity:

The world has never had a good illustration of the word liberty, and the American people just now, are much in want of one. We all declare for liberty, but in using the same word we do not all mean the same thing. With some the word liberty may mean for each man to do as he pleases with himself, and the product of his labor; while with others the same word may mean for some men to do as they please with other men, and the product of other men's labor. Here are two, not only different, but incompatible things, called by the same name, liberty. And it follows that each of the things is, by the respective parties, called by two different and incompatible names—liberty and tyranny.

What two ideas (to take another example) are more opposed than selfish and unselfish? Yet all of us know that so-called selflessness is often the most intense kind of self-assertion, and that acts of self-realization may nevertheless be free from self-seeking. Some persons who have become aware that all behavior, at least all voluntary behavior, is self-expressive, have hastened to assert that everything a person does is necessarily selfish. Were they to extend the meaning of their idea of selfish out into the field of overt operation they would discover that the conduct they designate as selfish includes very different types of acts, some of which have both their source and their goal in the acting self, while some, though they have their source in the acting self, are directed at a satisfaction or a good to be enjoyed by another. The subject was touched upon previously in this book, but it can do no harm to approach it from another angle.

Before the study of human psychology had reached its

present stage it was customary to think of human beings as combining two antagonistic elements, a physical body, the wants of which, being necessarily physical, were necessarily bad, and a spiritual soul, the wants of which, being always spiritual, were always good. The distinction between selfish and unselfish turned on the source, not on the intended effect, of behavior.

Theological thinkers like Jonathan Edwards were consistent from their point of view in claiming that a man might crave eternal salvation and struggle all his life to do the will of God utterly without avail, because his motive might be physical rather than spiritual. It might be a purely bodily desire, say to escape the torments of hell, as purely selfish or carnal as the lowest physical hunger, and so not to be honored of God, who looked only upon the source of conduct, not upon conduct itself. An exemplary life was no evidence at all of that inner spiritual motivation which alone gave moral quality to what a man did, as despicable behavior did not prove that the one responsible for it was cut off from God's grace. There was simply no way of really judging between goodness and badness by observing the doings of men. "In these mischievous days," St. Augustine used to say of the life on earth, "many reprobates live amongst the elect; both come into the Gospel's net, and both swim at random in the sea of mortality, until the fishers draw them to shore, and then the bad are thrown from the good."

Today this dualistic notion of human nature is not the vogue. It certainly is not the opinion of psychologists. All acts are assumed to have one source, the organism which is

the man. Every act is regarded as expressive of the self,
unselfishness no less so than selfishness, self-denial as
truly as self-assertion. If there is any distinction to be made
between them—and of course there is—it must refer to the
character of the *action*, not merely to the self from which
it proceeds. Unless this is done, selfishness and unselfishness
will be vague if not meaningless ideas, or selfishness will
tend to mean someone else's kind of self-expression whatever form it may take, and unselfishness will be one's own
kind of self-expression, especially if it happens to be ac-
companied by a sense of personal loss.

An American newspaper which modestly claims to be
the greatest in the world, and which conducts itself on
self-assertive and self-seeking principles difficult to equal,
at the same time disparages opposing persons, ideas, or
movements as basely selfish. Granted that the accusations
are sometimes hypocritical, deliberately made to win a
purely selfish advantage through the use of noble sounding,
but morally empty, phraseology, they are probably more
often due to psychological and moral confusion. In general,
the editorial pronouncements of this periodical show the
writers of them to belong with those who have never
stopped to set off selfishness against unselfishness in the
light of specified practice.

iii

Nicolaus Berdyaev, in his book, *The Bourgeois Mind*,
has made an interesting analysis of another very common
idea. He contends that the words Capitalism, Communism,
Fascism, Democracy, which in the minds of most of us

stand for so many antagonistic ideas of social organization, are in fact more alike than they are different. The respects in which they vary from one another are in his view superficial. Basically, they are all examples of the Bourgeois Mind. In each of them men are animated by the desire to make the most of human existence through the increase of ownership and possessions. Each is a scheme of life demanding continuous class war between the few who control and the many who are controlled. Each means a society of masters and slaves. "In every people or nation which has assumed the form of democracy," so Mr. Berdyaev declares, "there is indubitably class war, and the 'general will' of the people is a conventional fiction. There are, of course, national and state interests which transcend the classes and which must be protected if society is to live, and class power is called on to safeguard at least a minimum of these interests. But democracy, formally understood, hides the actual strife among parties and frequently becomes an instrument whereby one class exercises predominant power: a political masquerade."

As Mr. Berdyaev sees things, there are two fundamentally opposed conceptions of life in its economic aspect. One is the bourgeois way, in which each man is expected to act as a unit competing with every other unit for the biggest share of a limited stock of economic goods; the other is the Christian way, according to which the individual belongs to an organic whole or a co-operative commonwealth within which each member is to engage in furthering a superearthly plan of activity. Capitalism, Communism, Fascism, Democracy, are so many varieties of the first, the acquisitive type. They are all anti-Christian in their plan of living. The differences between them are negligible surface appearances in contrast with that which goes to the heart of the matter and sets them off, one as much as the other, from the Christian commonwealth, the only valid, tenable, decent human society.

The correctness of Mr. Berdyaev's analysis of the situation may be doubted, but this doubt does not carry over to his implied suggestion that in order to discover the meaning of the ideas in question it is necessary to work out their significance in practical behavior.

iv

All this has direct bearing upon our subject. Atheism is one of the most emotionally combustible words in the vocabulary. And the feelings it kindles are of so repellent a nature that most people, no matter what they believe or do not believe, refuse to regard themselves, or have anyone else regard them, as atheists. Nor will they make any effort to determine the conduct implications of atheistical beliefs. Consequently, the whole subject will be easier to understand if we delay the direct examination of atheism long enough to analyze a closely related idea, namely, materialism, which does not arouse the same emotional disturbance.

Materialism resembles atheism in having two distinct meanings, one designating a metaphysical creed and the other an attitude toward life. That is why we are talking about it. These meanings may be associated but need not be. Materialism as a theory of the cosmos is believed to have originated with Leucippus many centuries ago. It was more fully stated by his famous pupil Democritus, and distilled and handed down in one of the great poems of Roman antiquity, the *De Rerum Natura* of Lucretius. Mr. Santayana has spoken of cosmic materialism as perhaps the greatest single conception that the human intellect has achieved.

According to this theory the world in all its seeming variety and wealth of qualities is composed underneath of one kind of substance which alone is real, the kind we call matter; not only the physical world but the mental world and the mind itself. And the law that governs this all-embracing realm of matter is resistless, mechanical force. Cosmic materialism has fascinated some of the greatest minds of the past, and even today many thinkers believe it to be the final truth.

Now a view like this naturally has an effect upon the life plans of those who hold it. But by no means the same effect upon all. Some will simply try to free themselves from a sense of dependence upon anything in the natural order or beyond it which can be thought of as caring for them or their destiny, and they will then go resolutely forward in the endeavor to make the life they share with their fellow men as humane, beautiful, and enjoyable as conditions permit. Others will pattern their scheme as closely as possible after a pitiless and morally indifferent physical universe. Democritus chose to do the former. Thrasymachus the latter. And their examples have been followed down to the present.

This brings us to the materialism which is primarily an

attitude toward life, and only incidentally, if at all, a metaphysical interpretation of the cosmos. A materialist in this more popular sense is well described in Alexander Meiklejohn's words: "To be a materialist is to think of men, to deal with them, in external terms, as if they were 'things.'" This seems to me to put the position exactly. The materialist of this type is dominated by the material aspects of experience, by money, property, power, and the like. He is cynical about human nature, hard-boiled in human relations, careful to get the advantage in every bargain.

Perhaps logically this type of materialism should always go with the other type and never appear without it. It happens, however, that there is no such relation between them. People who look upon the physical world as a pure mechanism are more likely than not to be actuated by human sympathy and social imagination. And it is a sad truth that many people who would resent being called materialists in reference to the world as a whole, people who insist that without belief in a divine purpose human society would be a "den of ferocious wild beasts," are crassly materialistic in the moral sense. There are people, and they are very numerous, who are strongly opposed to cosmic materialism as a theory, on the ground that it is destructive of all that is worthy in life (a charge which, as we have seen, is not justified), yet who devote themselves to making the everyday world relentlessly materialistic in fact.

V

Now to atheism. We remind ourselves that it is one of the ideas most certain to stir up feelings of repulsion and to stir them up profoundly. Few people have tried to decide what atheism means, yet most of them have learned that hardly anyone cares to be known as an atheist even though he is without any positive belief in God. One reason for this is the disrepute associated with the very name. To be thought an atheist is to be the object of a suspicion that one is all manner of things which are strongly disapproved of by decent people.

Theism, on the other hand, is very appealing. The inferences drawn as to consequent beliefs and practices are of the socially approved kind. The feeling tone of the word is therefore very agreeable. Belief in God may be so weak, indefinite, or abstract that it can only be called theistic by courtesy, or it may refer to nothing more divine than the noblest qualities of human nature, nevertheless the "believer" will hold to the term theism because it makes him feel more comfortable to do so. A Chicago taxicab driver phrased the common feeling very nicely: "I don't know anything about it, but I'll be damned if I'll call myself an atheist."

Matters grow worse the farther we look. The slightest acquaintance with God-ideas is disconcerting, if we really desire to know what people mean when they speak of belief or disbelief in God. Socrates, one of the most God-conscious of human beings, was condemned as an atheist;

Jesus, whose every thought would seem to have been God-centered, was crucified because his theism was atheism to others; Spinoza, later to be spoken of as "God-intoxicated," was persecuted and reviled for atheistical teachings. What enormous quantities of human blood the earth has been made to drink by theists who slaughtered men and women as atheists because their theism was of a different kind! Rabbi Solomon Goldman, without aiming to be exhaustive, has enumerated some forty-five conceptions of God in Hebrew literature alone. How many kinds of atheists does that make? William Blake went so far as to call anyone an atheist who believed in the real existence of a physical world.

For us just now the thing of importance is that atheism, like materialism, has a metaphysical or cosmic and a moral or social denotation. It may refer to the universe at large or to the human scene. It may be primarily a denial that "there is a divinity that shapes our ends, rough-hew them how we will," or an assertion that nothing in the experienced world is of value; that intelligence, human affection, character, good will, social idealism are amiable delusions. Atheism may be disbelief in a Divine Purpose at work behind or within the whole of things, or it may be disbelief in greatness of purpose in man's life; disbelief in truth, love, justice, beauty, any of the great ends which, for innumerable persons, are sublimated in the concept of God. Joseph Wood Krutch, speaking of the cynical devaluation of love by certain contemporary writers, is profoundly right: "We have grown used . . . to a Godless universe, but we are not yet accustomed to one which is loveless as well, and only when we have so become shall we realize what atheism really means."

We must therefore make a distinction between what we may term *cosmic* and *ethical* atheism, and try to decide which of them is the more destructive of the highest human potentialities.

vi

Let us develop this distinction a little. In a troubled night during the World War, when civilized man seemed bent on self-destruction, Franklin K. Lane wrote of his religious doubts in an intimate letter not intended for public consumption as so many were at the time. Fortunately it is now available with others equally sincere in *Letters, Personal and Political.* "I am trying hard," said Mr. Lane, "to believe something that might be called the shadow of a religion—a God that has a good purpose, and another life in which there is a chance for further growth, if not for glory." However, as he faced certain inescapable aspects of life he tended to fall back upon what he called the "philosophy of a purposeless or else a cruel God." He experienced a "sinking of the heart, a goneness, a hopelessness—not even the pleasure of a resignation." Speaking of a friend, he says, "Old Sid's cold mind has worked itself to a decision that there is no purpose and no future, and finds a place in the ultimate; having reached the cellar he finds the satisfaction of rest. I can't get there for my buoyancy, the holdover of early training or perhaps my naturally sanguine nature will not permit me to hit bottom, but forever I must be kept floating, floating nowhere. Happy the man who strikes the certainty of a rock-bottom hell, rather than one who is kept floating midway—that is a purgatory worse than hell."

Mr. Lane was apparently never able to bring this search to a satisfactory conclusion. He did not on that account surrender his faith in those ideals of personal conduct and those aspirations for his country which he dreamed of seeing realized, and in the furtherance of which he sought for evidence of God's existence and a life after death. "Suffer the illusion to come unto me," he replied to those who questioned the reality of social idealism, "for of such is the kingdom of heaven." And in those hope-filled hours at Rochester, Minnesota, when, after a serious operation he believed himself on the way to recovery and new usefulness, he wrote the moving passage which suggests the character of his social idealism. It is part of an unfinished fragment telling whom he would have sought out if he had "passed into that other land":

But for my heart's content in that new land, I think I'd rather loaf with Lincoln along a river bank. I know I could understand him. I would not have to learn who were his friends and who his enemies, what theories he was committed to, and what against. We could just talk and open out our minds, and tell our doubts and swap the longing of our hearts that others never heard of. He wouldn't try to master me nor to make me feel how small I was. I'd dare to ask him things and know that he felt awkward about them, too. And I would find, I know I would, that he had hit his shin just on those very stumps that had hit me. . . . Yes, we would sit down where the bank sloped gently to the quiet stream and glance at the picture of our people, the negroes being lynched, the miners' civil war, labor's hold-ups, employers' ruthlessness, the subordination of human-ity to industry,—

He did not live to finish the thought. Death overtook him even as he believed himself to have escaped. He died keenly interested in the social ideals which some who claim to be sure of God's existence treat as fiction.

Franklin K. Lane was uncertain whether he could honestly be a theist or not; Malcolm Muggeridge is certain that he can be. If there is a more confirmed theist in the world I have not heard of him. But he, too, has his troubles. They grow out of the behavior of ostensible theists. "Men in their history," he says, "like individuals in their lives, fluctuate between religion and materialism"; between "a conviction that life is mysterious and more than its phe-nomena, part of a whole, dimly glimpsed here on earth, but ultimately to be comprehended," and "a conviction that life is its phenomena, and that they provide the only basis for evaluating it." Mr. Muggeridge is "most convinced of the truth of religion and the falsity of irreligion or material-ism." Why, then, is he troubled? I quote from an article by him in *Time and Tide*:

I ask myself what this civilization which is to be saved—some say against Fascism, some against Communism, and some against both—amounts to. It has a Christian Church. The head of the Roman Catholic branch of this Christian Church, the Pope, blesses the Spanish General who has laid waste much of his own country, caused large numbers of his fellow countrymen to be massacred and killed in battle, and associated himself with a Government whose trusted supporters constantly execrate the teachings of Christ.

Another branch of this Christian Church, the Anglican, gets large revenues from and has become identified with a necessarily corrupt, worldly, and hypocritical State; while occasional stragglers belonging to the same organization, without forfeiting their right to officiate at its services and minister to its congregations, acclaim what is done in the name of a philosophy which denies not merely Christ, the founder of their religion, but the validity of all religion as it ever has existed or might exist.

Such writings as these show how necessary it is to determine which atheism is referred to when the word is used.

vii

The wide difference between cosmic and ethical atheism is evident in this curious fact. Well-known men who are far apart in their beliefs about God may be almost indistinguishable when it comes to enlightened interest in the ethical advancement of mankind. Bishop McConnell is a theist; H. S. Jennings is at best an agnostic; Julian Huxley is an outspoken atheist; John Dewey prefers to be neither a theist, an agnostic, nor an atheist. Yet each of them— bishop, biologist, or philosopher—is committed to very similar ideals of social progress. Each is opposed to ethical atheism. A slight examination will show this to be true.

It is a fundamental mistake, writes Bishop McConnell in The Christian Century, to regard the commandments, "Thou shalt love thy God with all thy heart" and "Thou shalt love thy neighbor as thyself" as two commandments. "They are not two, but one." We have come to a pass in human affairs, Bishop McConnell believes, where "mystical unity with God, God remaining undefined or a God of social passivity, amounts to nothing." So too of God conceived as an Absolute above all human striving, "the source of all beauty," "the fount of reason," "the center of all power in the universe." If this is all that theological or philosophical thinking can make of God, Bishop McConnell is not sure "that it is especially worth while for men to think overmuch of God, *just now*." His position is amplified in the following paragraphs:

Just now the main question concerning God is as to whether we can think of him as morally responsible in the use of his power in dealing with the billion and a half persons supposed to be living at any one time on the face of the earth. Let us withdraw for contemplation—withdraw into desert solitude, if need be, for the sake of fashioning a nobler idea of God, if we do so for the sake of coming out of the desert with the nobler idea taking the form of a deeper responsibility on the part of the divine for the right outcome of human affairs.

The actual process followed in humanity's moralization of the idea of God is the seizure, usually by a prophet or seer, of some larger or finer ideal of human life as binding upon God as well as upon men. Then the adjustment of this moral insight to the conception of the divine gives that divine itself new force for human life.

These are brave words for a religious leader to print. Only an exceptional interest in humanity and an integrity equally exceptional would make them public. And they hit the mark. They indicate what the issue turns upon. They help to make clear which meaning of atheism is the one that has serious consequences for our time.

Mr. Jennings would prefer not to use the term God. Gods and goddesses he speaks of as reflecting the highest characteristics in men, as devils represent the worst in men, animals, and insects. He declines to believe in any power supposed to have existed before biological life began its progressive course to which the direction of that course can be ascribed. Of belief in God, taken in this sense, he has written frankly in his book, *The Universe and Life:*

In part, it is a reflection of wishes, the outgrowth of a desire for an all-wise, all-powerful protector and father. In the practice of science, the tendency to base convictions upon wishes is one of the chief errors to be avoided: it does not lead to verifiable truth; on the contrary, it leads to demonstrable errors.

As this biologist sees the situation, the thing of superlative value is not life in conformity with the supposed commands of the wished-for protector and father, but a life of "fullness, variety, and adequacy." The highest aim of morality is to spread forbearance, generosity, good will, and love of truth, virtues which he believes have not kept pace with advances in practical efficiency. And for the furtherance of these aims men are dependent upon themselves and the resources at their disposal:

It is only experience, it is only living itself, that discovers what things in life are of value. What life, in direct experience, finds satisfactory, is satisfactory; what life finds valuable, is valuable. The worth while includes all those satisfactions and experiences of life that are discovered to be good, as food is discovered to be good by a hungry creature; and that do not yield later consequences of evil that overbalance the good.

Mr. Huxley puts it in this way:

I do not believe in the existence of a god or gods. The conception of a divinity seems to me, though built up out of a number of real elements in experience, to be a false one, based on the quite unjustifiable postulate that there must be some more or less personal power in control of the world.

What does he say as to the consequent value of life? Does his disbelief in "the existence of a god or gods" carry with it what we have called ethical atheism? Not at all. Without belief in cosmic theism, "men and women may yet possess the mainspring of full and purposive living, and just as great a sense that existence can be worth while as is possible to the most devout believers." He could not very well say this more emphatically:

I believe that life can be worth living. I believe this in spite of pain, squalor, cruelty, unhappiness, and death. I do not believe that it is necessarily worth living, but only that for most people it can be.

I also believe that man, as individual, as group, and collectively as mankind, can achieve a satisfying purpose in existence. I believe this in spite of frustration, aimlessness, frivolity, boredom, sloth, and failure. Again I do not believe that a purpose inevitably inheres in the universe or in our own existence, or that mankind is bound to achieve a satisfying purpose, but only that such a purpose can be found.

Mr. Dewey, as I have said, rejects theism, agnosticism and atheism. He finds the evidence insufficient for the belief in a particular supernatural or superhuman Being. Nor does he think such a Being morally or religiously indispensable. But while we can get on, indeed get on better without such a Being, we do need, he thinks, what he terms "natural piety," or "the sense of a connection of man, in the way of both dependence and support, with the enveloping world that the imagination feels is a universe." And we need, especially is a distracted age, a clear and intense conception of "the natural forces and conditions— including man and human association—that promote the growth of the ideal and that further its realization." Atheism and agnosticism, this philosopher believes, lead men to regard the natural environment as indifferent or even hostile to them. Ideals are then "mere rootless ideals, fantasies, utopias," to be realized, if at all, only in defiance of nature and of natural human desires. "Use of the words 'God' or 'divine' to convey the union of the actual and ideal," he hopes, "may protect man from a sense of isolation and from consequent despair or defiance."

Obviously, Mr. Dewey's objection is to ethical atheism. He is well aware that his refusal to give up the word God is likely to be interpreted as endorsing the belief in a divine cosmic Being. His book, A Common Faith, although explicit in its denial of theism, has been interpreted as a defense of it. He takes the chance of being thus misunderstood rather than the other chance of being misunderstood to hold that man's ideal endeavors are not sustained by the world in which we live. The word God stands for "those factors in existence that generate and support our idea of good as an end to be striven for. " It "denotes the unity of all our ideal ends arousing us to desire and actions." It stands for "the ties binding man to nature that poets have always celebrated."

Here then we have four eminent men who differ as regards the theistic interpretation of the cosmos, but are in essential accord in their conduct allegiance. Theist, atheist, agnostic, and adherent of none of these cosmic views, each is intent upon encouraging active co-operation of man with man, and men with processes of physical nature and the social order, to the end that, individually and collectively, we may attain to a fuller realization of the good life.

viii

A tantalizing phase of the problem grows out of the fact that a person whose chief objection is to ethical atheism may insist that what he is against is cosmic atheism. The most clean-cut example I know of is Upton Sinclair. It was the report that Mr. Sinclair is an atheist, widely circulated during the closing days of his political battle for Governor of California, which is believed by competent observers to have turned the tide against him. Some were honest in spreading the report; but some, I am reliably informed, did it to hold well-paying jobs on venal newspapers. The lie could not have succeeded had the two kinds of atheism been clear in the public mind.

In his book, *What God Means to Me*, published after the campaign was over, Mr. Sinclair declares himself to have

been a believer in God since boyhood. But his theism is
primarily ethical or social. Had the book been available
during the campaign, many would still have voted against
its author on theological grounds. To them he could only
be a nonbeliever or atheist because he does not believe in
their kind of cosmic God.

The impression must not be left that Mr. Sinclair dis-
believes in a God of the cosmos, for he expressly states the
contrary:

So it is that I believe in a *personal* God: a power operating at the center of this universe, which creates, maintains,
and comprehends my personality, and all other personalities, those which were, and those which are, and those
which have yet to be; a power which causes my being—
otherwise it would not be; which sustains my being—otherwise it would cease; which understands my being—otherwise I should not conform to my pattern, but would become a chaos.

He believes in this personal cosmic God, and he promises to give a scientific proof of his existence. If he does this
anywhere I have missed the place. So far as I can discover
he never seriously undertakes it. Why should he? For the
thing that matters to him is not something outside in the
universe, but something inside at the core of his own being. It is a "still small voice in the heart," as he says, "a
sense of the worth-whileness of what I am doing," an "impulse to develop our faculties," a freedom from the pessimistic, self-refuting doubt which to give way to "is to be
mentally sick, and part of a mentally sick age."

These attitudes are his evidence for God. That is why he can honestly say, "I believe those things about God which make it possible for me to develop my own powers, and thus to serve God better." He can believe that it makes no difference whether you say you *discover* God or *make* God, for the two phrases mean the same thing. The cosmic interpretation given to this inner psychical process or experience seems to him relatively unimportant. "If my materialist friends," he declares, "prefer to say Nature, or Universe; if my philosophical friends prefer Elan Vital with Bergson, or Life Force with Bernard Shaw, or Cosmic Consciousness with Bucke, or Oversoul with Emerson or First Cause with Plato, or Noumenon with Kant—that is all right with me."

It is all right with him, but it would not be if he took cosmic theism seriously enough. Mr. Sinclair is not that kind of a theist. His theism, as I have said, is primarily ethical and social, and it is from this ethical theism that his cosmical theism, such as it is, derives. How else is one to read what must be a final quotation from his book?

This God whom I preach is in the hearts of human beings, fighting for justice, inside the churches and out— even the rebel groups, many of which reject His name. A world in which men exploit the labor of their fellows, and pile up fortunes which serve no use but the display of material power—such a world presents itself to truly religious people as a world which must be changed. Those who serve God truly in this age serve the ideal of brotherhood; of helping our fellow beings, instead of exploiting their labor, and beating them down and degrading them in order to exploit them more easily.

ix

A good many people are inclined to dismiss this subject
as a purely academic one. They are not the people who care
what the deeper motives are that move men to action. For
it is not a purely academic question. Let us make one more
comparison with special reference to practical attitudes.
James Weldon Johnson was frankly nontheistic. What was
the conduct aspect of his nontheism as set forth in his
extraordinary book, *Along This Way*? Arthur Brisbane was
theistic in his newspaper column. What did his theism
mean when applied to international relations? His Eminence William Cardinal O'Connell is an ambassador of
God on earth. What side did he take in a crucial struggle for child welfare in Massachusetts?

Toward the end of Mr. Johnson's autobiography he
makes this statement:

I do not know if there is a personal God; I do not see
how I can know; and I do not see how my knowing can
matter. What does matter, I believe, is how I deal with
myself and how I deal with my fellows. I feel that I can
practice a conduct toward myself and toward my fellows
that will constitute a basis for an adequate religion, a religion that may comprehend spirituality and beauty and
serene happiness.

As far as I am able to peer into the inscrutable, I do not
see that there is any evidence to refute those scientists and
philosophers who hold that the universe is purposeless;
that man, instead of being the special care of Divine Provi-
dence, is a dependent upon fortuity and his own wits for
survival in the midst of blind and insensate forces. But to

stop there is to stop short of the vital truth. For mankind and for the individual this state, what though it be accidental and ephemeral, is charged with meaning. Man's sufferings, his joys, his aspirations, his defeats, are just as real and of as great moment to him as they would be if they were part of a mighty and definite cosmic plan.

This says it all and says it beautifully. Compare the social *idealism* of this program of life, based on a *nontheistic* outlook, with the social *materialism* of another program, announced by one who talked theistic language. The two sets of paragraphs are from Arthur Brisbane's newspaper column, and they appeared about two weeks apart:

(1) In American churches, Sunday, August 18, will be a day of prayer for peace in Africa, and safety for little Ethiopia, which confronts war with powerful Italy.

That is the right United States interference in foreign affairs. The prayers will reach their destination, and the supreme being to whom they are addressed knows what is best, and has power to arrange matters in Ethiopia as He chooses.

To pray: "Lord, possessor of omniscience and omnipotence, we leave all in your hands," is right.

To send a million young American men, and several thousand million American dollars to meddle in hot Africa would be wrong.

(2) The French Government, through Premier Pierre Laval, tells England that Italian rule over Abyssinia would be beneficial even to Abyssinians. It certainly would be beneficial to the world at large to have control of a vast fertile section of the earth's surface taken from savagery that in some parts adheres to the hippopotamus cult and eats hippopotamus flesh.

Every good reason for the whites taking North America from the Indians applies to Italy taking Abyssinian territory from its present rulers, and it is silly to be hypocritical about it.

The mockery of the prayer, "Lord, possessor of omniscience and omnipotence, we leave all in your hands," does not need to be pointed out. It means too obtrusively, "We leave all in your hands that we can't bother to take." And, as the last quoted paragraph advises, "it is silly to be hypocritical about it." What Mr. Brisbane preached in spite of, indeed with the help of, an ostensible reliance upon a "supreme being" who "knows what is best, and has power to arrange matters in Ethiopia as He chooses," is the right of the stronger to march where he dares and take what he wants from the weaker, who cannot prevent him. Theism of this sort is surely hard to differentiate from ethical atheism.

Suppose the question is asked whether this is a typical example of theism, whether it is not, on the contrary, the perfunctory theism characteristic of men of action who are dominated by materialistic ambitions and are consequently prone to forget the claims of God upon them. Well, that is of course just the point. God is spoken of as if his will were central to human affairs when, in point of fact, it is only the echo of a rumor that disturbs the outskirts of living. The alleged theism is a matter of words; it is not a program of faith and action.

The theism of a cardinal of the church is naturally more revealing than the theism of a journalist, for in his case we may assume the interest in God to be paramount, which

is not necessarily true of a columnist on a newspaper. I
take the liberty to quote a number of paragraphs from an
article by Carl Knudsen in *The Christian Century* entitled,
"The Cardinal Wins." I have reason to believe in the
trustworthiness of Mr. Knudsen's report:

The embattled forces of Massachusetts have won another valiant fight against the child. Led by His Eminence
William Cardinal O'Connell, and well supported by the
Boston press, the brave defenders of righteousness have
definitely set the land of the Cabots and the Lodges against
the child labor amendment . . . His Eminence, the
Cardinal, basking in the sunlight of the Bahamas, has reason to believe that his long vacation is well earned, for it is
everywhere conceded that the rejection of the amendment
in the legislature was a victory won by one man and only
one—our friend, the cardinal.

The struggle for ratification was led by the Massachusetts federation of labor. The legislative agent of that organization, himself a Catholic, presented an appeal to the
committee on constitutional law which would have done
credit to any professor or clergyman in the state. He presented unassailable economic arguments; he presented a
long list of eminent advocates of the amendment; he kept a
remarkable poise while the legislature heckled him with nit-
wit questions concerning the "sanctity of the home" and
the "nationalization of children"; he rose to a moving
peroration which made even his bitterest opponents sit
up and ponder. If ever logically unassailable argument was
presented before a legislative body, it was in this instance.

But Robert Walt might as well have been talking to
the statue of Edward Everett Hale out on the common.
. . . The penetrating proamendment argument of Dr.
John A. Ryan, director of the department of social action

of the National Catholic Welfare Conference, and of the Reverend William A. Bolger, head of the economics department in Notre Dame University, failed to register. The cardinal had spoken!

What about the human appeal? Such revelations as were made by Miss Helen Wood of the Connecticut department of labor should have melted the icicles off the coldest heart. Commercialized agriculture being exempt from N.R.A. codes, the tobacco industry of Connecticut has ridden to prosperity on the backs of boys and girls eight years of age and somewhat older. Children must work under cloth which is spread over the fields to maintain tropical temperature. "It is a common experience," says Miss Wood, "to see children working from 54 to 60 hours a week in temperatures ranging from 98 to 120 degrees. Children are employed by the plantation managements because there is less likelihood of their damaging the plants as they pass through the fields—and above all else because their services cost so little." Similar conditions, some bad enough to remind one of Oliver Twist, are to be discovered in the sugar beet fields of the west and the onion fields of Ohio.

The child labor amendment is of course a proposal on which even socially minded people may differ. The fact remains that when the theism of His Eminence William Cardinal O'Connell took the form of action in this case it was on the side of those who were willing to sacrifice children's welfare. His theism did not mean a lively concern for their health and education and happiness. It meant at best an interest in the destiny of their "souls." Possibly this is what Jesus meant when he said, "Suffer little children to come unto me, and forbid them not, for

of such is the kingdom of heaven." I do not so interpret
what he said. Possibly it was interest in the "higher" welfare
of children which caused the Catholic-controlled press to
array itself, as Mr. Knudsen reports, against the child labor
amendment along with Cardinal O'Connell. Possibly, but
not probably. The more likely explanation, judging by what
was done, is that the Boston newspapers were thinking of
advertisers, and that Cardinal O'Connell was thinking of
Roman Catholicism. This is what faith in God meant in
the way of practice. And I think involuntarily of a warning that dates from the time when Christian theism was
more primitive. It speaks of those who are willing to betray the helpless, and it says, "It were better that a mill
stone were hanged about their necks and they were cast
into the depths of the sea."

Speaking for myself, and in moderation, I detect no
trace of the divine in the theism of either the columnist,
the Boston newspapers, or the Cardinal, as disclosed in
these instances. It is rather in such dedication to the human cause which is evident throughout the autobiography
of James Weldon Johnson that I find a spirit which, but
for the fact that the word has been ruined by its other
associations, I should be happy to call divine: a spirit of
dedication to "a religion that may comprehend spirituality
and beauty and serene happiness," arising out of "man's
sufferings, his joys, his aspirations, his defeats."

x

Perhaps it is desirable, even if not strictly necessary, to
conclude the chapter with a summarizing statement of its

main theme. Viewed with respect to resulting conduct, atheism may have reference to the superhuman or to the supremely human. It may be disbelief in a Cosmic Being at work in the universe and in history, seeing to it that mankind shall not suffer ultimate defeat; or it may be an unconscious or a deliberate disregard of the aspirational side of the human struggle. Harry Emerson Fosdick's doctrine that disbelief in God is a rationalization of the evil in human nature is one of those errors which thrive in language but cannot stand exposure to fact. Truer words than Dr. Fosdick's were spoken by Judge Holley at the funeral service for Clarence Darrow, the most widely known atheist in America:

The heartless call has come, and we must stagger on the best we can alone. In the darkest hours we will look in vain for your loved form, we will listen hopelessly for your devoted, fearless voice. But, though we lay you in the grave and hide you from the sight of man, your brave words will speak for the poor, the oppressed, the captive, and the weak; and your devoted life inspire countless souls to do and dare in the holy cause for which you lived and died.

Are we to say, then, that cosmic atheism has no effect on behavior? No, not that. All beliefs have some effect on behavior; they make some difference in the conduct of the believer. Beliefs about the cosmos have consequences and they may be very profound. But the point is that only by making sure of the conduct meaning of theism or atheism in a given case is it possible to determine what these consequences are. "Vanity of vanities, all is vanity," we read in Ecclesiastes. This is surely the quintessence of atheism, if there is such a thing; but throughout the poem in which it appears a cosmic God is constantly assumed to exist.

The reason why many people refuse to think of themselves as atheists is not that they are theists, but that they understand atheism to commit men to a way of life of which they strongly disapprove. Their cosmic outlook, if frankly stated, would be atheistical. But this seems to them of purely academic interest compared with a correct appreciation of their ethical and social convictions.

We have found a most striking illustration of this mood in Mr. Dewey. He defends the use of the word God to designate "the natural forces and conditions—including man and human association—that promote the growth of the ideal and that further its realization." Whether we agree with him or not on the desirability of this usage—personally, I do not—we can all join him, all of us but those whose attitude has been described as *ethical* atheism, in aiming to keep alive the temper of mind which he seeks to encourage. We need a sense of community with the environing world and with our fellows. We need to recognize continuity between ideals and actuality. In no other way can we keep idealism healthy and realism sane.

There are such goods, says Mr. Dewey, as "values of art in all its forms, of knowledge, of friendship and love, of growth in mind and body," which exist concretely and experimentally, but in embryonic form. "Many persons are shut out from generous participation in them; there are forces at work that threaten and sap existent goods as well as prevent their expansion." And there are forces in nature and human nature which, if properly united to each other, can bring these valued goods into more general and secure enjoyment. It is the betrayal or neglect of these beneficent forces which Mr. Dewey calls atheism, and it is with atheism of this kind that he refuses to have anything to do. In this refusal he should have the support of all of us, whatever we may believe regarding God.

xi

A question must repeatedly have occurred to the reader of this chapter. Is there after all a God or is there not? That question will be considered in the succeeding chapter. Whatever the correct answer to this is—my own answer will presently be given as frankly as I can give it—the conclusion so far arrived at will stand. The deeper meaning of atheism must be sought in everyday conduct, not in metaphysical views. We end as we began. The meaning of an idea is what it refers to in behavior. We may avail ourselves of another quotation from the New Testament. The earlier quotation was attributed to the brother of Jesus; we may end with words attributed to Jesus himself:

And why call ye me Lord, Lord, and do not the things which I say?

Whosoever cometh to me, and heareth my sayings, and doeth them, I will show you to whom he is like:

He is like a man which built an house, and digged deep, and laid the foundation on a rock: and when the flood arose, the stream beat vehemently upon that house, and could not shake it: for it was founded upon a rock.

But he that heareth and doeth not, is like a man that without a foundation built an house upon the earth; against which the stream did beat vehemently, and immediately it fell; and the ruin of that house was great.

There are many who talk the words of cosmic theism and act the deeds of ethical atheism. They are shocked by the merest *suggestion* that the *universe* may be purposeless, but are not shocked at all by the *fact* that the world of affairs is purposeless for millions of human beings. Life is degraded and spoiled not only by those who crave vulgar satisfactions, but by those who, conscious of their respectability and culture, their adherence to "spiritual ideals," refuse to assume any active responsibility for what is done in business, industry, politics, or in any of the numerous practical relations which make up so large a part of almost every man's life. Frequently with good intentions, and always with noble sentiments, they chip away the rock upon which a worthy house of man must be built. If they succeed in their designs the house will fall, and the ruin of that house will be great.

❧ XI ❧

THE EXISTENCE OF GOD

In the foregoing chapter the question of God's existence was not discussed, although it is undoubtedly the first to occur to the mind whenever atheism is mentioned. The reason for this omission was indicated in the chapter itself. Atheism has other meanings than disbelief in a supreme cosmic being, and some of those meanings are of the utmost human significance. The more important problem was found to be how to get a human exemplification of "divine" attributes, rather than how to prove the existence of a divinity within or behind the cosmos. Nevertheless the question whether a God who realizes his purposes on the scale of the universe and in the best interests of mankind exists, is distinctly relevant. Its temporary neglect may be advisable for reasons of greater clarification in the end, but it cannot be neglected permanently. All the more is this true since scholars of ability and integrity insist that *cosmic* atheism must unavoidably end in what we have called *ethical* atheism. Let us now consider the question of God's existence.

i

Some years ago on a bluff overlooking a beautiful stretch of the Ohio River, I came upon a natural bridge left along the edge of the bluff by the wearing away of the soil behind it. Rains, draining down the hillside, had formed a watercourse under the bridge into which fragments of sod, twigs, old leaves, and pebbles had washed from the top and sides. In patches of these deposits tiny toadstools were growing, with seedlings of yellow poplar, silver maple, chestnut oak, and grasses of various kinds—as if life were snatching a brief respite from death by clinging to bits of earth temporarily halted in the inevitable journey down the hillside into the river.

A prehistoric man, stopping to speculate on these phenomena, could avail himself of a handy explanation. One god made the hills, another washed them away, a third backed the seeds in their struggle against the wasting environment. It is well known that long before the beginning of recorded history man had arrived at the idea of distinct forces to account for what happened in the world about him, and had humanized these forces by making them into personal beings analogous to himself. During the Homeric period primitive theism gave rise to an assemblage of divinities that for splendor of conception will always be remembered as an astonishing creation. All the orderly processes of nature and of human nature, as well as catastrophic and unpredictable occurrences, were thereby brought into an intelligible and uplifting scheme of polytheistic explanation.

This hierarchy of gods retained its standing so long as men were satisfied with telling tales about their world. Very early in the Occident, and still earlier in the Orient, thinkers appeared who desired to give a factual account of things. The Ionians embarked upon systematic investigations of an essentially scientific character, to be followed by the Athenians, who were as if designed for the task. They hit upon the revolutionary idea that everything is ultimately composed of some identical substance and is ruled throughout by the same law. Soon the atomists entered upon the scene, to explain hills and rivers and growing plants as transitory aggregates of material particles, thrown into the perceived patterns only to be disintegrated and thrown into other patterns by blind, resistless forces: not only hills and rivers and growing plants, but animal bodies; not only animal bodies, but minds and souls; not only nature and human nature, but all that was regarded as divine. For the atomists were daring thinkers. They boldly climbed the dread heights of Olympus and demanded the surrender of the whole bench of gods. The gods, in spite of their august mien and the sublimity of their abode, were not allowed to be different in kind from the motes of dust that dance on the floor of a sunbeam.

Stated in the language of later times this marks the beginning of the warfare between theological and scientific views of the world. And a thing happened at the outset of the conflict which has happened again and again down the centuries and is happening today. Although theism was undermined by new beliefs resulting from inquiry into observable facts, and from radical social changes, it was not surrendered outright. The breach between the growing rational and social temper and the inherited theistic ideas was provisionally healed by a compromise. Theism was redefined, intellectually purified, and so made acceptable to many who were disposed to reject the gods in their earlier, cruder forms.

Credit for this refinement of theism belongs to classical Greek philosophy. It has been said indeed that Greek philosophy originated in this very undertaking. At any rate, philosophy provided an intellectualized theism which could be substituted for the anthropomorphic theism of the current religion. The theistic principle was not merely saved from destruction; it was given the highest intellectual respectability.

ii

Our country supplies its own striking example. As one stands on Copp's Hill where those stout defenders of theistic faith, Increase and Cotton Mather, lie buried, and looks down on the busy life of the city and out over the animated bay, one finds it difficult to form a mental picture of the neat little Boston and the pleasant countryside they saw when they stood in the same place some two hundred years ago. It is still more difficult to revive the theistic frame of mind which then prevailed in New England, or, rather, which had prevailed until then. For it was the fate of the Mathers to live in a time when the idea of God was undergoing drastic transformation. The God whose all-seeing eye was fixed upon individual men and women, the God who sent comets and thunderbolts to admonish and frighten them, who punished them with diseases, snatched their children away, tripped up their ventures, ruined their crops, sank their ships at sea, that God was losing his authority. A new God was replacing him, one who had staked out the world, set it in order, started it going, then left it to run itself, returning occasionally to mend what had gone wrong in his absence.

The Mathers had their troubles choosing between the two, especially Cotton Mather, who prided himself on keeping abreast of new ideas. Looking backward they spoke a word for the one; looking forward they spoke a word for the other. And before Cotton Mather had ended his labors Jonathan Edwards was ready to lead the reaction against the liberalizing forces at work in the Puritan colonies. Soon he had become the fiery Calvinist, voicing in theology the conservative social tendencies which were rising in the commonwealth about him in opposition to the growing spirit of political independence. Great numbers were persuaded to believe in an absolutely sovereign God who had predetermined literally everything cosmic and human, all of it with perfect indifference to its effect upon man. But Edwards lived to know men who were to win renown in the American Revolution. Having risked their lives and fortunes in a struggle with earthly tyranny, they were not inclined to worship a cosmic tyrant.

Further changes followed just as inevitably. The men and women who crowded into the developing cities, who suffered from the social consequences of the newly intro-

duced factory system, or who pushed westward into the
wilderness, found the God they needed in the compas-
sionate, friendly, and morally disposed Heavenly Father of
the Methodists and Baptists. As for the more intellectual liberals, they turned to the genteel and humani-
tarian deity of the Unitarians. By the time of Emerson,
many of the educated had come to think of God as he did.
God had become an impersonal ethical process operative
in the universe. Those who, like Orestes Brownson, lived
closer to the deplorable realities produced by the rapid expansion of industry and commerce, saw God as their leader
in the battle for social justice.

Thus on the restricted stage of New England, and in a
short span of history, a succession of God-ideas held sway.

Such redefinitions have succeeded one another these
two thousand years, not to mention what had taken place
before the critical period in Greece. The change was sometimes brought about so gradually that it was almost unde-
tected. Again it took place with suddenness and with con-
vulsive effect over wide areas of life. Here and there
organized religion was powerful enough to suppress the
slightest threat to the reigning meaning of God; or religious groups, claiming access to a superior source of truth,
have been relatively successful in holding themselves aloof
from secular events; but in spite of these obstructions, improvements in knowledge of the world and changes in the
general manner of living have continually modified theism.
This accounts in part for the great variety of God-ideas, as
it does for the increasing vagueness or abstractness of those
ideas. Both are results of a general unwillingness to give

up believing in God, combined with the feeling that the believer must, somehow, remain responsive to his social and intellectual milieu.

iii

Here then is an impressive phase of human history. Periodically, belief in gods or God has had to reconstruct its object to keep it in sufficient accord with the changing status of culture. It is of course possible to make light of this continuous redefinition. God, in his full reality, it may be argued, is humanly incomprehensible. As knowledge increases we are able to get a better idea of God, and the succession of new definitions is evidence that this has been done. The reality, God, has remained unchanged. It is our concepts of him that have changed. They have come nearer and nearer the truth.

Before we admit that this argument is conclusive let us observe the difference in the effect of redefinition on a comparable idea. Naturalism has changed as theism has. Mr. Whitehead's God differs no more profoundly from the Homeric gods or the Hebrew Lord of Hosts, than Mr. Einstein's universe differs from that of Democritus or Newton. The fact of importance, however, is not the change itself, but the trend of the change in relation to daily practice. Redefinitions of naturalism have been paralleled by the extension of naturalistic explanations to an ever widening field of practical activity, and by a correspondingly extended reliance upon naturalistic method. Redefinitions of theism, on the contrary, have involved the exclusion of theistic explanation from one sphere after another, and a growing disinclination to employ theistic method anywhere. *Naturalism has gained and theism has lost in power over man's lives.* In the one case redefinition has registered advance; in the other case retreat.

This difference is the fact of importance, and I do not see how it can be denied. Nothing is more obvious or amazing than the steady weakening of living faith in God, I mean in a God of any kind. Early man believed the gods to be real in the same sense that he believed the mountains, forests, or waterfalls to be real which were their dwelling places. For a long time spirits lived in drugs and wines and made them potent. They were believed to be of the same order of fact as the potency itself. But man is curious and curiosity is relentless. Hence the discovery was made that a reported god may be a myth. It became known that this or that god might be disregarded. Once initiated, skepticism regarding theistic explanations could not be halted. In the end it destroyed the theism of the ancient world.

Nor could it be stopped by the change later on from polytheism to monotheism, or in modern times by refinements in monotheisms. And we must remind ourselves that this had wide practical repercussions. Dependence upon human effort more and more replaced dependence upon God. One domain after another was taken from God's empire and brought under human supervision. Today his prerogatives are acknowledged in a very limited region of life.

Some years ago Nancy Barr Mavity made a critical observation which seemed to me then and seems to me still pertinent. "The one thing needful," she wrote, "is not that we should find blanket terms under which we seem to agree, but that we should drag out our disagreement into the clearest possible light, and so find out what we are talking about. Not only our language, but our intelligence, suffers from preferring vague unity to distinct differentiation." Her criticism applies with special force to the present theme. If there is a word that has spread a wider blanket over disagreement than the word God, it has not come to my attention.

The explanation is simple. Redefinitions have not been due to new intuitions or insights. They have been, with rare exceptions, the work of intellectuals who were busy adjusting a traditional concept to the demands of accumulated learning. The task that absorbed them was to stretch the blanket term God over newly discovered intellectual discrepancies. The result has been the piling up of redefinitions, one upon another, until the life of the word has been all but smothered out of it. What we have left of God in the most pretentious definitions now current is little if anything more than the original word. The vital meaning of God in human experience has been refined away.

Man thus seems to have gone far in the direction of not believing in God. If this is really a fact, what good can come from ignoring it, and consequently failing to make provision for the serious hazards it has brought? Personally, I can think of no question more in the human interest to ask than this: What has been the effect of turning away from hoped-for divine aid, and relying instead upon human initiative and effort?

Well, what is the answer? That in proportion as men have ceased to lean on God, they have not only learned to bend mechanical forces to good use and to control the physical conditions of human well-being, but they have opened up undreamed-of resources for the satisfaction of the noblest desires of which they are capable. In the securing of food, clothing, and shelter it has proved to be better to proceed as if the existence of God were irrelevant. The advance of medical science in safeguarding life, caring for bodily and mental health, and putting up a winning fight against diseases that had decimated mankind for centuries, is perhaps the most conspicuous example. It is not theism to which we must ascribe the development of medicine. Medical progress has had to fight against theistic prejudice. It was likewise theistic prejudice that stood in the way of a hopeful treatment of psychic disorders, of sex and population problems, of antisocial propensities, and similar difficulties.

Whenever men and women have been able to act as if there were no divinity to shape human ends, and have themselves assumed responsibility, they have discovered how to turn their abilities to good account. Is it likely that this process will be reversed in the future? I am convinced that we are nearer the beginning than the end of it, as helpless to change this general direction as we are to prevent ourselves from getting older. What we can do is to try to go forward intelligently, as in growing older we may try to grow wiser.

iv

Not believing in God has worked well. It has worked better than believing did. It is responsible for a realistic

acquaintance with our world and a better understanding of
human nature. This would seem to furnish evidence, of a
kind usually considered good, that there is no superhuman
being who cares what becomes of mankind. And the vast
majority of people have apparently been convinced. They
show it by the way they live day in and day out. They go
about their business from morning to night taking no coun-
sel of God. True enough, they would not dream of admitting it and they are offended if anyone else does, but such
paradoxical behavior is not unusual. Their refusal to be
called unbelievers, like their continued attendance upon
church services, though they do not subscribe to the church
creed, merely shows that something holds them back from
openly admitting what they take for granted six days of
the week and most of the seventh. What is it that holds
them back?

One thing that holds them back is human mortality.
Much of the persisting theism is crisis theism. Many people, even of those who ordinarily give no thought to God,
and who never lift a finger on behalf of the values of life
most intimately associated with his name, are transformed
into theists when confronted by the fact or thought of
death. They cannot admit that death is the ruin of life, and
since the existence of God is required to save it from being
just that, a sufficient belief to meet the emergency lingers,
though inert, in the background of their minds. I admit
that it is a shallow belief, one that does not pervade their
lives but comes forward only to attend funerals, weddings,
and like occasions, yet it may be singularly genuine while
it lasts. It lifts the believer for the moment, however tempo-

rary his belief, above the struggle for material advantage. He is made tender toward failure. A mood of reverence is awakened and a sense of the mystery of life. In a word, he lives for the time being in his better impulses. And when the theistic mood has retired again to the outermost fringe of interest, which it often does with shocking suddenness, the good words that were spoken for God in the interim echo and re-echo in memory. It is these echoes which hold many people back from accepting an explanation of the world which leaves out God, and makes them feel that anyone who faces death in the same nontheistic spirit as he faces life must be exceptionally hardhearted, if not down-right vicious.

No one would claim, I trust, that belief in God is a necessity for creatures who know that they must die. For one thing, few people are called upon to undergo the ordeal of their own death. As a rule they are planning to be alive when unconsciousness overtakes them, and when they die they know nothing about it. Since men have foresight and imagination, however, it is not enough for them to know that they will not experience dying, if they also know that the time will come when they will be dead. It is usually taken for granted that unless they are supported by the hope of immortality it is a kindness not to allude to their last hours.

Statistical evidence is not available one way or the other. If it were, we could show, I believe, that a certain personal quality, more than any belief a man holds for or against theism, determines his behavior in the expectation of death. I wonder whether the commander of a regiment could tell by the behavior of soldiers under fire, who was a believer and who was not. I wonder whether a sea captain whose ship is sinking could divide his sailors into the two classes. I wonder whether the confirmed criminal who walks with a firm step to his execution is sustained by theistic faith or by the same psychic hardness, reckless nerve, and need for display which made a life of crime attractive. And as for bravely bearing the death of others, I have never witnessed greater fortitude than that of devastated hearts for whom there was no balm in Gilead.

The crucial test of how a man will meet his own end is reserved for one who is snatched by the powerful arm of the law, and as he believes unjustly, out of active, sincere preoccupation with social reform and is condemned to die at a stated hour. By that test Bartolomeo Vanzetti, who was not upheld by faith in God, but by the vision of a social ideal for which he felt he was giving his life, and by the loyalty of friends, will bear comparison with Socrates. Since we are considering the possibility of meeting death without divine aid, it is well to recall the statement of Vanzetti when he was sentenced to die:

If it had not been for these thing, I might have die unmarked, unknown, a failure. Now we are not a failure. This is our career and our triumph. Never in our full life could we hope to do such work for tolerance, for justice, for man's understanding of man as now we do by accident! Our words —our lives—our pains—nothing! The taking of our lives —lives of a good shoemaker and a poor fish-peddler—all! That last moment belongs to us—that agony is our triumph.

V

Another reason for the retention of theism is man's low opinion of himself as a moral being. Thousands who leave God out when engaged in practical pursuits, or in following the promptings of desire, are careful to keep him on hand for the sake of ideals. They feel that God is needed to validate and enforce the moral life. This they believe is especially true of "the masses." Without God, man is a purely natural creature and must act, so they think, like any other animal, though he may express his animality with superior shrewdness. A naturalistic attitude may suffice, indeed must suffice, when the need is one of feeding and housing men, keeping their bodies clean and healthy, increasing their efficiency as producers of material wealth; it can do nothing to make men decent human beings, and it is worse than useless in the attainment of moral character. Generosity, ethical idealism, civic-mindedness, interest in moral growth can be expected from none but those who are inspired by God.

To say it in another way, the higher life, however conceived, does not pay in its own terms, so that unless men believe in a God who makes good the losses incurred in living it, no one will find it attractive. A general acceptance of a nontheistic philosophy, so the argument runs, would "eat all nobility out of our conception of conduct and all worth out of our conception of life."

Here we have one of those persistent half-truths that manage to outlive repeated refutation. "But men are better," said Emerson, "than their theology. Their daily life gives it the lie. Every ingenuous and aspiring soul leaves the doctrine behind him in his own experience, and all men feel sometimes the falsehood which they cannot demonstrate." *Aspiration is much older than man's acquaintance with the gods, and it does not die when faith in them is lost.* A natural discontent with objects less perfect than they can be imagined, and the pursuit of idealized objects that stir the feelings, are the vital forces at work in men's upward striving. The visible results at a given time may seem slight; they are not slight when estimated over years and generations and centuries.

Evidence is everywhere about us, in the community where we live, in the street that runs by our door, in our own hearts. Men are aroused to adore supremely, to triumph over the cold hard misery of life, to serve and die without reward. I remember Justice Holmes and the Law, Jane Addams and World Peace, La Follette and the People. I think of Flaubert and his worship of Beauty, of "The Worst Journey in the World," made by three heroes to fill a gap in the evidence for Evolution. I stand with Captain Ahab on the deck of the *Pequod*, scanning the horizon for Moby Dick. I follow a lantern through the darkness and the churchyard to the tomb of the Capulets with its testimony to the power of romantic love. So my mind wanders on—for there is no end to the number and variety of examples of supreme devotion—wanders on until lost in the thicket of life. There I find devotion, heroism, self-sacrifice, loyalty to causes. What is it but this original virtue in human beings that faith in God draws upon to give itself vitality?

No; the conclusion cannot be withstood that greatness, from every point of view, has been achieved by individuals and by whole peoples in the absence of faith in God. Men can and do develop great conceptions of conduct, can and do devote themselves to social causes with enthusiasm and self-sacrifice, without counting on help from higher powers. Co-operative faith in the intelligent use of natural and human resources has provided a sufficient incentive to high-minded conduct.

The number of those who have adopted this platform as a working hypothesis for themselves, and are solicitous that it be tried on the largest possible scale, is growing. Say against these men and women what we please, we cannot truthfully say that they are the riffraff of human nature. In my judgment theirs is the only dependable type of idealism left to man in the modern world.

vi

Perhaps the most plausible argument to be made against the foregoing considerations is that after all a study of the world in which we live discloses the slow working out of a great ethical purpose. And what can such a purpose be but the will of God? The evidence, however, does not, I think, support this interpretation.

In the first place, selection of the goal of natural events is premature. Suppose we were able to prove that a definite tendency is observable in the evolution of life on our globe, and suppose we could argue from tendency to intendency, neither of which we are in a position to do, we would still be unable to clinch the argument. We have not seen the *drama to the end.* Once it looked as if it were designed for fishes; then for reptiles; then for lower mammals. Now it may look as if designed for man. But the play is not over. The curtain has not dropped. How can we talk about the climax of a performance of which we have witnessed only the opening scenes?

What have we actually observed? Has everything moved in a steadily maintained direction toward man as the culminating goal? Evolution has been an incredible spendthrift of life. Highly organized creatures have been developed again and again only to be pushed up blind alleys and left there to die. If there is a God whose method has been Evolution, his slogan must have been, "We'll fight it out along this line if it takes a billennium!" But, unlike Grant, he has always surrendered.

In this maelstrom the human species, as Thomas Huxley said—and he knew something about the subject— "plashed and floundered amid the general stream of evolution, keeping its head above water as best it might, and thinking neither of whence or whither." If the great scene we look upon, with its waxing and waning of suns, its appearance and disappearance of plant worlds, its rise and fall of animal dynasties—if all this or any part of it is the working out of a divine purpose, "friendly to man's intellectual, moral and religious education," this purpose is well hidden.

What if we disregard Evolution and examine human history? Do we then observe the unfolding of a divine plan? Do we find demonstrable proof of a Power not ourselves that sides with the ethical best? Does it thwart the wrongdoer and circumvent the morally indifferent? Do we, or do we not, see "the wicked in great power and spreading himself like a green bay tree"? What happened to Socrates? To Jesus? According to the best authorities, they gave their lives to God and in the hour of their need he deserted them. They are conspicuous examples, but the fact which they illustrate is a commonplace of experience.

So far as the course of human life testifies, there is no indication that anything or anyone superhuman is bent upon the triumph of humane or ethical principles. *It seems to be up to us and us alone.* And since on the appearance of things man is forced to make shift with such powers as he can discover in himself and in his social and natural environment, why not be open and aboveboard at least about the appearances? Why not admit that for the practical realization of the good life we are obliged to act as we do in tilling the ground or baking bread, that is, to rely upon experimental knowledge to find out what it is we want and how to get it?

This surely offers a sufficient program for the most aspiring soul to work at. It has the added advantage of providing an escape from the chief risk of the ethical life, the danger of being victimized by our ideals. And we are less easily deceived by the type of leadership that would beguile our eyes from what we want to "higher things," in order that someone else may help himself to what he wants of things high or low.

If it is impossible to demonstrate the working presence of a divine ethical purpose in the world, there are, in the second place, certain demonstrable facts which make the existence of any such purpose very doubtful. I avail myself of a statement made by Bishop Ernest William Barnes in one of the profoundest books I have read, *Scientific Theory and Religion*. I do this because Bishop Barnes cannot be suspected of twisting the facts against the theistic position, and because his writings are sincere not only in the usual sense that he refuses to say what he does not believe to be true, but in the far more unusual sense of taking the trouble to assure himself that he is justified, in view of the evidence at hand, to say what he does. The statement is this:

The whole process of creation now appears to be non-moral. There is no evidence to lead us to infer that variations in the genes are directed towards ends which in our judgment are good. In such variations there seems, in fact, to be no ethical quality whatever. They have led to odious parasitism, to the carnage of the jungle, to the microbic diseases which cause such suffering to humanity, to those animal appetites which are useful in the struggle for survival and are the basis of sin in man. This, the immoral, brutal, lustful side of creation is as characteristic as the parental self-sacrifice, the adventurous curiosity, the instinct for truth, the enthusiasm for righteousness, the beauty of form and the physical well-being which equally result from the evolving process.

In such facts as these "we are confronted," Bishop Barnes points out, "by a dilemma from which there is, at present, no escape." And he makes this further remark which, coming from him, should have a salutary effect: "Verbal dexterity and the skilful use of those evasive phrases which are too common in modern theology might seem to offer escape to some: but to the man of science evasion is high treason against truth." To which I add that unless theism can find a solution for just this dilemma, the best we can in truth say for the cosmos is that up to date it has not prevented the human experiment from being tried. Anything more is too much.

vii

For the reasons adduced in this chapter, and such as these, I have for myself arrived at an affirmative faith in the nonexistence of God. The affirmation is important. One may be *without* a belief in the *existence* of God or *have* a belief in the *nonexistence* of God. The two are not identical. Each is associated with distinctive further beliefs and distinctive individual and social commitments. What I desire to make clear without taking space to elaborate the point, is the tentative, undogmatic, yet outspoken character of the belief in question. It is essentially a kind of faith, but the kind of faith we act on in daily life when we call a doctor or drive an automobile, in fact when we take any step whatever, a faith that is rooted in tested experience. It is militant, though not belligerent; convinced, but aware of difficulties in holding the position; an aggressive belief that is tempered by appreciative understanding of the motives and claims on the other side.

But why make so much of the deflection from God? Why draw attention to it at all? Why not let it go quietly on, if it is going on, and occupy our minds with something else? Is it really so important to be aware of what is happening to theism?

Yes, it is; and for this reason among others. By tradition

God has been the foundation of truth, goodness, beauty, humane feeling, and pretty much every virtue. The weakening of this theistic foundation endangers them all. Presently they will come down in a heap unless solidly placed upon another base. To ignore the crumbling away of the sacred underpinning upon which our whole structure of values has rested, or to observe it with cynical indifference, meanwhile to do nothing toward providing a footing for idealism in secular life, is to assist the tendencies which, if they go far enough, will destroy aspiration itself.

The drift from God is not an academic theory but a living fact. It is a movement of vital human interests. Theism is subjected to frontal attack by men and women who have ceased to be theists. It is attacked from the rear by the young who have grown up in a world where God had already lost his sovereign position. Shutting our eyes, mincing words, making up other definitions, will not stop what is going on. Can any thoughtful person wish to remain ignorant of an issue so momentous? Will he not rather insist on knowing about it, that he may lend his aid, big or little, to agencies of human betterment that may replace those which are slipping away?

viii

Affirmative faith in the nonexistence of God is thus intended as a positive attitude toward life. Its correlative is a marching interest in the well-being of mankind, material and spiritual. All that has already been accomplished has been due to Man's innate desire to improve his conditions. This likewise accounts for the elevation of his dominating interests and their expansion to include more of the happiness of others. I know of course that God has taken innumerable forms—a giant with the long beard, a cosmic objectification of the best human impulses, a purely abstract formula needed to make a logical demonstration click throughout.

Mr. Dewey believes it necessary to decide whether we are talking about *the* God or *a* God; whether we mean "the God of Abraham, Isaac and Jacob; of the Aristotelian metaphysics; of the Homeric Olympus; of the Athanasian creed; of Islam; of St. Thomas Aquinas; of Spinoza's Ethics; of Rousseau's Savoyard Vicar; of Kant's Critique of Practical Reason, to mention a few of the possibilities." He may be right. For my part, I do not choose among them. At bottom all of them seem to me to go back to primitive psychological reactions which we have been forced to outgrow in other realms. Put your fingers on the pulse of the most learned argument for God and you feel the heartbeat of primitive man's anxiety, his eagerness to get help from superhuman beings to deal with forces which appear too strong for him alone. Remove the verbal wrappings from the God proffered to contemporary men and women by leading theologians and philosophers, and his lineage is apparent. He bears a strong resemblance to his predecessors born out of social crises in the past, whose ancestors are traceable to their ancestors, until we reach the misty divinities of the first men we know anything about. The creativeness of early men in forming God-ideas moves me to wonder and admiration. But when I think of analogous productions today, I recall a sentence from F. H. Bradley: "It is better to bury a de-

lusion and forget it than to insult its memory by retaining
the name when the thing has perished."

ix

Among the most arresting sayings I have read is this:
"The gods are a splendid company. It is a great pity that
they are not better known." These words come from a
chapter on the nature of the gods in A. E. Haydon's book,
The Quest of the Ages. Mr. Haydon tells how the gods
were born and how they died and passed out of the lives
of men. "Graves of dead gods," he says, "mark all the high-
ways of the world."

Gods have died; but the quest which called them into
being is still alive. Those who deliberate about the problems this quest creates almost invariably begin with the
search for some universal principle which may be used to
validate particular experiences. If it is a question of thinking, they must first make sure of a theory of logic; if a
question of morals, they must first establish an absolute
standard; if a question of religion, they must first define
God and prove his existence.

Life has taught me to pursue an opposite course. It has
taught me to take the *particular situation* as authentic; to
interrogate *it* for light and leading. Every particular situation is of course interwoven with other situations. It reaches
out as it were around itself and into the past and future.
But a circle does not lose its center because it has a circum-
ference. It was everyday thinking that eventually gave rise
to logic; everyday habits and customs that developed into
moral principle; everyday efforts to live the good life that

led to the idea of God. It was not the other way around. Programs of living have been, as they are now and will be tomorrow, the output of loyalty to specific better alternatives offered in acting, feeling, and thinking.

In these critical days it is tragic to see men who mean to work for the best life attainable, sublimate their hearts' desire into a cosmic reality, mistake it for a helpful God, and so turn away from the physical world and the flesh and blood from which they must finally draw every blessing their brief and troubled existence can yield.

Men look to God, however God be defined, because they seek in him satisfaction of wants, worth of living, assurance of what they passionately desire and despair of finding in man or the human venture. I want them to find what they seek. Theism, however, will not help them. It sets ideals of excellence before men which are not made in *their* image but in the image of a being who, by hypothesis, is above driving impulse, unacquainted with vacillating and conflicting desires, and never harassed by doubt or misled by ignorance. It addresses itself to a mood which must be superinduced. All through life outcroppings of the natural creature in his physical, intellectual, and cultural wholeness must be resisted.

The authority of theism is therefore not that of expanding human life. Theism is prohibitory and repressive. Its inevitable tendency is to divide human nature into physical and spiritual elements and to work for the triumph of the latter over the former. It aims at the death of the natural man, as if to improve the fruit of the vine you had to sever it from its roots in the ground.

X

In the examination of some questions we so nearly agree as to the data that are relevant, and the reasoning that is to be employed, that we can reach a decisive conclusion, one way or the other. It need hardly be said that we have been discussing a different kind of question. I expressly disclaim any notion of having established nontheism with finality. No reasonable doubt remains in my own mind, but the existence of God is a question which, by its very nature, cannot be decided conclusively. I have tried to make clear that the weight of the evidence seems to me to be against it, and I leave it at that.

One further word may be needed to protect the position against another misunderstanding. I have argued that plain human nature and the surrounding world are sufficient for the realization of individual and social greatness. By this I do not mean that everyone, just as he is, is all that he should be, or that the ideals to which we give allegiance are ideal ideals. This whole book is a contention for the contrary view. It nowhere states or implies that "All's right with the world."

And I have not meant to suggest that man is equipped to "master nature," and is sure, given time, to create a perfect society which will not pass away. That, too, should be clear from what has been said. Unclouded assurance of life's significance is not to be had, no matter in what direction we look. Perfect satisfaction is unattainable, whatever the power on which we rely. If we must get on in a cosmos where we have no friend but each other, it is not because this is our free choice, but our inescapable condition. By deliberately accepting it as such we may be able to convert an allotted fate into something like a voluntary assignment, and work out the happiest possible human destiny.

This—not more and not less—is what I have meant to say. Men and women have no one to turn to but themselves and each other; but they do have themselves and each other, and if they turn to themselves and each other in good faith and with intelligence they will be surprised by the idealistic fecundity of the human mind and heart, and by the ideal possibilities of the natural environment upon which they may draw to enrich and elevate their lives.

xi

Nothing is said in this chapter in defense of the notion that to surrender faith in God means also to surrender everything which historically has been associated with that faith, especially every form of nonrational attitude and practice. I have not said, and I have no intention of saying, that the nontheist must limit his interests to what can be weighed and measured, intellectually delineated, or presented in some embodied form with clear outlines; that he must never allow himself to stray into the land described by Virginia Woolf, where words "fold their wings and sit huddled like rooks on the tops of the trees in winter." On the contrary, the nontheist I have in mind is pledged to uncommon moral independence in the face of the two commanding voices of our time—the strident voice of business and the proud voice of science. He prizes attitudes of mind and heart that transcend practical demands and elude intellectual formulas.

Let the first be a feeling of oneness with the unending procession of living forms that has marched and marches with unresting feet through time, stepping from death to death, but itself not dying. This feeling is naturally and properly most poignant as it touches the surging life of mankind. A certain variety of interest in man is almost universal—interest in his thrift, his morals, his politics, his religion. Another interest is correspondingly rare, one which does not end where practical purposes end, but finds something perennially fascinating in man as man. It is of this interest I am speaking, the interest in the individual not as a letter in an alphabet, but as an undeciphered word in a possible sentence of weight and beauty. "Surely," as Henry Beston says, "there are few moods of the spirit more worthy of our care than those in which we reverence, even for a moment, our tragic and bewildered kind."

And there is the primitive, elemental sense of community with the all-sustaining earth. Thoreau's ability to convey this sense in words made him immortal. Who that has felt its vague, dumb rapture has not been aware of the profound influence on his spirit? A man may be much out of doors and remain a stranger to nature's ways, or he may open a hospitable imagination to the revolving year and come under the influence of a redemptive intimacy. He may follow the sun in its journeys through the seasons; may drift with rivers to the sea; may smell the winds and the rains and note the never-ending play of life all about them. As he does, his spirit will be lifted above pettiness and distraction and rendered immune for the time to the fever frequently made identical with civilization.

A mood of reverence for "our tragic and bewildered kind," and an elemental sense of community with the all-sustaining earth which our fathers had and we have lost, these two—and a third. Most of us believe that life must be nailed down along all its edges lest some act or thought or dream tear loose the fabric of values woven by tradition, and civilization, fluttering in the wind of impulse, is little by little torn to shreds. It seems to me better to admit that in things which matter most we are compelled to leave something at loose ends. The world would be a vastly better place if all of us, and especially our leaders, were more ready to admit the ancient and eternal truth—I don't know. But whether we admit it or not there is always an unexplored beyond, always mystery.

A conscious awareness of this mystery does healing work on the inward man. It is the healing work of acknowledged ignorance in the revered presence of that which eludes comprehension—the incomprehensible in each other, in the life we are called upon to live, in the great cosmic setting that reaches from our feet to the infinities. Benjamin Blood was acquainted with the feeling. "Behind the proudest consciousness that ever reigned," he said, "reason and wonder blush face to face."

These are qualities of experience that may be counted upon not only to work against drabness and vulgarity, but to provide a positive source of inner renewal analogous to that found in the best forms of theism. We have practical tasks to care for. We have economic, political, moral, and educational problems to solve. Our sense of human solidarity is weak. We are too quick to rise against each other. We have still to find civilized means to settle international conflicts.

These are basic obligations. The man who intentionally slights them and leaves to other people all responsibility for improving the social order he enjoys the benefits of is not playing a man's part. Yet life at its best includes not only the performance of duties but emancipation from duties. We need to keep a window open toward the uncharted. We need to follow trails leading beyond workaday walls to heights from which we catch glimpses of wide vistas.

❧ XII ❧

"WALK TOGETHER CHILDREN"

i

We have reached the concluding chapter of this study of The Human Enterprise. Suppose, before we stop, we try to discern, even if it must be dimly, the meaning of the long struggle through which the human race has come to the present. Possibly we may get from it a sense of something irrepressible in man on which we can count as we face the future.

Fifty or sixty million years ago when the great reptiles were lords of life, and the earth was as if made for their use, small mammals appeared in what is now Wyoming. They were insignificant-looking creatures. The reptiles would have called them vermin. In spite of their diminutive size they were peculiarly fitted to survive, equipped as they were with a greatly enlarged brain case in proportion to the size of the body, eyes capable of stereoscopic vision, and grasping forepaws. They were forerunners of the primates.

As in other instances of animal origin in North America the venture proved abortive. Prior, however, to their extinction on this continent, numbers of these primate pioneers had migrated over the Alaskan land bridge to the Old World and over the Isthmus of Panama to Central and South America. In time genera of monkeys evolved in Vera Cruz, Brazil, and elsewhere on this side of the Atlantic, and in Egypt, Africa, India, and Europe on the other side. Primitive apes, too, came into existence and branched off in diverse directions. A most remarkable early proliferation of the monkey and ape lines occurred in the Sivalik Hills of Northern India. The wealth of fossil remains discovered along these outlying slopes of the Himalaya Mountains includes dog-faced monkeys, short-tailed baboons, and apes allied to modern chimpanzees and gorillas.

In some such active center of biological evolution the transition from anthropoid ape to subman must have taken place, three or four million years ago. The region of the earth in which the decisive steps were taken is not agreed upon. It may have been near the Caspian Sea or northeast of Tibet. Possibly it was in the heart of Africa or somewhere in that vast continent, much of it now submerged, which once extended from East Africa through India and Java to the Philippine Islands.

The exact locality is in doubt, the fact is not. Wherever they may have originated, hordes of submen were roaming far and wide over the earth probably a million years ago. Separated by seas, deserts, forests, or mountains as they came in time to be, they developed distinctive characteristics. They followed paths that ultimately led to destruction, but also paths that opened out into amazing achievement. Toilsomely they advanced toward the true human type.

Discoveries of the last seventy-five years make it possible
to form some idea of their evolutionary procession—the
ape-man of Java, who had learned to walk upright; Piltdown
men, with an almost human cranium but a simian jaw;
Pekin men, acquainted with fire; Heidelberg men, chinless
as apes, but with human teeth; Neanderthal men, having
a skull capacity equal, if not superior, to the lowest human
races now existing; men of the Reindeer Age, who had acquired the large frontal brain and the well-developed association centers of the present human species.

ii

With the coming of the Reindeer Men *homo sapiens*
had arrived. Unheralded and leaving no sign whence they
came, these remote ancestors of ours arrived in Europe
twenty thousand or more years ago. Their progenitors had
doubtless been moving toward the human level for hundreds of thousands of years. In such races as the Cro-
Magnons, they had become impressive creatures, tall, of
commanding carriage, and with foreheads that had lost the
heavy browridges of their apelike forebears. They retained
from the remote past ferocious and brutish traits in contrast with highly developed manual dexterity and marked
psychic capacity. They were expert hunters armed with
effective weapons. They could prepare and sew hides. They
had acquired a language and they buried their dead with
some thought of the continuance of life. Their work in
sculpture and line drawing, their paintings, made with a
few pigments they had discovered, show highly developed
powers of observation and marked artistic skill.

For a long time the progressive stock lived side by side with the more backward Neanderthalers and perhaps other submen. There may have been interbreeding, although it is more likely that the superior and the inferior races waged war on each other and gave no quarter. Bones found in ancient cave deposits bear witness to bloody conflicts and cannibal feasts. Whatever the cause may have been, the submen disappeared. Long before the beginning of written history the backward stocks had been exterminated or pushed into remote corners of the world, and the progressive races had responded to the command, "Be fruitful, and multiply."

Unnumbered centuries of upward movement, of which this account conveys the merest inkling, thus stretch back of the appearance of civilized man. The material aspects of the long journey are unrecoverable except for the weapons and implements found strewn along the way, the scratches on cave walls and ceilings, and the pathetically small collection of human bones. On the immaterial or psychic side evidence is scanty indeed. What fears and hopes, what pains and pleasures these early men experienced we can only try to imagine.

As the student of human history works his way back to the farthest borders of civilization he beholds, rising out of the haze of prehistory, the towers and walls of communities. Men are already gathered in the alluvial deltas of the Tigris and the Euphrates, and in the rich valley of the Nile. The nomad has largely given up his wandering. Not only has the movable retreat, half cart and half tent, been left behind for a settled abode, but so has the early subterranean structure, half cave and half hut. Men dwell in houses similar to those in use today. They are no longer solely dependent for food on wild plants and wild animals. Fields of cultivated grain ripen under the sun and the fruits of agricultural labor are garnered into spacious granaries; while the ox, the ass, the dog, the goat, the horse, the camel, have been trained to lighten human toil and to help assure a steady supply of food. Artisans have learned to make durable vessels of clay, beautiful furniture, weapons and tools of copper. Fine art and music have developed. The various occupations have been organized as a communal enterprise, regulated by custom and stabilized by inherited tradition. And the unpretentious gods of earlier times have grown into awesome beings that are trusted to give aid and protection to the community.

iii

What an enormous distance man had already come and what driving purpose to advance he had already shown when the historian first catches sight of him! The advance had of course cost a price. Looking back from where we are, habituated to our way of life, we cannot tell whether the price was or was not too high. The freedom of the savage to go his own way at his own hazard had to be sacrificed. Large numbers of people had to live under some form of centralized authority. Burdens had to be borne which were absent from the more roving and individualistic life that had passed away. Forced labor, wars of conquest, race hatreds, class antagonisms, acquisitive ambitions, and the various kinds of envy which differences in social status tend to incite, these were part of life in populous cities, rich in material goods, adorned with stately architecture, supported by far-flung commerce, controlled by political and religious institutions.

In the course of time the burdens which communal life entailed bore down heavily on the unlucky many, while the lucky few escaped. Evidence of this comes to us from the oldest societies. In Iran an elaborate theory of good and evil seems to have developed out of the injustice suffered by the workers at the hands of those who exercised power over them. In Babylon the famous code of Hammurabi was based on the frank recognition of social inequality. And according to J. E. Breasted's highly significant conclusion, ancient Egyptian writings, which must be dated at least four thousand years ago, are social tracts composed as "campaign propaganda" in a "crusade for social justice." The social idealism of the time was, in his view, inspired by the hope of Messiah, a righteous ruler who was to come and "usher in a golden age of justice for all mankind."

The meaning of these facts is unmistakable. Organized society, an early social invention of man, was deflected from its possible function as a means to general human happiness. The assemblage of men in large aggregates afforded an opportunity for the enrichment of the life of a social class through the exploitation of the great majority, and either the temptation was too strong to be resisted, or the rulers of these aggregates saw no other or better way to proceed.

This is not to say that man's reaching out for a satisfying life had been conquered. It is unconquerable. When it is blocked, and no way can be found around the obstruction, the time will come when the whole social arrangement will be overthrown. The literature of ancient Egypt shows that the existing social arrangement was expected to last forever. An Egyptian Pharaoh had these picturesque words inscribed on his tomb doors: "Eternity is afraid of them." The kingdom over which he ruled doubtless seemed to him as ageless as his tomb. Social injustice, however, grew unbearable. The oppressed arose and destroyed the social order in which they struggled as they thought in vain. Mobs raced through the streets robbing and destroying. They tore up legal documents, trampled upon them, and strutted about "as if they were the Nine Gods." "Every man," it was said, "hath his face downcast against his brethren." Persons of rank were dragged out and murdered. Impregnable tomb doors were thrown open. The indestructible kingdom was destroyed as by a cataclysm of nature.

Some of the outcries of despair and disillusion which this social revolution called forth are transcribed in Adolph Erman's *The Literature of the Ancient Egyptians*. There are many like these:

Nay, but gold and lapis lazuli, silver and turquoise . . . are hung about the necks of slave-girls. But noble ladies (?) walk through the land, and mistresses of houses say, "Would that we had something that we might eat."

Nay, but laughter hath perished and is no longer made. It is grief that walketh through the land, mingled with lamentations.

Would that there might be an end of men, no conception, no birth! Oh that the earth would cease from noise, and strife be no more!"

Possibly out of this very upheaval, or, if not out of it then out of another one, a new idea was born which was profoundly significant not only for the then existing emergency, but for the whole human enterprise. Mr. Breasted has named it "The Dawn of Conscience." It was the thought of moral character, the conception of right as distinguished from wrong in the ethical sense. In its inception this idea seems to have reflected a great purpose. It was meant to curb the lust for power which the gathering of human beings in large numbers had released. But like the earlier contrivance, organized society, ethical conduct was in time diverted from its best use. It was misapplied to advance restricted interests, sometimes the basest interests.

Just how this happened cannot be determined. Ruins are cryptic. Some students claim that the suppression of the common man was the intended objective from the beginning. They believe that the idea of morality was invented for that purpose and no other by those who aimed to exploit their less sophisticated fellows. This interpretation will always appeal to some people, especially to such as are in the habit of deciding complicated questions by disregarding their complexity. All we are reasonably certain of is that as the idea of moral character came under the influence of secular leadership, so that the distinction between right and wrong could be used as an effective means for perpetuating the existing order of things, it was so used. Moral aspiration was encouraged in the many by powerful minorities as a means of advancing themselves and their class, and the many, who had their own schemes to put over, often found moral slogans helpful in turning the trick. We may disregard these complicating factors providing we remember that from the birth of the idea of moral character it was the aim of religious and secular authority to define its meaning, and providing we avoid the oversimple notion that the origin and spread of moral ideas must be ascribed to hypocritical priests and self-seeking laymen.

The idea of moral character was a discovery of human beings and was therefore imperfect at best. Imperfect human beings had to put the idea to work. Existing customs, also imperfect, were resistant to change then as now. These factors had their effect. But they should not conceal the driving purpose to elevate conduct out of which moral idealism was born. This moral idealism is the thing to be kept in view, even while we admit that neither then nor since have its full social potentialities been realized. Secular life and secular leadership were doubtless in part responsible for this, but the direction in which religion developed was even more responsible. By a succession of sublimations the good life was translated into otherworldly terms, so that justice and righteousness in practical dealings became of less and less importance in comparison with "higher" interests, then of no importance whatever. Secular interests were consequently left to work out their own development, until practical success and moral achievement were confined to separate, and finally to antagonistic, realms of behavior.

iv

The spiritualizing tendency appears to have taken its rise among the very people who originated the idea of character. For a long time it did not occur to men to associate their gods with ethical problems. A god was not thought to concern himself with right and wrong. He had other business to see to. Social strife in Egypt led to the desperate step of calling on the gods to take the side of social justice. There was nothing illogical in this extension of divine helpfulness, for if a god could be counted on to help fight enemies outside the state, why not enemies inside the state? But a god of war, of fertility, of this, that, or the other thing which might be desired, is not necessarily a god of righteousness. Centuries of intellectual and ethical development were required to reach the stage where moral attributes could be associated with divine power.

When the union of the two had been brought about, a new orientation was given to right and wrong. Right and wrong lost their original human reference. In Persia, the conflict between the good and the bad was lifted out of the human setting into the cosmos. It was seen as a struggle between mighty superhuman powers, of which the earthly struggle was a puny duplication. In Athens, where an ideal of moral excellence had been reached which, for inclusiveness of interests and the harmonious relationship of personal and civic aims, has never been surpassed, foremost thinkers transfigured the good into supersensible immateriality, and evil into a pure negation. In India the very differentiation between good and bad purposes was deprived of meaning. Every earthly aim was looked upon as bad; the one and only good end was the extinction of all desire.

These spiritualizing traditions trickled into Palestine and there, merging with Hebrew tradition and current revolutionary social movements, eventually inundated the West. No one can say how differently Occidental history might have developed, and how greatly altered our scheme of life might be today, if instead of somber Christianity it had been the sunlit Confucianism of China that flooded the Occident. Nor is there any way of telling what might have happened if Jesus had not been crucified at the beginning of his career, or if Saul of Tarsus, on the way to Damascus, had not suddenly seen a strange light.

As things turned out, the world-denying currents gathered momentum as they spread from Palestine. Their confluence produced institutionalized supernaturalism. The western world passed under the control of a religious organization which for a dozen centuries drew to itself the aspirational outreachings of all who lived in the West.

According to church doctrine, man's life on earth was Jehovah's plan for populating a heavenly community. Earthly cities were the means of establishing a City of God. Many were called to struggle in the one in order that a few might be chosen to attend upon God in the other. For this reason was the cosmos created and history unfolded. Men of all races were to live and die that this plan might be carried out. They were to forget the squalor and misery of their present surroundings; they were to bear hardship like good soldiers in the country of the enemy; they were to school themselves to look upon the City of Man as an evil and accursed place. It was their privilege to spread this social theory as "tidings of great joy" to the "heathen that sit in darkness."

The early Christian phase of the human story is as

complex and elusive as any that can be studied. An incredible amount of excellent work has been done to collect, classify, and interpret the facts, but the subject remains in many respects unclear and probably always will. This much we may claim to know, that the religion of which we are speaking had back of it the positive, strenuous force of man's purpose to advance, and that unfavorable conditions deflected it into channels which prevented its possibilities from being realized. Humane feelings, artistic talent, loyalty to principle, good impulses of all kinds were directed away from investment in the activities connected with making a living. Church religion was more and more committed to the preservation of doctrinal or material property, until it proved willing to sacrifice human interests and human beings themselves.

v

Man knew how to get around the attempt to restrict his life to a piece of himself. Roguish gargoyles looking down from cathedral gutters suggest that the "old Adam" had not been entirely suppressed. Behind the conventional acquiescence in world denial we may, if we look, see a passionate courting of life. Though we cannot revive the past, we can evoke an image of the past from the records that remain. We learn that while ecclesiastical power had spread over one area of activity after another, the natural man had not heeded St. Paul's admonition and died. The natural man had remained very much alive. When the way was opened, as by the Crusades, the travels of Marco Polo, or the voyages of the explorers, in a word, whenever and wherever there was opportunity, the virility of mankind burst forth in exultant activity. Even supernatural religion was tempted to admire out of the corner of its eye the satisfactions of a rejuvenated life on earth.

Revival of earthly interest drew sustenance and courage from Greek literature. Perhaps it did more. Still, medievalism was not pushed aside by a power gained from acquaintance with literature. The power was incomparably more compelling. The new magnitude of commerce, improved means of communication, growth of cities and of wealth, by altering the medieval man's manner of living, his employment, his means of satisfaction and amusement, his economic and social status, altered his outlook on everything.

At such times some men will look about for intellectual justification of impulses and desires. The ancient classics were able to provide this. They could give exalted expression to the cultural demands of the exuberant age. The influence of the Greek spirit which had flowed underground for centuries, perhaps refreshing an individual here and there, streamed into the open again and life turned green along its course. Even today one who enters as a student into Greek history bears away a lifelong and beautiful memory. What the impact of Greek ideas must have evoked in the medievalists who were prepared for it, what its flights and profundities and artistry must have meant to those whom it liberated, we moderns can scarcely appreciate.

vi

It was in the sixteenth century, and especially in the seventeenth, that the reassertion of natural humanity reached a climax. Then was undertaken the most daring project which had yet been attempted to improve man's state on earth. It had its beginning in a deliberate, concerted effort made by a succession of unusual minds to "see things as in themselves they really are." Something of the sort had been initiated in Greece, in China, probably elsewhere, but the time was not ripe for it. By the seventeenth century everything was ready for a new start. Acquaintances with empirical fact had greatly increased, numerous practical inventions had been made, pioneers like Leonardo and Paracelsus had stimulated the naturalistic impulse, humanistic programs, like that of Erasmus, had touched the imagination of educated men. The world was on tiptoe for some great event when modern science was born.

The distinguishing characteristics of these early scientists was their determination to discover truth through the study of the physical world. They had faith that in this way, rather than by fitting ideas together into a rational system as the scholastic thinkers had done, a solid foundation could be laid for human betterment. They were uplifted by the conviction that at last, after ages of failure or only moderate success, the means to true knowledge had at last been found in the experimental study of nature. All kinds of mechanical contrivances would be invented. Grinding toil and poverty would be done away with. There would be relief from physical and mental suffering. Universal well-being and the Golden Age would follow in due time.

We who live in the twentieth century, in the direct path of the scientific advance, need not be told that the daily life of mankind has been greatly ameliorated by what men of science have achieved. There are people who make light of these achievements, but even they are usually careful to take advantage of them. Science has not only added to physical comfort, improved bodily and mental health, relieved mankind of numerous fears, broadened and civilized the general attitude toward life, but has provided the human race with an instrument for brightening existence for ages to come.

In the scientific temper of mind human intelligence has, so far at least as we can now see, reached its highest efficiency, and in scientific inquiry at its best the human spirit has attained to a purity of aspiration unsurpassed by any other form of devotion. To the honest scientific worker, as P. W. Bridgman has said, as well as to many who are not scientists, scientific integrity appears "as the last flowering of the genius of humanity, the culmination of a long cultural history, and the one thing that differentiates man most notably from his biological companions." In his article, "The Struggle for Intellectual Integrity," which appeared in *Harper's Magazine*, December, 1933, Mr. Bridgman speaks of science with the authority of intimate acquaintance: "Once the scientific worker has started living the life of intellectual honesty, he finds growing within him the realization that he is in the power of something much more than merely a tool by which he may get the

right answers. . . . He finds something fine in the selflessness involved in carrying through a train of thought careless
of its personal implications; he feels a traitor to something
deep within him if he refuses to follow out logical implications because he sees that they are going to be unpleasant;
and he exults that he belongs to a race which is capable of
such emotions." Still, as we have seen, many people, including scientists, contemplate future scientific progress with
uneasiness.

vii

One legitimate ground for uneasiness at the moment is
the spectacular utilization of science in the service of sheer
might. The danger in this use of science is as obvious as
it is incalculable. In its contemporary form it is a new thing
in the world, one that has so profoundly changed the
hazards of life for the individual and for society that it is
impossible to find a parallel in the past. Another ground
for uneasiness, equally legitimate and more closely interwoven with all our everyday processes and activities, is the
exploitation of scientific research for commercial ends. The
same age that saw the beginning of modern Science also
saw the beginning of modern Business. With each generation they have been drawn closer together. Today in their
organized, co-operative unity they constitute perhaps our
greatest institution of potential good and harm.

There is always a gap between a scientific discovery or a
mechanical invention and its practical utilization. Finan-
ciers, entrepreneurs, and the men we used to call Captains
of Industry bridge this gap. It is this alliance between

science and business, "science in action, or militant science," as it has been called, that has created the problem which the early scientists could not foresee. Some industrialists— Henry P. Kendall was an example—think of industry and commerce "as social instruments to be used in such ways that people may be developed and human values enriched." Others have the one aim of the Chicago businessman whom President Hutchins quotes as announcing: "Our only motive is to make a profit." The president of the Philadelphia Electric Company assured his hearers at a recent meeting of educators in New York City, that "businessmen of today are more conscious than ever before of their responsibility to society at large. They see themselves as trustees for the joint interests of the four parties recognized as essential components of present-day business—workers, stockholders, customers, and the public." A steel magnate in Detroit, on the other hand, denounced programs aiming at a greater degree of economic justice as "weird and fantastic man-made laws, which seek to turn aside God's eternal forces."

It would be extremely difficult if not impossible to decide with any accuracy which of these quotations is most representative of the group for which it speaks. At all events the present and future social meaning of science is closely bound up with the alliance that has been brought about between scientific investigation and business ambition. It is a conspicuous example of man's ability to design and put to work great social instruments. But since it is an instrument it can be misused. Some persons in every community make a better and some a worse use of it. To some persons life is a series of business transactions. Their acquisitive intensity distils a poisonous essence and injects it into every human relation. Compared with ruling individuals of this type, armed as they are with the implements and weapons provided by science, those who ruled in other days were gentlemen and amateurs in the wielding of power.

The problem, however, is not set for us by extraordinary individuals alone, but by the pattern of life in which we are all implicated. The malady that has to be cured is a general business-mindedness; therefore a symptomatic treatment of flagrant individual eruptions does not reach the seat of the trouble. Adequate therapy makes it necessary "not to denounce, not to ridicule, but to understand"—to understand, and I would add to Spinoza's words, to do what we can that things are changed for the better. Men must differ in occupation, in what they need and in what they desire beyond their needs, yet underneath they are united in the human venture and must succeed or fail together. It cannot be the course of wisdom blindly to sharpen and deepen our differences though we wreck the machinery on which civilized life has come to depend.

viii

As populations have concentrated in cities, as hungers developed that had not been dreamed of and as the multiplying desires were satisfied out of the growing store collected in all the corners of the world from the never-resting machinery of trade; as one mechanical triumph has followed another and each spectacular project for harnessing natural forces has made way for a greater; as these things have happened, men have been drawn, as if by an accelerating centripetal force, into a stupendous producing-distributing mechanism. It would be useless to argue against this outcome as if we could be persuaded to turn away from it. We cannot be persuaded to turn away from it, because we are part of it, and are conditioned to want what it supplies. And it would not be well for us if we could be persuaded; for although the business mechanism may be misused, it can supply the resources basic to civilized living in a measure not possible before.

We cannot prosper in the fullest and finest sense, I take pains to repeat, if the occupations essential to our very existence are regarded as being inherently devoid of ethical quality, necessarily committed to purely materialistic aims. Those who do the work of feeding, clothing, housing, transporting us, the millions who in one way and another add to the comfort and convenience of living, do more than that. They contribute to life's dignity and beauty. Many of them, although never putting the idea into words, look upon their calling as part of the general effort to make life more livable. Were the inarticulate but practically applied idealism of such merchants, clerks, secretaries, laborers, farmers, to die out, it would be a greater social calamity than if our articulate experts in idealistic theory were reduced to silence.

This is a fact which does not get the understanding it should. It must of course be seen in relation with another fact, well stated by Robert Brooks: "No eulogies of the achievements of business can offset the roll call of industrial pathologies. . . . In addition to producing goods, modern business also produces chronic unemployment, avoidable industrial accidents, disease and unrest, old-age dependence, business cycles, and fantastic inequalities in the distribution of the national income." That is to say, in the most spectacular social institution of our day we observe once more the combined effect of incredible propulsiveness, inventive genius, and the deflection of the invented instrument from its highest usefulness.

ix

No one can tell the story of man's rise and development without omitting innumerable important episodes; nor can he tell it in perfect faithfulness to the relative significance of those he includes. His account unavoidably takes on a dramatic emphasis which gives it a subjective slant. The best any author can do is to recognize the inevitableness of the storyteller's bias, to guard against its distorting influence, and to present his version as openly and clearly as he can.

In the simplified picture of this chapter three things stand out prominently and they grow in impressiveness as they are considered. The propulsiveness of mankind is one of these, a propulsiveness which no obstacle or catastrophe has yet brought to a halt. Equally striking is man's resourcefulness, his seemingly exhaustless ability to invent mechanical, intellectual, and social instruments to help himself on. The third is the tendency of man's very creativeness to interfere with social progress. Tools, organizations, institutions draw people to themselves whose chief interest it becomes to perpetuate them and to enhance their prestige in the human economy. Thus groups are divided from one another by the pursuit of specialized life purposes. Equilibrium of a kind is established among them from sheer necessity, for without it society would fall apart into units which cannot exist alone; but it is in the main an equilibrium brought about by a form of struggle and survival which becomes increasingly precarious as specialization advances and the problem grows more and more complex.

We have reached a stage in the development of human interrelations when this accidental equilibrium will no longer do. We must move on from group-conscious to man-conscious planning, as earlier in history individual interests had to be enlarged to include group interests. Enjoyment or misery is always individual in nature, and to some extent what an individual enjoys or suffers will be dependent upon his own effort; but now as never before everyone is at the mercy of what happens in the wide world beyond the individual's control. This suggests the size and the character of the task to be taken in hand. As Mr. Bridgman has said: "No one who has not thought about it can realize how pathetically deficient we are at present in even the preliminary data which are necessary before a start can be made in living a rationally ordered life. The development of new philosophies, new psychologies, and new biologies are necessary." But we need not wait to find the preliminary data. Difficult as the task is we have more than enough knowledge to start with and it will be added to if we look for and apply it. "Real discouragement," as Mr. Bridgman has also said, "need not be faced unless it should prove after full self-consciousness of the situation has been awakened and time has been allowed for the terribly complex adjustments, that we are incapable of creating the opportunities that we need."

x

We have taken a cursory glance at the human story, at the evolution of man's animal progenitors millions of years ago, the emergence of submen, then of man himself, still incredibly far in the past, and, finally, the succession of remarkable social inventions through which the material and ethical level of daily life has been elevated. We have seen that the community, moral character, religion, science, business, each has contributed to social progress, but that *each has tended to become its own justification for being*, and so has been arrested in its development as an agency for the larger good of man.

This concluding chapter has therefore summed up and confirmed the position taken in the book as a whole. What we lack is not energy or idealism; it is a comprehensive and workable philosophy of life for those who are in it and of it; a philosophy which sees in the natural and social environments positive means for human advancement, and which aims to include all men and the whole man in its vision.

A philosophy such as this, at once realistic and dedicated to the attainment of the completest and most satisfying life, is by some modern thinkers made identical with religion. What it shall be called is of secondary importance. The thing of importance is that the mood shall grow upon us; that in the churches, the schools, the colleges, the public service, and thence outward until it permeates every calling and occupation, we grow in the consciousness of a common task in which all the functions of life are involved, and that we learn better and better the art of co-operative practice.

The endeavor has been well named by A. E. Haydon "The Quest of the Ages." "Seen in longer perspective," he finds it to be "the heroic adventure of earth-born man wrestling for self-fulfillment on a tiny planet swung in the vast immensities of the stars." It is the embodiment of a great hope, "the hope of a good life in a good world," a good life of comradeship and laughter and self-respecting work. "The fires of that hope," as he says, "were kindled in lowly organisms at the dawn of time. They blazed into impressive burning in man, the creator of culture." Through frustration and betrayal those fires have "remained an undying flame." It seems to me beyond dispute that neither religion, social idealism, nor philosophy can be separated from this undying flame and retain any vital meaning for contemporary men and women.

The deepest source of a man's philosophy, the one that shapes and nourishes it, is faith or lack of faith in mankind. If he has confidence in human beings and believes that something fine can be achieved through them, he will acquire ideas about life and about the world which are in harmony with his confidence. Lack of confidence will generate corresponding ideas. A man's opinion of mankind may seem to originate in knowledge of physical nature and society; I believe it to be derived from first-hand experience with his fellows. Consequently the growth of active division among men in recent years has resulted in social ideologies, national and racial theories, conceptions of the world in which we live, all of which rest on the premise that as realists men must regard each other as natural enemies who must settle their differences by cunning and might. It is of the profoundest importance that we see through these disuniting verbal or intellectual precipitates to the experiences of disillusion and suffering which caused men to lose faith in men, and started them on those courses of aggression which then divided them still more.

Historically it has been the mission of the religious spirit to overcome these destructive tendencies. Religious leaders have at times misled their followers. Organized religion has been guilty of hypocrisy and cruelty. The religious spirit, however, in and out of churches, has stead-fastly refused to accept a degraded, miserable, or hopeless life as proper to man. And it has provided individuals and groups with the imaginative and practical means of unify-ing their desires, thus making it possible for them to expe-rience the sense of security and the peace of mind which most persons must have to remain normal human beings. The question is whether in these days of testing religious people have the insight and the will to refuse the leadership of those in State, Church, Science, or Business, who, how-ever they may talk, are indifferent or hostile toward the one interest which, from the human point of view, transcends every other—an organization of affairs which will enable mankind to move step by step toward the fulfillment of life generously and nobly conceived.

xi

We have tried to look from a hill instead of from the clouds. It would have been easy to see all hope for the future of mankind blacked out. But it has looked black before, and men and women of courage have pressed on, confident that a brighter day lay ahead. "The things in civilization we most prize," as John Dewey has told us, "are not of ourselves. They exist by grace of the doings and sufferings of the continuous human community in which we are a link. Ours is the responsibility of conserving, transmitting, rectifying, and expanding the heritage of values we have received that those who come after us may receive it more solid and secure, more widely accessible and more generously shared than we have received it. Here are all the elements for a religious faith that shall not be confined to sect, class, or race. Such a faith has always been implicitly the common faith of mankind. It remains to make it explicit and militant."

No person of sensibility will think of a task of these dimensions without feelings of misgiving. He will sometimes wonder whether the whole struggle may not be doomed to failure. But he will take heart as he remembers those who have traveled the way before him. The march has been long and trying—a march not of forty years or forty decades, but of forty times forty centuries; a march through the wilderness of brute nature, through ice ages, floods, and earthquakes, through Black Deaths and World Wars, through terrors born of superstition and the cold ingenuity of reason, through selfishness, laziness, weakness of will—

on and on toward a Promised Land pictured by an unconquerable urgency in the human spirit.

The drive of that resistless march is in us and about us. It should give us hope. The attitude of mind needed in our world, by whatever name it may be known, is outspoken reverence for this long pilgrimage, and outspoken confidence in the men and women who march in it today. Out of the lives of unnumbered millions who have ceased from struggling and are at rest, and of the hopes of millions who still push on, the spirit of man calls to us, to each of us, whatever the Promised Land he seeks; calls to each of us and says, in the words of the pilgrims of darker skin:

Oh, walk together children,
Don't you get weary,
There's a great Camp Meeting in the Promised Land.

BIBLIOGRAPHY

A short bibliography is here given of some of the books and printed articles from which quotations appear in the foregoing chapters. It has seemed best to refer to these books and articles, rather than to give citations for the passages quoted, on the assumption that any reader who desires to go more fully into the discussion will do so most profitably to himself, and most justly to the authors concerned, if he reads a good deal more that it was feasible to quote.

A number of books and writings have been included in this bibliography from which no quotations were taken, but which I believe will be of special value to the serious student of the subjects covered.

None of the chapters in this volume has heretofore been published in its present form. The first chapter is based on an address delivered at a meeting of philosophical associations in New York City; the heading of the second chapter was previously used as the title of an article in *The New Humanist*; the chapter on man borrows from an article called "What Is Man?" printed in *The International Journal of Ethics*; Chapter XI is in debt to my contributions to the "Conversation," *Is There A God?* which was published originally in *The Christian Century*; but all this material has been so thoroughly revised and so expanded that even these portions of the book are new in form and thought.

I wish to thank the authors and publishers from whose works I have quoted, although specific permission was not asked because of the brevity of the quotations. The

371

following publishers have granted me permission to quote from the works indicated which are published and copyrighted by them. I wish to thank them for the privilege.

The American Mercury, "Why We Do Not Behave Like Human Beings," by Ralph Adams Cram.

The Christian Century, "The Cardinal Wins," by Carl Knudsen, and "The Whole Gospel of Christ," by Bishop Francis J. McConnell.

Doubleday, Doran and Company, *Virginia*, by Ellen Glasgow.

Farrar and Rinehart, *What God Means to Me*, by Upton Sinclair (Copyright, 1936).

Harcourt, Brace and Company, *Quack, Quack!* by Leonard Woolf.

Harper and Brothers, "Hymn to the Dark," from *The Fox of Peapack*, by E. B. White, and *The Quest of the Ages*, by A. E. Haydon.

Holt and Company, *Things and Ideals*, by M. C. Otto, and "Wilderness," from *Cornhuskers*, by Carl Sandburg.

The Houghton Mifflin Company, *Behold Our Land*, by Russell Lord, *Impressions and Comments*, Second Series, by Havelock Ellis, and *Letters*, by Franklin K. Lane.

King Features Syndicate, "Today," by Arthur Brisbane.

Alfred A. Knopf, *Decline of the West*, by Oswald Spengler, and *Tertium Organum*, by P. D. Uspenskii.

The Liveright Publishing Corporation, *On My Way*, by Art Young.

The Macmillan Company, *Labor and Administration*, by John R. Commons, and *New Pathways in Science*, by Sir Arthur Eddington.

The McGraw-Hill Book Company, *Rich Land, Poor Land*, by Stuart Chase.

The New Yorker, "Hymn to the Dark," from *The Fox of Peapack*, by E. B. White, printed first in *The New Yorker*.

W. W. Norton and Company, *Science and the Human Temperament*, by Erwin Schrödinger.

The Open Court Publishing Company, *Experience and Nature*, by John Dewey.

G. P. Putnam's Sons, *Apes, Men, and Morons*, by E. A. Hooton.

Science, "Conservation of Minerals," by C. K. Leith.

Charles Scribner's Sons, *The Great Amphibium*, by Joseph Needham.

Sheed and Ward, *The Bourgeois Mind*, by Nicholas Berdyaev.

Simon and Schuster, "Life Can Be Worth Living," by Julian Huxley, in *I Believe*, edited by Clifton Fadiman (Copyright, 1939).

Survey Graphic, "Twenty Years of Grace," by Morris Llewellyn Cooke.

The University of Chicago Press, *Frontiers of Public Administration*, by White, Dimock, and Gaus.

The University of Oklahoma Press, *Deserts on the March*, by Paul B. Sears (Copyright, 1935).

The Viking Press, *Along This Way*, by James Weldon Johnson (Copyright, 1933, by James Weldon Johnson).

The Yale University Press, *A Common Faith*, by John Dewey, and *The Universe and Life*, by H. S. Jennings.

READING LIST

Many points of view are represented by the books and
articles below. The student who wishes to analyze critically
the social thinking of our time will, I hope, find this list
helpful.

Barnes, Ernest William (Bishop of Birmingham), *Scientific Theory and Religion*, The Macmillan Company.

Benét, Stephen Vincent, *John Brown's Body*, Garden City,
Doubleday, Doran and Company.

Berdyaev, Nicholas, *The Bourgeois Mind*, Sheed and Ward.
Christianity and Class War, Sheed and Ward.
The End of Our Time, Sheed and Ward.

Bradley, F. H., *Appearance and Reality*, Sonnenschein.

Breasted, J. H., *The Dawn of Conscience*, Charles Scribner's Sons.

Brewster, Henry B., *The Prison, A Dialogue*, Wm. Heinemann, Ltd.

Bridgman, P. W., "The Struggle for Intellectual Integrity,"
Harper's Magazine, December, 1933.

Burtt, E. A., *The Metaphysical Foundations of Modern
Physical Science*, Harcourt, Brace and Company.

Chase, Stuart, *Rich Land, Poor Land*, McGraw-Hill Book
Company.

Cherry-Garrard, Apsley, *The Worst Journey in the World*,
The Dial Press.

Christian Century, The. I am under obligation to *The
Christian Century* for permission to quote from Bishop
McConnell's and Carl Knudsen's articles referred to
under their names, and also for the privilege of making use of my part of the discussion called, "Is There
A God?"

Chronicle of An Ancient Monastery. This chronicle, an extract from which was quoted in Chapter IV, was purchased by someone in the United States, but who the purchaser was has not been disclosed.

Cohen, Morris, *Reason and Nature* (especially the Epilogue), Harcourt, Brace and Company.

Commons, John R., "Utilitarian Idealism," *Labor and Administration*, The Macmillan Company.

Conklin, Edwin Grant, "Science and Ethics," *Science*, Vol. 86, pp. 595–603.

"What Shapes Our Ends?" *The American Scholar*, Vol. 6, No. 2, pp. 225–235.

Cooke, Morris Llewellyn, "Twenty Years of Grace," *Survey Graphic*, Vol. 24, pp. 277–282.

Cram, Ralph Adams, "Why We Do Not Behave Like Human Beings," *The American Mercury*, Vol. 27, pp. 41–48.

"The Limitations of Democracy," Rice Institute Pamphlet.

Dewey, John, *Experience and Nature*, Open Court Publishing Company.

A Common Faith, Yale University Press. Quotations in the text are from these books; I strongly recommend the reading, in addition, of *Human Nature and Conduct*, Henry Holt and Company and The Modern Library. "A God or The God," Mr. Dewey's critical book review of *Is There A God?*, *The Christian Century*, Vol. 50, pp. 192–196.

Dickinson, Emily, *Letters of Emily Dickinson*, Edited by Mabel Loomis Todd, Harper and Brothers.

Dykhuizen, George, *Soil Conservation, A Philosophical Viewpoint*, The Vermont Agricultural Extension Division.

Eddington, Sir Arthur, *New Pathways in Science*, The Macmillan Company.

Also his chapter in *Science and Religion, A Symposium*, no publisher given.

Ellis, Havelock, *Impressions and Comments, 2nd Series,* Houghton Mifflin Company.

"Harmony in Conflict," *The Nation,* Vol. 148, pp. 463–466.

Erman, Adolph, *The Literature of the Ancient Egyptians,* translated by A. M. Blackman, Methuen and Company.

Flexner, Abraham, "The Usefulness of Useless Knowledge," *Publication of The Squibb Institute for Medical Research,* Vol. 1, pp. 19–23.

Gilson, Etienne, *Medieval Universalism and Its Present Value,* Sheed and Ward.

Reason and Revelation in the Middle Ages, Charles Scribner's Sons.

Glasgow, Ellen, *Virginia,* Doubleday, Page and Company.

Hart, James H., "Humanism and the Snares of Materialism," *The New Humanist,* Vol. 4, No. 2, pp. 1–22. This article, a reply to Harry Emerson Fosdick's article, "Religion Without God or the Limitations of Humanism," is the most thoughtful and poetic argument for nontheistic religion which I remember to have read.

Haydon, A. Eustace, *The Quest of the Ages,* Harper and Brothers.

Hooton, E. A., *Apes, Men, and Morons,* G. P. Putnam's Sons.

Hutchins, Robert Maynard, *The Higher Learning in America,* Yale University Press.

No Friendly Voice, University of Chicago Press.

Huxley, Aldous, *Ends and Means,* Harper and Brothers.

Huxley, Julian, *Scientific Research and Social Needs,* Watts and Company.

"Life Can Be Worth Living," *The Nation,* Vol. 147, pp. 349–352. Later published in *I Believe,* edited by Clifton Fadiman, Simon and Schuster.

Chapter in *Science and Religion, A Symposium*, no publisher given.

Infeld, Leopold, *The World in Modern Science*, V. Gollancz.

James, William, *Pragmatism*, Longmans, Green and Company.

The Will to Believe, Longmans, Green and Company.

Jennings, H. S., *The Universe and Life*, Yale University Press.

Johnson, James Weldon, *Along This Way*, Viking Press.

Jones, Rufus, *The Testimony of the Soul*, The Macmillan Company.

Josephson, Matthew, *The Robber Barons*, Harcourt, Brace and Company.

Kerr, J. Graham, *Evolution*, The Macmillan Company.

Knudsen, Carl, "The Cardinal Wins," *The Christian Century*, Vol. 52, pp. 541–543.

Lane, Franklin K., *Letters, Personal and Political*, Edited by A. W. Lane and L. H. Wall, Houghton Mifflin Company. Personally, I find this book stimulating reading. It seems to me to be the kind of book which should be put before students in our High Schools and College in these times.

Leith, C. K., "Conservation of Minerals," *Science*, Vol. 82, pp. 109–117.

Livingstone, R. W., *The Greek Genius and Its Meaning to Us*, Oxford University Press.

Lord, Russell, *Behold Our Land*, Houghton Mifflin Company.

Markham, Edwin, "Earth Is Enough," *The Shores of Happiness and Other Poems*, Doubleday, Page and Company.

Mavity, Nancy Barr, "The Conditions of Tolerance," *The Unpopular Review*, Vol. 10, pp. 94–105.

McConnell, Francis J. (Bishop), "The Whole Gospel of Christ," a Christmas Sermon, *The Christian Century*, Vol. 51, pp. 1622–1625.

McIver, R. M., "Is Sociology a Natural Science?" *Publications of the American Sociological Society*, Vol. 25, pp. 25–35. To be read in connection with W. F. Ogburn's address (see below).

McWilliams, Carey, *Factories in the Field*, Little, Brown and Company. This book, "which tramples out the vintage of facts whence came John Steinbeck's *The Grapes of Wrath*," bears directly on the argument made in Chapters III and V of the present volume. It is a case study of commercial ruthlessness which deserves the widest possible publicity, especially among those who, like the present writer, hope to see practical-minded men and women participating in the shaping of social idealism. If it is impossible to rid society of the type of acquisitiveness which has the upper hand in the region studied by Mr. McWilliams, every attempt at a realistic idealism is doomed to fail. But the farm industrialists, big bankers, insurance and utility executives are not the whole people, even in California. I have a different kind of businessman in mind when I contend that social wounds must be healed from within.

Meiklejohn, Alexander, *What Does America Mean?* W. W. Norton and Company.

Miller, Dickinson S., "Free Will as Involving Determination and Inconceivable Without It," *Mind*, Vol. 44, No. 169, pp. 1–27. An illuminating discussion of a difficult but perennially interesting subject.

Muggeridge, Malcolm, Contributions to *Time and Tide*, an English journal of opinion, independent, and of high literary quality. See also his *Study of Samuel Butler*, G. P. Putnam's Sons.

Needham, Joseph, *The Great Amphibium*, Charles Scribner's Sons.

Man a Machine, W. W. Norton and Company.

Nettels, Curtis, *The Roots of American Civilization*, F. S. Crofts and Company.

Ogburn, W. F., "The Folk-ways of a Scientific Sociology," *The Scientific Monthly*, Vol. 30, pp. 300–306.

Osler, Sir William, *A Way of Life*, Paul B. Hoeber.

Planck, Max, *Religion und Naturwissenschaft*, Johann Ambrosius Barth.

Russell, Bertrand, *Problems of Philosophy*, Henry Holt and Company.

Saint Exupéry, Antoine de, *Wind, Sand and Stars*, Translated by Lewis Galantière, Reynal and Hitchcock. A remarkable book. Few such books are written in any generation. Eloquent with the truth of the human struggle and the indomitable spirit of man, it is the perfect antidote for those who have unwittingly swallowed the contemptuous cynicism of certain academic critiques of mankind.

Sandburg, Carl, "Wilderness," *Selected Poems*, Harcourt, Brace and Company. When I asked Carl Sandburg's permission to quote a portion of this poem, and told him that I wanted to try my hand at concluding verses with a somewhat different emphasis, he graciously replied: "I don't know what you're up to, but I'll take a chance."

Schrödinger, Erwin, *Science and the Human Temperament*, W. W. Norton and Company.

Sears, Paul B., *Deserts on the March*, University of Oklahoma Press.

Seaver, George, *Edward Wilson of the Antarctic*, E. P. Dutton and Company.

Sibley, William G., In "Along the Highway," *Chicago Daily Journal of Commerce*.

Sinclair, Upton, *What God Means to Me*, Farrar and Rinehart.

Smith, Logan Pearsall, *Trivia*, Doubleday, Page and Company.

Smuts, General J. C., "The Scientific World Picture of Today," Presidential Address, *Report of British Association for Advancement of Science*, 1931, pp. 1–18.

Soddy, Frederick, *Science and Life*, E. P. Dutton and Company.

Spengler, Oswald, *The Decline of the West*, Vol. II, Translated by C. F. Atkinson, Alfred A. Knopf.
Man and Technics, Translated by C. F. Atkinson, Alfred A. Knopf.

Stamp, Sir Josiah, "The Impact of Science Upon Society," Presidential Address, *Report of British Association for Advancement of Science*, 1936, pp. 1–26.

Stuart, M., *Francis Bacon*, Wm. Morrow and Company.

Thoreau, Henry, *Walden*, Houghton Mifflin Company.

Tomlinson, H. M., *All Our Yesterdays*, Grosset and Dunlap.
See also contributions to *Time and Tide*.

Uspenskii, P. D., *Tertium Organum*, Alfred A. Knopf.

Vaihinger, Hans, *The Philosophy of 'As If,'* Translated by C. K. Ogden, Harcourt, Brace and Company.

Wertheimer, Max, "Some Problems in the Theory of Ethics," *Social Research*, Vol. 2, pp. 353–357.

White, E. B., "Hymn to the Dark," From *The Fox of Peapack*, Harper and Brothers, printed first in *The New Yorker*.

White, Leonard (with Marshall Dimock and John Gaus), *The Frontiers of Public Administration*, The University of Chicago Press.

Whitehead, A. N., *Science and the Modern World*, The Macmillan Company.
Nature and Life, University of Chicago Press.

Wilder, Russell M., "Industrial Laboratories and Clinical Research," *Publication of The Squibb Institute for Medical Research*, Vol. I, pp. 15–18.

Willey, Basil, *The Seventeenth Century Background*, Chatto and Windus.

Williams, C., *Bacon*, Harper and Brothers. A biography of Francis Bacon written with exceptional understanding.

Wolf, A., *Spinoza, Benedictus de, Correspondence*, The Dial Press.

Woolf, Leonard, *Quack, Quack!* Harcourt, Brace and Company.

Woolf, Virginia, "A Conversation About Art," *The Yale Review*, Vol. 24, pp. 52–65.

Young, Art, *On My Way*, H. Liveright.

INDEX

Adams, H., 228.
Aquinas, 98, 100, 228.
Aristotle, 98, 109, 202, 208, 229, 240.
Augustine, 173, 245, 286.

Bacon, F., 174, 231, 233-239, 250.
Bargaining, collective, 275-276.
Barnes, Bishop E. W., 333-334, 374.
Bayle, P., 232.
Beard, C. A., 105.
Benét, S. V., 194, 196, 374.
Berdyaev, N., 287-289, 374.
Berkeley, 5, 6, 159.
Beston, H., 5, 341.
Blood, B., 342.
Bradley, F. H., 163, 374.
Breasted, J. H., 349, 351, 374.
Brewster, H., 75, 219, 374.
Bridgman, P. W., 358, 364, 374.
Brisbane, A., 305-306.
Brooks, R., 362.
Bruno, G., 70, 230.
Business, ideals of, 360-361.

Cardozo, Mr. Justice, 58, 175.
Chase, S., 188, 374.
Cohan, G., 52.
Cohen, M., 106, 375.
Commons, J. R., 122-123.
Compromise, defined, 148.
Conklin, E. G., 248, 375.
Cooke, M. L., 188, 375.

Cram, R. A., 215-217, 375.
Crane, S., 185.
Curie, P., 125.
Cusanus, 18.

Darrow, C., 311.
Debs, E. V., 25.
Democritus, 172-173, 290.
Descartes, 159 ff., 230-231.
Dewey, J., 26, 27, 170, 210, 222, 297, 305, 312-313, 336, 368, 375.
Dickinson, E., 116, 375.
Dimock, M., 108.
Dressler, M., 219.

Eddington, Sir A., 168-169, 242, 256, 375.
Eden, A., 140.
Einstein, A., 267, 278.
Ellis, H., 54, 135, 376.
Emerson, R. W., 23, 94, 161, 178, 203, 224, 328.
Erman, A., 350, 376.
Evolution, and man, 197 ff., 346.

Fosdick, H. E., 56, 311.
Frankfurter, Mr. Justice, 153.

Gaus, J., 108.
Gilson, E., 117, 376.
Glasgow, E., 165, 376.
Goldman, Rabbi S., 293.
Good, the, defined, 137.
Gregory, Sir R., 273.